CONFESSIONS OF A ONE-TIME CRONY CAPITALIST

WELFARE STATE UNDER ATTACK

AJAY S. KUMAR

Chennai • Bangalore

CLEVER FOX PUBLISHING
Chennai, India

Published by CLEVER FOX PUBLISHING 2024
Copyright © Ajay S. Kumar 2024

All Rights Reserved.
Paperback ISBN: 978-93-56484-79-5
Hardback ISBN: 978-93-56484-80-1

This book has been published with all reasonable efforts taken to make the material error-free after the consent of the author. No part of this book shall be used, reproduced in any manner whatsoever without written permission from the author, except in the case of brief quotations embodied in critical articles and reviews.

The Author of this book is solely responsible and liable for its content including but not limited to the views, representations, descriptions, statements, information, opinions and references ["Content"]. The Content of this book shall not constitute or be construed or deemed to reflect the opinion or expression of the Publisher or Editor. Neither the Publisher nor Editor endorse or approve the Content of this book or guarantee the reliability, accuracy or completeness of the Content published herein and do not make any representations or warranties of any kind, express or implied, including but not limited to the implied warranties of merchantability, fitness for a particular purpose. The Publisher and Editor shall not be liable whatsoever for any errors, omissions, whether such errors or omissions result from negligence, accident, or any other cause or claims for loss or damages of any kind, including without limitation, indirect or consequential loss or damage arising out of use, inability to use, or about the reliability, accuracy or sufficiency of the information contained in this book.

Dedication

To my parents and teachers who taught me to be sensitive as well as rational, to be receptive but be critical and to have clarity in thought and action.

ACKNOWLEDGEMENT

I owe my book to the intellectual climate my alma mater Sree Narayana Public School, Kerala, India provided in my most formative years. I am extremely grateful to the founder Principal Sri M.K Sasidharan for his academic leadership and to my beloved teachers Ms N. Savithry, Ms Leena K R, Mr V. Jayaprakash, Dr Suresh, Mr Rajesh P K, Ms Anitha Kumari C.R, Mr Anil Prasad, Mr C.P. Sunil, Mr Anil, Ms Hemalatha, Ms Jayarani, Ms Vineetha Vasudevan, Ms Vinoba C B, Ms Bindu, Ms Sumam and to a host of other inspiring teachers who knitted together the most conducive environment. The atmosphere was bohemian. Those were the best days of my life…

To them, I say, this is your book as much as it is mine.

The camaraderie fostered by my graduate school, Model Engineering College, Kerala, India is unparalleled. The institution instilled in me the courage to experiment. I am grateful to the faculty and my friends.

Indian Institute of Management-Kozhikode, is one institution that had a profound influence on me. It truly embodies the task of 'Globalising Indian Thought'. I owe to this great institution the frameworks that often I employ to make sense of the world around me.

I want to express my gratitude to

- Prof C.N. Somarajan who had faith in me that I could pull it off and encouraged my contrarian views. He fuelled and at times provided me a sense of direction for my endeavour when I wandered in the doldrums of indecisiveness.

- Pramod Alexander who in spite of his formal training in Engineering and Management has evolved into a military historian of repute, a great conversationalist, the intellectual combat with whom greatly benefitted me.
- Prof Sarangadharan, who provided clarity of understanding through his surgical strikes that struck at the core of my belief system.
- Dr Hycinth Sophia Paul , Dr Praveen, Mr Sunil Kumar who read through the entire script of one lakh words and offered me suggestions to improve.
- My Professor Dr Abhilash Nair of the Indian Institute of Management - Kozhikode whose devout belief in Gandhi greatly influenced me. It was Prof Abhilash who insisted that the book should rely on a theoretical approach, a daunting task to which I believe I was faithful.
- Creative Freelancers, who designed the book cover.

My friends and well-wishers Bobby Hussein, Rizwan, Jai, Anaz, Santhosh George, Pradeep, Alphus, Prasanth Sasidharan, Zachariah, Shivas Hameed, Samoj M Panicker, Sruthi P Vijayaraghavan, Seshadrinathan, Anitha, Jayakrishnan, Clifton, Harikrishnan S B, Geethanjali, Hareesh N G, Riji N Das, Sanu Krishna, Harikrishnan Nair, Indu Nair, Khaleel Rahman, Manoj James, Arun Sreekumar, Vaisakh G, Aravind, James Xavier, Naveen Krishnan, Mahima Samuel, Shajeena Shahul Hameed ,Gayatri, Pradeep Mohan Sankar.

The journey of writing your first book is often a long and solitary one! I wish to thank Coach Manju K Manohar for her vital help in finding a good publisher for my first book and for her useful tips regarding the marketing of my book.

Naghma, a dear friend and the visionary CEO of Foster Reads, who passionately endeavours to rekindle the joy of reading in individuals and aspires to construct the world's most extensive community of book enthusiasts.

Cleverfox Publishing has been a great inspiration for me. Right from its visionary leader Ranjan Mohapatra, everyone whom I associated with was a great source of inspiration. Never even once they were found wanting. The first points of contact, Devika Soni and E Vinodha who were instrumental in onboarding me, Project Manager Sumitha Menon, the Editor Maheshweta Trivedi Dey, the designer Arunav Moitra, and the production team led by Praveen Raj… All of them jelled so well in making my 'Confessions' reach you…

PREFACE

'Those who control the present, control the past and those who control the past control the future'.

The perceptions we harbour on our past come in the way of our deciphering of the developments of the present which impacts our understanding of its implications in the future. This book intends to be a blitzkrieg on all such wrongly conceived perceptions.

The well-documented bitter rivalry among the European nations for centuries, culminating in two World Wars, contrasts itself with the present bonhomie between them, that betrays no sign of faltering as is evidenced by the ever-increasing intensity of economic cooperation facilitated by a common currency and a sense of shared security between them as manifested by the ever-expanding military pact of NATO. It is unpalatable given the brief time frame in which the animosity between nations was replaced with a sense of brotherhood. While in East Europe, the Balkans especially, or in the entire Third World, the animosity, though not violent enough to culminate into the kind of wanton bloodshed the West European rivalry descended into, shows no sign of waning. It is unpalatable because our understanding of the rivalry which we take to be national, is fundamentally erroneous.

With the dawn of neoliberalism, the West reclaimed its former colonies to its East and South with unprecedented ease. Sovereign Welfare Republics, which had fought bitter battles to shrug off the colonial yoke to steer an independent path towards their tryst with destiny playing second fiddle to western Capital in its own enslavement and dismemberment is appalling. A change of government in these sovereign nations does not translate to a paradigm shift in the policies pursued. Unlike in the colonial days when the domestic Capital joined hands with the freedom movement, we find that in these sovereign nations, it is in league with western capital. There is more to it than meets the eye in the sudden muting of the inter imperialist rivalry of West Europe and the unprecedented bonhomie between the domestic Capital with the metropole.

In the present era of neoliberalism what is being intensely tutored and widely subscribed to by the unsuspecting citizens is the mantra that the interest of the nation is co-terminus with that of International Finance Capital. The most pressing demands of the broadest strata of the population hardly merit any attention in the inner councils of the government. Rarely does a government rise to the historic needs of the time. A Sovereign government harping on a policy of firmness rather than capitulation to the dictates of capital is increasingly becoming an exception.

The book seeks to address many such paradoxes by attacking the very notions which we have come to harbour.

The Genesis of the Book

Given the intellectual climate that prevailed in the 1990s, India like many other Third World countries which while being technically non-aligned had a very discernible Soviet slant, made a course correction and embraced the free-market ideology. With the unconstitutional dissolution of the Soviet Union there was nothing to lean on, intellectually as well as in the material sense. The discredited 'Soviet ideology' found no takers.

Why Confessions?

The narrative of the neoliberal think-tank that has been increasingly subscribed to since then is that the government is the enemy that stands in the way of our freedom and prosperity. The regulatory functions of the government stifle individual entrepreneurship. An impediment to human progress, the government should be reduced to a state of impotency. It is only in a free-market economy the blooming of the individual happens. I readily subscribed to the prevailing intellectual orthodoxy. Pursuing my studies in Technology and Management and embarking on a career as a Consultant, travelling and meeting people from around the world, I was constantly perturbed by the incongruence of what we had been tutored and the glaring facts that I came to reckon with. My interaction with the people from former Soviet Republics and those in East Europe was enlightening.

Mere knowledge of the forces at work will give us the power to predict. Goodwill, noble aspirations and rhetoric will serve no purpose to undo the wrongs unless it is backed by an action plan that is informed by the necessities and contingency factors. History will hold us accountable for not marshalling the intellectual energies in furtherance of the establishment of the Welfare State.

The book is a humble attempt towards this end. An attempt to **see the** world as it is, without ideological blinders that often take the rhetoric to the point of absurdity.

CONTENTS

Part 1 Capital's Abhorrence Of A Welfare State 1
- Chapter 1: The Scramble for Russia 3
- Chapter 2: What Was President Reagan's *'Evil Empire'* Like? 17

Part 2 WW II Renewed Onslaught on the Welfare State.....................23
- Chapter 3: Adolf Hitler: A Darling to the Western Capital... 25
- Chapter 4: Hiroshima-Nagasaki: A Message to the Soviet Union.. 47
- Chapter 5: The Soviet Union Could Have Won the War All by Itself. 59

Part 3 Concessions by Capital to Labour..69
- Chapter 6: Attempts of a Welfare State in the Capitalist West 71
- Chapter 7: John Maynard Keynes: The Man Who Saved Capitalism from the Capitalists 85

Part 4 Cold War 93
- Chapter 8: The Context of the Cold War 95
- Chapter 9: Iran's Tryst with Democracy Comes to an End 109
- Chapter 10: Guatemala Follows Suit.. 115
- Chapter 11: 'North Vietnam Attacks US'. US Had to Retaliate! 123
- Chapter 12: In POL POT US Seeks Revenge!............................... 137
- Chapter 13: 9/11 Chile: The Neo-Liberal Laboratory 143
- Chapter 14: Nicaragua: A Government is Democratically Overthrown!... 151
- Chapter 15: The Cold War: A Fact File 161

Part 5 Neoliberalism: The Beginning of the End of the Welfare State **169**
- Chapter 16: From Post-War Consensus to Washington Consensus 171
- Chapter 17: Neoliberalism on Either Side of the Atlantic 185
- Chapter 18: German Unification: The Colonization of the East by the West 197
- Chapter 19: The Greatest Geopolitical Disaster of the 20th Century 199
  - The Greatest Welfare State Abolishes Itself 200
  - Russia on Sale 210
- Chapter 20: Yugoslavia: NATO Obliterates the Last Holdout of Collectivism in Europe 225
- Chapter 21: Critique of Neoliberalism 229
  - New Avatar of IMF: The Inflation Monitoring Fund 230
  - An Open Letter to Milton Friedman 240
  - Balance Sheet of Neoliberalism 245

Part 6 The Real Crime of Cuba **259**
- Chapter 22: Cuba 261
- Chapter 23: Cuba Internationale 267
  - Military Internationalism 268
    - The Context of Angola 270
    - Namibia Marches to Freedom in 1990 273
  - Medical Internationalism 274

Part 7 The Sham of Multiparty Democracy **279**
- Chapter 24: The Blitzkrieg of Unstoppable Self-Propelling Capitalism Pulverises Institutions of Democracy 281

Part 8 The Way Forward **303**
- Chapter 25: The Road Ahead 305

INTRODUCTION

Patent for System of transmission of electrical energy

1897-09-02 Application filed by Nikola Tesla
1900-03-20 Application granted
1900-03-20 Publication of US645576A

1908 Marconi was awarded the Nobel Prize for his 'invention' of Radio.

Wither Welfare State?

Imperialism refers to the economic domination of one geographic region by another. The most obvious form it manifests itself is colonialism which involves the physical occupation of a region by a dominant power. The internecine conflicts between the European imperialist powers culminating in two World Wars mark a major phase of human history. This desire and necessity of exerting control over distant geographic swaths stem from the lust for raw materials and markets. Imperialism is an inevitable outcome of capitalism.

The Great Depression was the first major existential threat to capitalism. The depression precipitated the rise of fascist forces. Post-war, there was a realization that the welfare of the common man was a prerequisite to maintaining international peace and domestic tranquillity. The capitalist countries began transforming themselves into welfare States. In fact, under the Presidency of Franklin D Roosevelt, United States of America had begun its transformation into a Welfare State in the 1930s. With the institution of welfare measures across the capitalist countries in the aftermath of World War II, it appeared that Marx and Lenin had become obsolete.

The transformation of the capitalist countries to the welfare states was paralleled by decolonisation. The colonial powers surrendered formal power to the natives gracefully. The decolonisation was an epoch of immense consequence to the colonies. With sovereign governments, these former colonies took upon the task of ensuring the welfare of their citizens. In a rare display of camaraderie and bonhomie, the Soviet Union reached out to the former colonies. The socialist state stood behind the newly independent nations and provided the technical know-how to harness their natural resources, which until recently was plundered by the imperialist, for the benefit of the native population. Ever since the capitalist framework became entrenched in western societies, the free run of Capital stood checkmated on both fronts, i.e. domestic and international.

However, with the formal surrender of power to the natives in the colonies, imperialism refused to fade. It assumed a new phase. The metropole never intended to cede its empire to the natives in the truest sense. The former colonies were still on a leash from the metropole-a very short leash indeed. The metropole retained strong political and economic influence over its former colonies to ensure the steady availability of the resources, without which it could not sustain itself. The Soviet Union proved to be a stumbling block. The socialist state 'interfered' with Capital's unbridled raid over the former colonies. The Cold War between the Soviet Union and the West had imperialistic underpinnings.

Neoliberalism – A Frontal Attack on the Welfare State

Capital that was subdued was waiting in the wings. The late 1970s presented the most opportune moment for Capital to reassert itself. The stagflation, the coexistence of high rates of inflation and unemployment, found a scapegoat in the welfare system. Seizing the moment the two Heads of Governments on either side of the Atlantic, President Ronald Reagan (1981–1989) and Prime Minister Margaret Thatcher (1979–1990) systematically dismembered the welfare machinery in their countries in the interest of Capital. With the implosion of the Soviet Union in 1991, the 'Soviet menace' too had ceased. Neoliberal thoughts that championed the power of the market stood validated while the alternative was *'consigned to the dustbins of history'*.

The Object of the Book

The book aims to set the context in which the present world operates and discusses the possibilities for the future. It lays bare the Capital's abhorrence of the Welfare State. It analyses the means Capital employs to dismember the welfare machinery in every State.

The book explores the possibilities of restoring the citizen his rightful place in the inner councils of government. An enlightened population that insists on a democracy that is more authentic than procedural alone can make it happen.

PART 1

CAPITAL'S ABHORRENCE OF A WELFARE STATE

The '*Long March*' of NATO to the East

9*th* February 1990

'...*Not an inch of NATO's present military jurisdiction will spread in an eastern direction*.'
— **James Baker III, US Secretary of State**

10*th* February 1990

'*We believe that NATO should not expand its scope*.'
— **Helmut Kohl, Chancellor Federal Republic of Germany**

17*th* May 1990. '*The fact that we are ready not to place a NATO army outside of German territory gives the Soviet Union a firm security guarantee*.'
— **Manfred Woerner, Secretary General of NATO**

29th March 2004 *'Today, we proudly welcome Bulgaria, Estonia, Latvia, Lithuania, Romania, Slovakia and Slovenia. We welcome them into the ranks of the North Atlantic Treaty Organization'.*
 – President George Bush welcoming the new members to the NATO in its biggest expansion till date.

Chapter 1: The Scramble for Russia

> 'NATO has put its frontline forces on our borders, and we have the right to ask: against whom is this expansion intended? And what happened to the assurances our western partners made after the dissolution of the Warsaw Pact? Where are those declarations today'?
>
> – **Vladimir Putin, Munich speech**

Would the Soviet Union, a powerful state in the 1980s, have conceded to German unification without an assurance from the West on the eastward expansion of NATO, a military pact formed by capitalist nations with the sole aim of wiping it out of the World map?

There had been five waves of NATO expansion towards the East in violation of the assurances given to the Soviet Union. Even after three decades of ending the Cold War, which had birthed the military alliance, it is still expanding. The relentless *long march* of NATO towards the East against every assurance given in the euphoric days of German unification is very much in keeping with the West's obsession with the Russian mainland, which has forty percent of the world's known natural resources. In the early 20th century, Russia had all the pretensions of a sovereign power. It had a Tsar and a Tsarina. It had a nobility and an army. It entered into mutual assistance pacts with Britain and France. Russia had all the trappings of a world power. But, for all practical purposes, it was but a colony of the western Capital. Western industrialists, bankers, aristocracy and politicians enriched themselves by their huge investments in Russia. It was their most profitable backyard. While West Europe and the US marched into the industrial age, Tsarist Russia remained a medieval country of agriculturists and pastorals.

Genesis of a Welfare State at Times of War
The Promise of 'Peace, Land and Bread'.

> 'Russia has not reached that height of development of the productive forces under which socialism would be possible'
> – **Menshevik author Sukhanov**

> 'If for the creation of socialism, a certain level of culture is required (although no one can say exactly what that level of culture should be, for it is different in every Western European state), why could we not begin with the conquest by revolutionary means of the prerequisites for such a particular level of culture and then, based on workers' and peasants' power, move towards catching up with other countries'.
> – **Lenin**

Tsarist Russia had entered the World War as an ally of the British and the French against Germany. It entered the war on a mutual assistance pact inked with France. Every army is considered invincible in the national mythology. Russians too believed in their army's prowess. But in reality, the Russian army was no match for the better organised and one of the largest armies back then – the German army. The Russian army was suited for skirmishes with semi-barbaric armies at the best. It had fought a war with the tiny island nation to its east in 1905 and was routed. Tsarist Russia was never an equal partner to the western powers. The delegation of the Russian Duma which was making friendly visits to the French and the English could easily discern that the allies intended, in the course of the war, to *'squeeze all the live juice out of Russia'*. After the victory, the allies had calculated that the war-ravaged Russia could be its backyard. A Russia in tow to a victorious *Entente* was nothing but a colony.

The Russian army stood no chance against the superior German military might. Russian casualties swelled compared to other members of the *Entente*. Russia lost 25 million of its troops in the war, it accounted for 40 percent of the casualties of the *Entente*. War Minister Polivanov in 1915 stated in response to alarmed questions from his colleagues in the Cabinet as to the situation in the front, '*I place my trust in the impenetrable spaces, impassable mud and the mercy of Saint Nicholas Mirlikisky, protector of Holy Russia*'. Russian General Ruszky confessed a week later, '*The present-day demands of the military techniques are beyond us. At any rate, we can't keep up with the Germans*'. It was clear that it was hopeless to fight the Germans. Even in the methods of fighting, the Russians were no match to the Germans. There were large-scale desertions from the Russian army. The industrial workers took to the streets. By September 1915 they wanted peace by all means. Pressure to conclude a separate peace treaty with Germany was coming from many quarters. But the war was to prolong for years amid desertions from the army. With disgruntled soldiers from the front joining the rank and file of the protestors in Petrograd, the situation in Russia was ripe for a revolution. The domestic situation had become so volatile that there was a consensus in the Russian elite, which until then had been clamouring for the continuance of war, that Russia should conclude a separate peace treaty with Germany and bring an end to the war to stave off the imminent revolution.

The Sham of February Revolution

In February things took a violent turn and the Tsar abdicated. The political apparatus of the workers in Russia was caught off-guard. The leaders of the Soviet workers failed to rise to the historical demands placed on them. Perhaps the blue-collared workers could not come to terms with the reality that the time had come to be the masters of their own destiny. Bolsheviks were a tiny minority then and Lenin had been in hiding elsewhere for the previous 16 years. It is a matter of un-palpable irony that with the abdication of Nicholas II, though triggered by the upsurge of the working class, the Soviets of the industrial workers did not assume leadership of the government. *'Their hands trembled with fear'*. The Soviet handed down the power to rule them to the Russian Duma. In the absence of an appropriate political agency to channel the fury of the masses, the power came to reside with the Deputies of the Duma. As events unfolded, the workers were to pay a heavy price for being found wanting.

The Duma was elected to office by the enfranchised propertied class. The Duma, true to its class character, did not resonate with the needs and aspirations of the workers and peasants. The Provisional Government initially led by Alexander Ivanov and later by the legendary Alexander Kerensky made no effort to ease the suffering of the workers and peasants, as was desired by the working class. Yes, it takes time to undo the heap of centuries of wrong-doings. But an immediate conclusion of a peace treaty with Germany could have brought an end to the war and there-by saved thousands of lives. It did not happen. The war inherited from the discredited Tsar was to continue even under the Provisional Government that had come to replace it. With the power in their hands, the elite had changed their minds. Both Alexander Ivanov and Alexander Kerensky, instead of concluding a peace treaty, launched major offensives during their tenure at the helm of affairs much to the disgruntlement of the very workers and soldiers who had handed power to them. True to the character of its class the Provisional Government, answerable only to the Russian Duma, a representative body of the possessed class, continued the hopeless war with Germany. The hype of the war was necessary to take the wind off the sails of the revolution. War would rationalise the continuance of the military-bureaucratic apparatus of the abdicated Tsar. The pandemonium and the mayhem of the war could be used as a convenient tool to postpone the formation of the constituent assembly to draft a constitution. Alexander Kerensky to placate the Russian elite, who manned the *'military-industrial complex'* as well as the British and French allies, launched an offensive that has come to be known as the *'Kerensky offensive'*. Thousands of Russian soldiers perished in this ill-timed and ill-conceived misadventure. The continuance of the war which was resented by the workers, peasants and the soldiers made the Provisional Government extremely unpopular. The Provisional Government of Kerensky castigated everyone who argued to conclude a separate peace treaty with Germany. They wanted to fight the war purportedly to bring Germany to its knees, though they were fully aware of the virtual impossibility of it, given the dismal performance of the ill-trained, poorly clothed and poorly fed retreating Russian troops in the front. The elite stood to gain from the spoils of war and that explained their newfound patriotism. As Trotsky notes in his *History of the Russian Revolution*, 'Enormous fortunes arose out of the bloody foam'. In the State Duma and in the press, the profits made through war were published. The Moscow Textile Company of the Riabushinskys showed a net profit of 75 percent, The Tver Company 111 percent and the copper works of Kolchugun netted over 12 million Rubles on a basic Capital of 10 million Rubles. Obviously, the war should continue. The blood spilled in the front never bothered the decision-makers as there were profits to pocket in the rear.

With the abdication of Nicholas and with the institution of the Provisional Government, Russia had technically transformed itself into a Republic. The western powers had a rapport with this new Republic unperturbed by the change of power. As it turned out there was nothing revolutionary about the February revolution. It proved to be a sham!

As the war showed no signs of ending, the Soviet workers and peasants were getting restless and there was mayhem in the streets. Russia was pregnant with revolution one more time. The Provisional Government working on behalf of the propertied class undertook swift measures to protect its financial interests. The propertied class fearing confiscation of their properties sliced up their land holdings and real estate and transferred it in the names of dummies. At times it was transferred in the name of foreigners. Savings were siphoned off to western banks.

The 'October Coup'

'The history of a revolution is for us first of all the forcible entrance of the masses into the realm of rulership over their own destiny.'
— **Leon Trotsky**

October witnessed the toppling of the Provisional Government of Kerensky by the Bolsheviks. The Bolsheviks came to power promising *'Peace, Bread and Land'*. The immediate fallout of the 1917 *'October Coup'* was the unilateral withdrawal of Russia from the World War denouncing it as a capitalist war. It secured an armistice with Germany on 13th December. Foreign Minister Leon Trotsky, Lenin's trusted lieutenant and Second-in-Command and heir apparent deliberated the peace process on behalf of Bolshevik Russia and concluded a peace treaty with Germany on 3rd March 1918. The treaty signed at Brest-Litovsk, a Polish city under German control, imposed humiliating conditions on the Bolsheviks. Russia had to surrender a third of its agricultural land, a major chunk of its coal fields and industry. Fifty-five million Russians were to be ruled by the Germans. Peace (by all means) was what the Bolsheviks wanted.

True to their words, the Bolsheviks on assuming power abnegated Tsarist Russia's extra-territorial rights over China and Mongolia. The far-reaching reforms initiated by Lenin in every sphere of human endeavour, like the regularisation of working hours, institutionalising better working conditions, preferential treatment of expectant mothers, universal education, health care, housing and massive electrification were a sign of things to come. The first Welfare State was being established.

---

[1] *'If it brings peace, go wearing a petticoat'* wired back Lenin to Trotsky's query on the German insistence of a dress code for a meeting during the protracted peace negotiations in WW I.

Alarm Bells in the Western Capitalist Countries

'Kill the Bolshie. Kiss the Hun.'

— **Winston Churchill**

Was Russia ever a military threat? It was trounced by Japan in 1905. It suffered a humiliating defeat at the hands of Germany, which eventually lost out to the allies. This underscores the point that it posed no military threat to any.

In Russia, a competing socio-economic-political order had begun to take shape following the October Revolution. The industrial workers and peasants had taken control of the productive forces and heralded their own emancipation through political means. Mikhail Gorbachev, the last leader of the Soviet Union observed, *'The October Revolution undeniably reflected the most urgent demands of the broadest strata of the population for fundamental social change'*. The leader of the Bolsheviks, Lenin took a stand against colonialism and called for a *World Revolution*. This alarmed the privileged aristocracy of Europe and America, as they stood a chance of being evicted from the colonies and overthrown by their own working class. The British Secretary of State for War Winston Churchill worried that the *'civilisation is being completely extinguished over gigantic areas, while Bolsheviks hop and caper like troops of ferocious baboons'*.[2]

What they most feared was the demonstrative power of the competing social order that was taking shape. Socialist ideas had been circulating for decades, but in Russia, the *'Spectre of Communism haunting Europe'* was being realised. *'October'* had the potential of electrifying the famished working classes across the world into shrugging off the capitalist yoke. The Anti-Soviet foreign policy of the capitalist nations was fuelled solely because of the threat it posed in challenging the class equations in

---

[2] United States of America, Canada, Great Britain, Czechoslovak Legion, Greece, Serbia, Romania, Italy, Estonia, Japan, Australia, India, South Africa and China pounced on the young Bolshevik Republic to reverse the revolution.

the domestic front. Now that a precedence had been established, the capitalist aristocracy was facing an existential threat at the hands of its own working class. In December 1917, Leonido Bissolati, a Minister of the Italian government stated, *'The influence of the Bolsheviks has reached proportions that are not without danger for us. If in the near future the Russian government does not fall, things will go badly for us'.* In March 1918 Arthur Balfour, Prime Minister of Britain, summing up the results of the London Conference of Prime Ministers and Foreign Ministers of France, Italy and Britain wrote to President Woodrow Wilson, *'What is the remedy? To the conference, it seemed none was possible except through Allied intervention. Since Russia cannot help herself, she should be helped by her friends'.* In 1919, Woodrow Wilson cautioned, *'We must be concerned that this form of rule by the people is not imposed on us'.* Winston Churchill's words *'drown the child while still in the cradle'* epitomised the hatred of the capitalist class of European nations towards the Bolsheviks.

It is to be borne in mind that neither America nor any of the western capitalist nations were truly democratic those days, though they had the pretensions of being one. In these countries, only the propertied classes were enfranchised. Women did not have the right to vote. Many of them were right-wing dictatorships. Universal adult franchise, the cardinal principle of democracy, was implemented in Britain only in 1932. France adopted universal adult franchise in 1945 and America in 1946. Interestingly the Bolsheviks had incorporated universal adult suffrage in 1918 in their draft Constitution.

The Allied Invasion of Russia 1918–1922

On 4th March, the very next day the treaty of Brest-Litovsk was signed between Germany and the Russian Republic, the British troops were the first to land in Russia, seeking to prevent the spread of the *'Bolshevik infection'.* Soon the armies of 14 capitalist nations led by the US, France,

---

[3] With the Allied invasion of Russia, English and Russian army prisoners in German custody learned much to their dismay that once let free they would have to fight each other.

Britain, Japan, Canada, Serbia, Romania and Japan joined forces with the counter-revolutionary White forces. Tsarist Russia was a prized colony of western Capital. It was never to be lost to its native people. Counter-revolutionary forces backed up by the firepower of all great capitalist powers of the world fought a war on 17 fronts extending over a battle line of 7000 miles long. In the western front war was still being fought between allies and Germany. But in East Germany, despite the Brest-Litovsk treaty with Bolsheviks, even while fighting the allies, the German elite was working independently to dismantle the Bolshevik menace. The class rivalry dwarfed the national rivalries. The armistice the allies signed on 11th November 1918 with Germany which effectually brought an end to the Great World War and dismembered Germany from being a threat, enabled the allies to augment and concentrate their efforts to topple the Bolsheviks. Bolshevik Russia suffered many reversals in the war. Poland too seized the opportunity. Though never a part of the fourteen-member coalition, the Polish army invaded Ukraine and seized Kiev. Churchill, a sworn enemy of the Bolsheviks, spoke of building up and rearming a defeated Germany in order to fight communism.[4]

The war was severely resented by the soldiers of the allied countries. Many of them identified themselves with the Bolsheviks, for the Bolsheviks had secured for the Russians living conditions that were being denied to them back in their homeland. There were mutinies among the rank and file of the Allied forces.

The rationale, the invading nations provided was that Russian withdrawal from the war was in violation of the agreement between England, France and Russia, which viewed an attack on any one of them by the Germans as an attack on all of them and be repulsed together. Yet another rationale provided was that allied shipments of arms and ammunition for the

---

[4] Bolsheviks were a threat to the European 'work climate'.
Factories Act of 1819 stated that no children under the age of 9 were to be employed and that children aged 9–16 years were limited to 12 hours' work per day. But the Act was effectively unenforceable. Children below 9 continued to slog in the cotton mills and coal factories in inhuman conditions for long hours.

war were lying in the Russian ports and the invasion was to secure the ports to prevent them from falling into German hands. The European aristocracy was related to the Romanovs. The restoration of the Romanovs back into power was also highlighted as one of the reasons for the Allied intervention. But the continued invasion of Russia by the allies even after the liquidation of the Romanov family on 17th July 1918, and the German capitulation and armistice on 11th November 1918 flies at the face of their cited reasons for invasion. Why did the European aristocracy continue the aggression as late as 1922, though they were aware that the Romanov family had long been liquidated? Why did Republics like the United States of America and France, which came into being after violent armed struggles, fight a revolution keen on establishing a Republic?

Territorial ambitions too mattered. Great Britain wanted Caucasus and Kubam. France wanted Crimea and Ukraine. Japan and the US wanted Siberia and the Far East. It was a scramble for Russia. It took the new nation besieged by enemies from the East and West seven years to evict the invading armies. It was not until 1925 that the last of the Allied armies, the Japanese were flushed out of North Sakhalin. It was amidst the Allied invasion that 'The National Economic Policy' was unveiled in 1921. The Union of the Soviet Socialist Republic was proclaimed in 1922 while the Red Army was still battling the allies. The debilitating conditions that the young Republic went through were to leave a mark on it in the decades to come. The allied invasion instead of reversing the revolution strengthened it and coalesced the fighting Russians into a nation. The Bolsheviks could galvanize the entire population against the invading marauders. The very fact that under Bolsheviks the Russians could thwart the aggression by a coalition force of fourteen nations goes to the credit of the military skills and statesmanship of its leadership.

A frontal attack by the western powers at the behest of their capitalist class on the young Republic barely weeks into its existence is often dressed up as a civil war between the Red Guards and the White Guards by historians. Refusal on the part of the European nations to recognize the first Socialist Welfare Republic is reflective of their abhorrence of the egalitarian socialist cause. They tried in every way to bring the Soviet Republic to its knees. Failed armed aggression was followed by diplomatic isolation, trade embargo and even withholding supplies of food at times of famine. It was not until 16th November 1933, that the United States of America recognised USSR and initiated diplomatic relations. Incidentally, the United States only took a week to recognize Kerensky's government as legitimate. The fact that the USSR was admitted to the League of Nations in 1934 along with Germany summarizes the isolation it suffered.[5]

'October' and the Red Scare Across the World

During the WW I (1914–1918) Europe and the US witnessed near full employment of industrial workers. As the workers were in high demand the War ensured that they were paid well. Near full employment with adequate pay was unthinkable in a capitalist system during peacetime. It is ironic that capitalism could provide near total employment only at times of war.

But as the war was getting over, in the US alone, 4 million soldiers were being de-mobilised. 9 million war industry workers were out of work. Labour wanted to keep the higher wages and stable jobs that the war had provided. As a large number of them were being laid off the reserve army of labour swindled. It ensured that those who were lucky to keep their jobs had to take a severe beating on their pay for fear of losing it. The labour class was rendered a mere price taker. Inflation worsened the matters further.

Industrial workers were getting militant. There were clashes between Blacks and Whites, owners and workers, and between natives and foreigners. Even when one views the Bolshevik's novel social experiment

---

[5] Tsarist Russia was an ally of the West. Even the Provisional Government was acceptable to Western capital as long as it prolonged the war. Peace loving Soviet Russia was an international pariah.

in Russia without any doctrinal lens, it was convincing that ensuring a means of livelihood for every person was possible even in peacetime. The new Soviet experiment in a very short span of time had turned itself into a beacon of hope. This was the first time that there was a Red Scare in the US and Europe. Union leaders demanding stable jobs with decent pay were dubbed *'agents of Lenin'*. In the US alone there were 3600 strikes in a year. Bolsheviks had called out a World Revolution and it seemed imminent that the unrest in Europe and the US could serve as a vehicle for a revolution by the working classes. Fighting the Bolsheviks and not the raging influenza epidemic was the priority. The left-leaning industrial workers' demands were legitimised with the capitalist world plunging into the Great Depression while the Soviet Union was making giant strides.

'February' and *'October'* offer great lessons in this era of neoliberalism. It must be said the greatest revolution the world had ever seen, when the people took it upon themselves to usher in a new era, was the February Revolution. In the absence of a political apparatus, it fizzled out. Able and visionary leadership made *'October'* possible. *'October'* was undeniably the single most important catalyst for change in the nature of the capitalist state. It ensured the quickening of the pace of social progress all over the world. Social benefits, never even thought about in the industrial West, were being realized. Walter Lippman states, *'But we delude ourselves if we do not realise that the main power of the communist states lies not in their clandestine activity but in the force of their example, in the visible demonstration of what the Soviet Union has achieved'.* It was too dangerous to lag behind the communists.

> *'Hatred was always greater between classes than with nations'.*

As the Bolsheviks overthrew the Provisional Government, which had lost its legitimacy and had faced the wrath of the people, and took power and ended the war, the very privileged aristocracy who were until then xenophobic *'patriots'* wanting to fight the Germans tooth and nail and bring them to their knees against all odds, reached out to the German aggressors to upstage the Bolsheviks. The Russian aristocracy preferred to be ruled by an alien enemy than by the native Bolsheviks. This is reflective of the class character of the war. Even in this age of neoliberalism, we observe the domestic propertied class, making common cause with International Finance Capital, often to the detriment and impoverishment of the domestic population as such collusion is conducive to furthering their interests, unlike in the days of colonialism where they identified themselves with the freedom movements as they too were at the receiving end as the entire gamut of domestic economic activities were systematically pulverized and routed as a matter of policy to fetch the raw materials cheap and sell manufactured products dear.

Churchill's abhorrence for the Bolsheviks, a trademark of his class, was legendary. In January 1919, as the Secretary of State for War and Air, Churchill pursued with a missionary zeal and secured from the loosely organised Cabinet a go-ahead for the intensification of the British involvement in the Russian Civil War. British soldiers had entered Russian territory the very next day the Bolsheviks had concluded a peace treaty with the Germans. Churchill's insistence that the British intervention should be stepped up against all odds invited the wrath and distrust of the Labour Party. His relationship with the then Prime Minister Lloyd George became strained. At the Treaty of Versailles Churchill opposed harsh measures against the defeated Germany. He viewed the Germans as a bulwark against the Russians. His actions and utterances betray a sense of camaraderie with the defeated alien enemy than the Russians who were their ally. While he was in charge of demobilising the British Army, he cautioned against demobilising the German Army.

In the subsequent months when the Allied armies were routed by the Red Army, Churchill warned the Cabinet that a White defeat would allow the Bolsheviks to threaten Poland, Romania and Czechoslovakia. He proposed a *cordon sanitaire* around Russia. Years of embargo, sabotage and isolation were to begin. In 1920, after the last of the British forces had been withdrawn, Churchill was instrumental in arming the Poles to the teeth in the Russo-Polish War of 1920. Poland would not have dared to pounce upon Russia but for the firepower Britain had lavished on her.

No sooner had the Second World War ended in Europe, Churchill had made elaborate plans to take on Soviet Union a second time. He had his commanders draw up *'Operation unthinkable'*, a plan for the Allied invasion of the Soviet Union with the US troops still stationed in Europe and the surrendered German prisoners of war. War was still raging in the Far East as Japan had not yet capitulated. When the Cold War heated up in the subsequent years, as the Soviet Union emerged to be the champion of the newly independent Afro-Asian nations, Churchill stated in the British Parliament in 1949: *'I think the day will come when it will be recognised without doubt not only on one side of the house but throughout the civilised world that the strangling of Bolshevism at its birth would have been an untold blessing to the human race'*.

Chapter 2: What Was President Reagan's *'Evil Empire'* Like?

October Revolution of 1957

For a long time, Americans had been accustomed to being virtually unrivalled in scientific and technological achievements. But very soon the Soviet nuclear and space programmes took the world by surprise. Whereas in Tsarist Russia, people travelled by carriage, Bolshevik Russia took matters to space in 40 years.

Post-War, Russia was keen on rebuilding its war-torn country. It did not even cross the minds of Russians that the Americans were scared of them. The Soviet Union reeling under the devastation of WW II checkmated the US monopoly over the Nuclear bomb in 1949. The western World was stunned when on 4th October 1957 Soviet Union launched Sputnik, a satellite companion to the moon. Russia not only had caught up with the US in nuclear devices, but it had unilaterally inaugurated the space age and was setting milestones for the US to reach. On 6th December 1957, two months after the Soviet Sputnik, the United States made its first satellite launch attempt. Vanguard Test Vehicle-3 (TV-3) exploded in the launch pad during lift-off. Dubbed as the FLOPNIK it was a major embarrassment for the West in general and the US in particular. Yuri Gagarin's maiden journey into space on 12th April 1961 and the botched up Bay of Pigs invasion of Cuba orchestrated by the CIA, that soon followed it (17th–20th April), put the Russians leagues ahead of the Americans. The achievements of the infant Republic always under capitalist siege are known to many, but the vision and the industry that went into this are seldom studied.

---

[6] In March 1958 a US delegation visited USSR to study its education system and published a report on, 'Soviet commitment to education'.

The Soviet System Was Built on Robust Foundation

The Soviet Union was founded on sound principles. Its transformation from a pastoral-agrarian country still in the Middle Ages to a superpower within a span of decades braving the economic and political isolation was phenomenal. The Soviet system improved the lives of its citizens by every single measure of well-being known to social science. The Soviet Union which lagged behind the capitalist nations by an epoch at the time of its coming into being in 1922 was soon inaugurating new frontiers of human achievement leaving the capitalist nations trailing behind it. In the 1930s when the entire capitalist system plunged into, what had come to be known as the Great Depression, the Russians were marching ahead in every walk of life. It increased its industrial production five times during the Great Depression from 1929 to 1939, while the world economy shrank. That the Soviet economy knew no recession let alone depression in its seventy-four years of existence acknowledges the robustness of the fundamentals of the Soviet planned economy.

The very attempt of 15 Sovereign Republics that occupied one-sixth of the planet's surface comprising close to 200 nationalities with their own unique languages, culture and belief systems that stretched from Asia to Europe across 11 time zones to federate themselves into an atheistic nation over which the sun never set was a novel experiment in nation- building. It was the first Republic that instituted a universal adult franchise as early as 1918. It was the first nation that took upon itself the task of wiping out hunger, homelessness and illiteracy among its entire population. Free education up to the highest level possible helps a person to identify, nurture and tap into one's talent. To be able to identify and fulfill one's calling is the most rewarding experience for a human being. It is the real flowering of freedom. The free choice of one's profession based solely on one's inclinations, aptitudes and capacities helps the person give oneself to it. This optimizes the creation of the *wealth of the nation*. The Soviet Union was the first completely literate country.

The Soviet success in assimilating the totally dissimilar nationalities into its fold is a lesson in nation-building that is worthy of emulation, especially in these times of ethnic strife. The Russian language and Russian culture were never imposed on the rest of the Republics, unlike during the Tsarist days. The individual languages and cultures were encouraged to develop and prosper. Education was imparted in the mother tongue. It was borne out of a growing realization that the highest intellectual and scholastic progress could be made only when learning is done in the mother tongue. The government machinery at the most granular level fully acknowledged the existence and the relevance of ethnicity and catered to the aspirations of each ethnic group. It tapped into the conventional wisdom that developed over the years. The Soviet system functioned as a unified whole, not by negating the multitude of nationalities, but by recognizing and nourishing the same by imparting autonomy to each cultural entity as a matter of state policy and assimilating them into it.

Soviet Commitment to Education

'Give me 4 years to teach the children and the seed I have sown will never be uprooted'

– Lenin

'Soviet Union would conquer the whole world in the classroom'

– Nikhita Khrushchev

The US-UK led fourteen nation coalition's armed attack on the young Republic had a long-lasting impact on the policies pursued by its leaders. There was a growing realization among the Soviet leadership that only a well-endowed citizenry could influence global decisions, not necessarily for global hegemony but to meet the existential threat it faced. Pitted against the colonial superpowers which they did repel at a heavy cost right in its infancy, Soviet Republic threw the full weight of its system behind total education. Lenin declared *'Russia cannot be saved by a good harvest in a peasant economy, nor by light industry for consumer goods. Heavy industry was essential, to be subsidised by the state, and unless we find them, we are lost as a civilised state, let alone as a socialist state'.*

As an instrument of government policy, education received paramount importance in the Soviet system. Given the excruciating circumstances, Soviet realism successfully replaced belief in God, encouraging the Soviet citizen to defend his nation against the God-fearing capitalist. In 1960, Soviet authorities founded the *Peoples' Friendship University*. The purpose of this institution was to give an opportunity to young people, especially those with unprivileged background, from Latin America, Asia and Africa.

Women Empowerment

'The progress of a society can be judged by the status of the fairer sex'.

The Soviet Union guaranteed equal rights to women. The right to vote, education, equal pay and the right to defend the country came to fruition at a very early stage in the republic's evolution. The Soviet Union had the first woman ambassador. The first woman in space was Valentina Tereshkova another Russian. 80 percent of doctors and 40 percent of Engineers in the Soviet Union were women. Women flew warplanes during WW II. No other nation in the world stressed the need for women's empowerment. The Soviet system was very keen on emancipating women from traditional roles and placing them at par with men.

Women had the right to vote as early as 1918 decades before the *'capitalist democracies'* enfranchised their women. The Soviet system expanded state support to institutions that would free women from traditional roles and bestow on them an economic role. Organisations, where women worked, had provisions for laundry, crèches, kindergartens and nurseries. Maternity leave if required extended up to four years. Vladimir Lenin referred to the nurseries and kindergartens as *'the sprouts of communism'*. According to him, these facilities *'could actually liberate a woman, in reality diminish and eliminate her inequality to a man through enhancing her role in social production and social life'*.

Influence of the Soviet Union on the US and the Rest of the World

> *'Everybody talks of planning now, and of Five-year, Ten-year and Three-year plans. The Soviets have put magic into the word'.*
> **– Jawaharlal Nehru**

National Defence Education Act 1958

Post-war, Americans were complacent, as the country had turned itself into the financial capital of the world. With the launch of Sputnik, the Americans found themselves lagging behind the Russians in the Space race. A war-devastated Soviet Union getting ahead of the richest nation on Earth brought into focus the efficacy of the Soviet education as well as the serious shortcomings in the US system.

In the US federal aid to education had always been hotly contested by the Congress. During the previous three Congresses, the Senate had passed legislation for federal funding of education. All three bills were administered a quiet burial in the House by Congressional apathy. Sputnik triggered a national sense of unease. It became apparent that the Americans lagged behind the Russians in science and technology. Some disgruntled Senators seized the moment. The Senate once again mooted the idea of an education bill. To get it enacted they called it *National Defence Education Bill*. But then, why defence? In the Cold War era only defence mattered for the US establishment. The line of argument in defence of the bill was that placing a satellite in space was demonstrative of the prowess of rocketry of the Soviets which translated to a decisive advantage for them in missile technology which had implications on the defence of the country that could not be glossed over. Federal funding in education in America owed as much to Sputnik as to the savvy legislative tactic of some senators.

The *National Defence Education Act* (1958) was a watershed in the US education. It established the legitimacy of federal funding of higher education and made substantial funds available for low-cost student loans, boosting public and private colleges and universities. An increasingly larger number of American students found education affordable and joined the curriculum. By the 1980s Americans started to outsmart the Russians and the decisive advantage the Russians enjoyed started to wane even by their own account. But as fate would have it all this was to end with the inauguration of Ronald Reagan into the Presidency of the United States.

The Soviet experience of leap-frogging from a primitive pastoral and agricultural nation to a position, envied by the very Capitalist West which was in its hot pursuit ever since its inception, through the planned and systematic use of science was a great vicarious learning experience for the Third World.

No wonder President Reagan called the Soviet Union *'Evil Empire'*.

PART 2

WW II RENEWED ONSLAUGHT ON THE WELFARE STATE

> 'If we see that Germany is winning we ought to help Russia and if Russia is winning we ought to help Germany and that way let them kill as many as possible, although I don't want to see Hitler victorious under any circumstances'.
> – **President Harry S Truman**

> In World War II the USSR lost 1 in 7 of its citizens, the UK lost one in 127 and the USA lost one in 320'.
> – **Vladimir Putin**

---

[7] Harry S Truman then a Senator from Missouri stated on the floor of the Congress on 23rd June 1941 a day after Nazi Germany launched an attack on the Soviet Union.

Chapter 3: Adolf Hitler: A Darling to the Western Capital...

Bankrolled him to the Chancellorship of Germany to take on the Soviet Union

> "If land was desired in Europe, it could be obtained by and large only at the expense of Russia, and this meant that the new Reich must again set itself on the march along the road of the Teutonic Knights of old, to obtain by the German sword sod for the German plow and daily bread for the nation. For such a policy there was but one ally in Europe: England".
>
> **– Adolf Hitler, Mein Kempf**

> 'We regard the agreement signed last night and the Anglo-German Naval Agreement as symbolic of the desire of our two peoples never to go to war with one another again. We are resolved that the method of consultation shall be the method adopted to deal with any other questions that may concern our two countries and we are determined to continue our efforts to remove possible sources of difference and thus contribute to assuring the peace of Europe'.
>
> **– From the Anglo-German declaration signed by British Prime Minister Neville Chamberlin and Hitler the day after the Munich Pact (30th September 1938)**

Conventional scholarship on the events leading up to WW II had been that Hitler was a maniac bent on world domination and sought to take revenge for the Treaty of Versailles which imposed on the Germans untold miseries and national humiliation and that the European powers who were weary of another World War chose to appease Hitler. The non-aggression pact Nazi Germany inked with the Soviet Union on 23rd August 1939, paved the way for the German invasion of Poland on 1st September 1939, and the start of WW II. As Hitler's troops marched into Poland from the West, the opportunistic Stalin who was in league with Hitler and buoyed by the pact inked a week ago attacked Poland in its hour of crisis from the East. As per the secret protocols contained in the pact Stalin together with Hitler set about redrawing the map of Europe. German troops rammed through the Central, East and Nordic Europe. While Stalin annexed Finland, Latvia, Lithuania and Estonia. Germany after neutralising France to its West attacked its own ally Soviet Union on 22nd June 1941, which sent shock waves in Kremlin as that was the unkindest cut of all.

Except that it wasn't.

Why was 1st September 1939, the day Germany invaded Poland, chosen as the day on which WW II began? Why was 12th March 1938, the day Hitler invaded Austria, forbidden by the Treaty of Versailles, not reckoned as the beginning of the Second World War? Or 15th March 1939, the day Hitler invaded Czechoslovakia in its entirety in violation of the Munich Pact? Why was 7th July 1937, the day Japan invaded China not reckoned as the date WW II began? 1st September 1939, was chosen by historians for the sole purpose of implying that the German-Soviet non-aggression pact inked the previous week on 23rd August 1939 was the precursor to the war. The German aggression of Poland from the West is often pitted against the Red Army's march into Poland from the East. Poland, a belligerent state in the inter-war period is painted as the victim at the hands of Hitler and Stalin as it serves the twin purpose of demonizing Stalin and absolving the western leaders of collaborating with Hitler in his onslaught against the Second Polish Republic. In fact, the Red Army marched into Poland to reclaim territory it had lost in the 1920 Russo-Polish War. By the time the Red Army entered Poland on 17th September the entire Polish leadership had fled from Poland and taken refuge in Romania. England and France had vowed to protect the sovereignty of Poland but did nothing towards this end except a declaration of war against Germany. Paying lip service!

Weary of Another War?

The European powers were never weary of another war. The armies of capitalist countries never betrayed any sign of weariness in the 1930s. Even before Germany had capitulated, the allies had taken upon themselves the task of liquidating the nascent socialist Republic of Russia in March 1918. After the abject surrender and dismemberment of Germany, the allies unleashed the full fury of their armies on that budding Republic. The armies of the capitalist countries were also fighting resistance movements in their colonies. In the post-WW II era of decolonisation, the French sought to retain their colonial possessions in the Indochina and towards this end they were ready to shed blood. In 1950 an attempt to unite Korea which came to be divided at the 38th parallel during WW II witnessed the mobilization of a 16-member coalition force. Then came *Vietnam* No sooner had the Cold War ended, the US opened a new front in the Gulf. The US had no qualms of opening a warfront in Afghanistan even before the Iraqi question had been settled. Armies of capitalist countries as it is even today are in a perpetual state of readiness to be pressed into service at short notice and shall be so in the foreseeable future.

Appease a Thoroughly Devastated and Dismembered Germany?

The Treaty of Versailles had relegated Germany to an underdog and coupled with the reparations it was required to pay, It was reeling under the worst crisis in its entire history. The high rate of inflation nearly paralysed Germany. The fact that it was being dictated the terms of a treaty to which it was not even a party was a matter of national humiliation! In addition to the treaty's harsh treatment of the German military, it had a crippling effect on the economy. The Great Depression was the last nail in the coffin of that pulverized nation. The Treaty had almost dismembered Germany. The victors had instituted inspection teams to religiously monitor and report on any minor violation of the Treaty. Such were the prohibitive provisions of the Treaty, that the native industry was relocated to neighbouring countries.

> **The Western powers preferred to pact with Hitler while the Soviet Foreign Ministers Litvinov and later Molotov were pleading with them to form an alliance against Nazi Germany**
>
> Four-Power Pact (Germany-Italy-Britain-France) (15th July 1933)
>
> Poland-Germany non-aggression pact (5th May 1934)
>
> Anglo-German Naval Pact (18th June 1935)
>
> Munich Pact (30th September 1938)
>
> Anglo-German Declaration (30th September 1938)
>
> Franco-German non-aggression pact (6th December 1938)
>
> Latvia-Germany non-aggression pact (7th June 1939)
>
> Estonia-Germany non-aggression pact (7th June 1939)
>
> Lithuania-Germany non-aggression pact (22th March 1939)
>
> Norway-German non-aggression pact (31st May 1939)
>
> Denmark-German non-aggression pact (31st May 1939)

It Was Never Appeasement. It Was Outright Collaboration.

Hitler was appointed Chancellor of Germany on 30th January 1933. On 22nd March, fifty days after his coming to power, Hitler established the first concentration camp in Dachau. The West chose to ignore it. 1933 marks the last year the Treaty of Versailles remained operative. In 1934, less than a year after Hitler's ascension to power, Germany was admitted to the League of Nations. Throughout the 1920s and 1930s British politics was dominated by Right Wing Conservatives. The Soviet Union was making giant strides in every walk of life while the capitalist nations with all their colonial possessions in the continents of Africa and Asia under their kitty were thoroughly famished by the depression. The Soviet model stood vindicated. Even in the US and Britain, there developed a consensus that the government should have a decisive say in the working of the economy. In the US it was New Deal time. The tide of history had turned left. The soldiers who returned from the front were jobless. That was when the first Red Scare engulfed the West. The spectre of communism that was being realized in Russia in all probability had a chance of finding material expression in the western hemisphere. It alarmed the propertied right wing. The right-wing British establishment considered Germany as the lesser of the two evils. Britain sought to use Germany as a bulwark against the rising tide of Bolshevism in Europe. Many British Conservative politicians including former Prime Ministers were hosted by Hitler. Hitler in just two years of his coming to power had cultivated considerable social capital in the conservative political establishment that Britain was to take the lead in arming Nazi Germany to the teeth. Hitler's anti-Jewish pogrom was glossed over. Hitler was being propped up to liquidate the Soviet Union in its entirety, a task that the capitalist powers had tried in the aftermath of WW I, a decade earlier.

---

[8] Henry Ford was awarded the Grand Cross of the German Eagle on 30th July 1938 on his 75th birthday by Adolf Hitler.

1935 Anglo-German Naval Pact and the German Rearmament

On 16th March 1935 Hitler announced massive rearmament. In June 1935, Britain entered a Naval Pact with Germany. By the pact, Germany could discard the prohibitive restrictions placed on its Navy by the allies in the Treaty of Versailles. The British did not even consult France or Italy, let alone take their consent or take them into confidence, prior to inking the deal with Germany. German Navy in violation of the Treaty of Versailles was restored with British connivance. Buoyed by the British support and goodwill Hitler started violating the provisions of the Treaty of Versailles with impunity.

Germany started to build submarines, U boats and torpedoes. It Introduced conscription beefing up the German army Wehrmacht close to a million in clear violation of the Treaty of Versailles that had restricted the German army to 1 lakh. Germany initiated production of Tanks, armoured vehicles, arms and ammunition at an unprecedented scale and built the German air force Luftwaffe from scratch to outnumber the combined fleet strength of Britain and France. The Versailles Treaty had restricted Germany from having an air force

So massive was the scale of re-armament that the economy was jump-started from the depths of the depression to a path of recovery. Germany was the second country after Japan and the first in Europe to emerge out of the Great Depression.

France which had to face the brunt of the German army in WW I had sufficient reasons to be alarmed. Her overtures to Britain were snubbed. Britain even dithered in entering an alliance with France in the event of a war with Germany. Such was the British collaboration with Nazi Germany that France, an ally of Britain reached out to the Soviet Union, which it despised, in 1935 and inked a treaty of mutual assistance. In the event of an attack on France by Germany, the treaty mandated the Russians to declare war on Germany. French felt the Germans could not afford a war on two fronts and that the treaty would deter Germany from any military adventurism.

7th March 1936: Re-militarization of the Rhine

German divisions occupied Rhine land, a territory bordering France that was demilitarized by the Treaty of Versailles. The outright violation of the Versailles and Locarno treaties went uncontested by the international community.

12th March 1938: Anschluss

The Treaty of Versailles prohibited the annexation of Austria. But, on 12th March 1938 Hitler invaded Austria and annexed it to Germany (A majority of Austrians were in favour of it and Hitler himself was an Austrian).

30th September 1938: Munich Pact aka Munich Betrayal

Following the annexation of Austria, Hitler turned his attention to the Sudetenland, the industrial heartland of Czechoslovakia. Hitler, unlike Austria had never claimed Czechoslovakia until then. The pretext was that the province had a substantial German population and hence should be handed over to Germany. It was the first time Hitler had raised a claim for a piece of territory that was never a part of Germany.

The Czechs wanted to fight but wanted an assurance from France and Britain that they would come to her aid as was formally agreed upon. It had Europe's second-strongest defensive line facing the German border. Czechs had a well-trained, well-equipped army, an equally modern and robust armament industry and a vibrant economy. In short, Czechoslovakia was a formidable enemy of Nazi Germany in its own might. With Anglo-French support the Czechs were confident that the Nazi onslaught could be checked. In retrospect, it appears to be true. In the Nuremberg trials of war criminals Field Marshall Keitel was asked if Czechoslovakia would have been attacked had the western nations come to Prague's rescue. He said, *'No. We were not that strong from a military perspective'*.

In the 1930s the continent of Europe was filled with right-wing fascist governments. Britain, France and Czechoslovakia were the rare examples of Parliamentary democracies that stood out. Britain and France were allies of Czechoslovakia and were bound to help the tiny country which was politically very similar to them. But the fate of Czechoslovakia was doomed since the day Hitler aired his claim over the *'Sudeten'* part of it. The western colonial powers were determined to direct Hitler's ambitions towards the East. The British Prime Minister Chamberlain went to Munich with the plan of giving Hitler what he wanted and then send him to the East. The two western powers Britain and France preferred to betray Czechoslovakia and enter into league with Nazis towards its dismemberment.

Great Britain, the USA, Italy and Germany signed the egregious Munich Pact on 30th September 1938. The government of Czechoslovakia was not invited. The Czechs referred to the Pact: *'About us without Us'.* The USSR was not invited to the Munich deliberations. The British Prime Minister Chamberlain referred to the treaty as the *'Peace of our time'.* Chamberlin inked a separate treaty with Hitler the following day of the Munich Pact. The Anglo-German declaration in the context of the Munich Pact was a clear indication to accommodate Hitler and pit him against the Soviets to the East.

The argument that France and Britain chose to appease Hitler and avoid war is not tenable. To accede to Hitler's demand and to hand over Sudetenland with 3 million people and a huge amount of industry amounted to arming Hitler. The argument that Britain and France hoped to appease Hitler whom they had let to re-arm to megalomaniac proportions by ceding an industrial belt in Czechoslovakia flies at the face of it. The Munich Conference utterly destroyed Czechoslovakia as a fighting force. All her major defensive lines as well as almost 90 percent of all her industries were lost to the Nazis by the pact.

March 1939

Five months after the Munich Pact German army divisions occupied the country in its entirety in violation of the Munich Pact. Czechoslovakia was wiped off the World Map. Surprisingly, the West did not express disapproval of this blatant breach of an international agreement.

Stalin Was The Last to Pact With Hitler

> 'With the pact, Soviet Union warded off a united capitalist attack on it'.
>
> – **Winston Churchill**

> 'What did we gain by concluding a non-aggression pact with Germany? We ensured a country a state of peace for a year and a half and the possibility of preparing our forces to fight back if Nazi Germany risked attacking our country contrary to the pact'.
>
> – **Joseph Stalin**

Whenever an idea becomes formidable to contest an attempt is made to misrepresent the same and discredit it. Western historians often draw an inaccurate parallel between Stalin and Hitler. The non-aggression pact inked between Nazi Germany and the Soviet Union, on the eve of World War II, the secret protocols for carving out spheres of influence, the *'well-timed'* attack on Poland from West and East by Nazi Germany and Soviet Union followed by slicing that sovereign nation between them form a convincing narrative towards this end. The intent is to hint if not establish, that the Soviet Union was as evil as the Nazi Third Reich and therefore equally condemnable. This blurs the uncritical and impressionable mind.

It also absolves the western powers of collaborating with Hitler to take on the Soviet Union and turning a blind eye on the extermination of the Jews on an industrial scale which the Fuhrer embarked on within weeks of coming to power. Ironically, the Soviet Union's repeated overtures towards the West in forging a collective security alliance against Germany until the eleventh hour and the West's consistent rebuttal hardly find any mention in this western narrative which is the staple diet even for the historians of the very Third World, whose cause the Soviet Union always championed. The Anglo-French betrayal of its own allies Czechoslovakia and Poland in the face of German aggression stands carpeted in this narrative.

The Context of the Nazi-German Non-Aggression Pact

> *'Chamberlain and Daladier had gone to Munich. Whom did we get here? Admiral nobody'*
>
> – **Joseph Stalin**

Munich marked the beginning of Hitler annexing a territory that was never a part of Germany or not taken away from it by the Treaty of Versailles. The connivance of the West in aiding and abetting this annexation of its ally Czechoslovakia by its *'arch-rival'* Nazi Germany alarmed the Soviet Union. Stalin was perturbed that the USSR was excluded from the deliberations leading to the Munich Pact inked on 30th September 1938 by Great Britain, France, Italy and Germany which authorized the transfer of Sudetenland of Czechoslovakia to Germany. The Soviet Union wanted to intervene on behalf of the Czechs as the Eastward march of Hitler had to be stopped at the earliest and as farthest as possible from its own borders. Poland refused passage to the Red Army to come to the aid of the Czechs. Thanks to the Munich Pact Poland too got a slice of Czechoslovakia. Poland was to pay dearly for its opportunism. The Munich betrayal convinced the Soviet Union that the West would forsake its commitments to its Eastern allies without any qualm. The subsequent dismemberment of Czechoslovakia in its entirety in March 1939 confirmed Stalin's fears. The League of Nations had become defunct. Lenin had forewarned that the League was a unification *'on paper only; in reality, it is a group of beasts of prey, who only fight one another and do not at all trust one another'*. Lenin was right. The 1931 Japanese invasion of Manchuria and the 1935 Italian invasion of Abyssinia (Ethiopia) went unchecked. Japan and Italy had violated the territorial integrity of two-member states of the League. The USSR was convinced that the League of Nations did not have the teeth to ensure world peace.

The western betrayal was symptomatic of the animosity that the West harboured towards the Soviet Union since the failed external aggression on the young Republic. It was becoming apparent to the Soviet leadership that Hitler was just an instrument in the hands of western Capital to take to its logical conclusion the West's unfinished agenda: The liquidation of the Soviet Union. With the Munich Pact, the die was cast. The shape of the *'Iron Curtain'* in this part of the European theatre was pretty much decided by the betrayal at Munich. From that point on, no force on earth could stop Adolf Hitler till the Red Army checkmated the Nazis at Stalingrad in 1943.

Hitler's expansion to secure *'lebensraum'* or living space for the *'superior'* German race was primarily to the East of Germany. He was keen on invading the rice fields of Ukraine and the oil fields of Baku. Since the rise of Hitler in Germany in 1933, Stalin, fearful of a German onslaught had been making overtures towards the West in forming a collective security to contain Nazi Germany. With the signing of the Anti-Comintern Pact by Nazi Germany and Japan in 1936 it became apparent that an invasion from the East and the West was imminent. In the words of Soviet Foreign Minister Litvinov, *'It can scarcely be doubted that in the present international situation no war wherever it may break out can be localized and no country can be certain that it will not be drawn into the war once it has begun. The*

Soviet Union is therefore interested not only in its own peaceful relations with other states but in the maintenance of peace generally'. The Soviet Foreign Ministers, Litvinov and later his successor Molotov, reached out to the West for a military pact. Signalling the possibility of a two-front war in the event of any military adventurism from Nazi Germany towards it was to deter Germany. Great Britain and France were dilly-dallying with the prospect of inking a pact with the Soviet Union even though Hitler made it no secret that he was on the verge of invading Poland. He had by then invaded Austria and Czechoslovakia and wiped out the two countries from the map. He was amassing his troops close to the Polish border. Far-right sympathies prevailed in the British Cabinet which led to a myopic cold-shouldering of the sincere Soviet overtures.

1939 had been a difficult year for the Soviet Union. The nation that extended from Europe to Asia was facing an existential threat from Germany from the West and a belligerent Japan in the East. The Japanese threat from the East was formidable. The disastrous war with the island nation in 1905 left nothing for the Russians to be complacent about. Occasional skirmishes between the two nations escalated into a full-scale war in 1939. Besieged by hostile nations to which it had conceded humiliating defeats and loss of territory in the recent past, the Soviet Union desperately wanted an alliance with the West.

The popular opinion in Britain was that she should form an alliance with the Soviet Union. The general wisdom was that Germany could not afford a two-front war. Shaping a two-front coalition against Hitler in 1939 seemed to be the only option to stop him.[9] The French population was also in favour of such an alliance. The Press in both countries were upbeat about an alliance with the Soviet Union. British Prime Minister Neville Chamberlain and French Prime Minister Eduard Daladier finally reached out to Moscow.

---

[9] In the national polls in June 1939 conducted by the British Institute of Public Opinion, 86% of the British favoured an Anglo-French-Soviet military alliance to contain Germany.

The British Prime Minister Neville Chamberlain, an aristocrat despised the Soviet Union. He was instinctively hostile to the USSR for ideological reasons. Daladier, who served as the French Prime Minister from 1938 to 1940, was keen on a pact with the Soviet Union. This interest in a pact with the Soviet Union arose from France's growing concern about Nazi Germany's aggressive expansionism and the threat it posed to Europe's security. The country had entered a Mutual Assistance Pact with USSR in 1935 alarmed at the Anglo-German Pact. But as fate would have it the British government was determined to undermine the verdict of their own people.

From 15th June to 2nd August 1939, the British, French, and Soviet representatives gathered in Moscow to discuss the formation of an alliance. It took two months of arguments to agree in principle that all three powers would give each other and any state bordering Germany (Estonia, Latvia, Lithuania, Poland, Romania, Turkey, Greece and Belgium) a guarantee of military help in case of German aggression. Meanwhile, Hitler continued to amass his troops along the Polish border, and war seemed imminent.

The diplomatic discussions ended on the 2nd August, and were to be followed by discussions between the military missions of the three countries in Moscow. Although air travel was common in those days, the Anglo-French team came by a slow-moving merchant ship. The French and the English military missions departed Tilbury on 5th August and arrived in Leningrad on 9th August. This lack of a sense of urgency from the Anglo-French was symptomatic of their approach to the forthcoming negotiations. The talks began only 3 days later, on 12th August. The Russians discovered that Admiral Drax, the leader of the British delegation, had no protocol papers authorizing him to negotiate with the Soviet Union. It was clear that the British delegates would not be able to make any decisions on the spot and would have to refer everything back to London. The French delegation, on the other hand, did have the power to negotiate on all military questions but was not authorized to sign any agreement with the Soviets. The Soviet Union was represented at the negotiations by none other than the Soviet Minister of Defence Marshal Kliment Voroshilov himself, Stalin's close associate. It appeared to Moscow that London and Paris never wanted a military alliance with them and were manoeuvring the USSR into a war with Germany, while Britain and France stood on the sidelines. The Soviet leadership felt snubbed by the prospect of negotiating with officials of no consequence. Moscow grew suspicious because, given the kind of insignificant posts they held, the members of the delegation could afford to be away from their countries for an indefinite period of time. The urgency of coming to a mutually agreeable actionable agenda and concluding a pact was visibly missing. Furthermore, Chamberlain was using the possibility of cooperation with the USSR as a means of putting pressure on Hitler and Mussolini to come to an agreement. Chamberlin could never contemplate a military pact with the Soviet Union.

The Soviet Union wanted to engage Nazi military might as close to Germany as possible, and on 14th August, Voroshilov put the question to the Anglo-French military mission: *'Would the Red Army be allowed to cross into Poland and Romania in the event of German aggression'*? However, the British and the French military missions were non-committal, stating that in the event of a war breaking out, Poland and Romania would invite the Soviets in. Moreover, these two countries being sovereign nations the Anglo-French military missions could not give an assurance on their behalf to the Soviets. They were of the view that Moscow should obtain such an assurance from these two sovereign nations. Voroshilov reiterated that since Poland and Romania were Anglo-French allies it was up to London and Paris to secure the right of passage to the Red Army through their territories. For the Russians, right of passage into Poland and Romania was contingent upon any treaty with the West as they viewed it was the benchmark of an effective military alliance and a sign of the West's seriousness about the formation of a military coalition against Hitler. Moscow was very clear about what it wanted from the West: A war-fighting coalition against Nazi Germany on its terms or no alliance at all. Given the animosity that existed between Moscow and the West ever since the allied attack following the revolution, Moscow insisted on very concrete and actionable measures. The largely fruitless attempts to forge security alliances with the West coincided with the West's warming towards Hitler during the previous five years ever since Hitler became the Chancellor. As a result, Moscow became precise in its demands. Quite understandably there was to be no retreat from this inflexible position, neither under the Soviet Foreign Minister Litvinov nor under his successor Molotov.

Stalin halted the discussions on 21st August as they were getting farcical. Two days later, on 23rd August, German Foreign Minister Joachim von Ribbentrop flew to Moscow. Thus, was born the Nazi Germany-Soviet Union Non-Aggression Pact. Stalin preferred a concrete deal with Hitler, rather than the continuation of farcical talks with London and Paris. Hitler wanted to ensure Soviet neutrality during the Polish campaign. Stalin on his part wanted to buy time. In Britain, the *Evening Standard* in the light of the prospects of a military alliance not getting anywhere hinted at the troubling prospect of a German-Soviet accommodation: *'We may yet see the German lion and the Russian lamb lie down together'.*

Russian 'Stab in the Back'

Stalin is often chastised for the conquest of the eastern province of Poland in accordance with the secret protocol. Russian troops entered Poland from the East only 16 days after the German onslaught from the West. By 17th September, the day Russian troops entered, it was clear the western European nations had deserted their ally to their East. Britain and France in spite of their declaration of war against Germany did not engage the German forces. By that time the entire military and political leadership of Poland had fled to Romania, abandoning its people, who continued to fight against the Nazi invaders. It is to be borne in mind that Russian troops occupied the territory it had lost to Poland in the 1920 war. Prominent British politician and statesman D. Lloyd George emphasized, *'The Russian armies occupied the territories that are not Polish and that were forcibly seized by Poland after the First World War ... It would be an act of criminal insanity to put the Russian advancement on a par with the German one'*. Fearful of a German onslaught Stalin wanted a strategic depth in the West with Nazi Germany. The territory restored should be viewed to be a buffer between Russia and Germany.

It should be borne in mind that Poland was a belligerent state and in the 1920 Russo-Polish war had annexed huge tracts of Russian land. It was in league with the 14-member US-led coalition that attacked Russia in the aftermath of the Bolshevik revolution. It was also the first European state to ink a pact with Nazi Germany as early as 1934. When Hitler invaded Czechoslovakia in March 1939, the Czechs wanted to fight and the USSR wanted to come in aid of its ally. However, Poland refused passage through its territory to Russian troops. It also prohibited flying rights to the Russian Air Force over its air space.

Secret Protocols to Carve Spheres of Influence

After the end of the WW I, a huge part of Europe had become fascist or pro-fascist or totalitarian, including Italy, Spain, Portugal, Hungary, Bulgaria, Romania, Yugoslavia and the Baltic States of Lithuania, Latvia and Estonia. The Treaty of Versailles had created numerous conflicts and tensions, as the borders of the new nations were randomly set by the victors. The USA too had its vision of a Europe, and President Woodrow Wilson had come to Versailles with a book of recommendations. French Marshal Ferdinand Foch who served as the Supreme Allied Commander gave a prophetic description of that Treaty: *'This is not peace. It is an armistice for twenty years'*.

Given the circumstances, Stalin was obsessed with building a line of buffer states to ensure that the mainland Russia did not fall to the aggressor. For this purpose, he wanted Russian garrisons in Latvia, Lithuania, Estonia, Finland, Romania and Poland. Stalin's annexation of Latvia, Lithuania and Estonia should be seen in the light of Soviet Union's need to build buffer against Germany. After all the Baltic states had inked pacts with Nazi Germany and were in league with it.

Poland Paid The Price For Its Role In Munich Betrayal

'It was not that simple to get the consent from Great Britain and France in Munich on including in the agreement Poland's and Hungary's claims for Czechoslovakia as well'.

> **– From the record of Adolf Hitler's conversation with Jozef Beck, Foreign Minister of Poland dated 5th January 1939**

Poland paid the price for being an accomplice of Hitler during the Munich betrayal. Poland was supportive of the dismemberment of Czechoslovakia. At Munich, Poland's and Hungary's claims over Czechoslovakia too were entered in the Pact.

The French Premiere Daladier remarked, *'Not only can we not count on Poland's assistance, but we are also unsure whether Poland will not strike from behind'.* He asked whether the Poles would let Soviet troops through. The Polish envoy Lukashevich replied in the negative. Daladier then asked if they could let Soviet planes fly across the Polish skies, and he replied the Poles would fire at them.

After Nazi Germany annexed much of Czechoslovakia in the autumn of 1938, Hungarian forces (aided by Poland) swiftly overran the Carpathian Ukraine. In the same period, Poland and Hungary annexed Zaolzie, Southern Slovakia and Carpathian Ruthenia, in the autumn of 1938. Polish and German troops were fraternizing after the march. As German troops entered Czechoslovakia Polish troops entered Slovakia and occupied it.

The War with Finland (30th November 1939–12th March 1940)

Finland used to belong to the Russian Empire until the Bolshevik revolution. Lenin granted the right of self-determination to the national minorities including the right to secede. In December 1917 Finland availed itself of this opportunity and declared independence. The relationship between the two states was uneasy thereafter, necessitating a non-aggression pact in 1932.

Though the non-aggression pact with Germany was inked on 23rd August 1939, Stalin was convinced that a German attack was imminent. German troops had conquered Poland in September 1939. It was clear that it was only a question of when and not whether German troops marched into the Soviet Union. Stalin detested the Finnish leader Gustaf Mannerheim. Stalin distrusted the ambitious Hitler and was worried about a joint German-Finnish attack on Russia. He was very much concerned about the security of Leningrad in the face of a German advancement. Leningrad was the second biggest city of Soviet Union and a Naval base just 20 kilometres from the Finnish border. Russia requested Finland to cede some part of its territory bordering Leningrad to it in lieu of Russian territory elsewhere, very much consistent with the Russian need for strategic depth against Germany. It was to build a buffer in the event of an attack. The Fins flatly refused. While Hitler *'blitzkrieg-ed'* through Poland it was *'sitzkrieg'* on the western front. Beyond a declaration of war against Germany the Anglo-French troops did not engage the Germans. It was a phoney war. The Anglo-French reluctance to come to the aid of its own ally Poland in the wake of the German onslaught and the phoney war on the western front were sufficient reasons for the Soviet sense of insecurity.

The Soviet Union attacked Finland on 30th November 1939. Stalin feared British and French intervention on the behalf of Finland if the war prolonged. Sweden entered the war on the side of the Finns. It was a bloody war that the Russians managed to win at a huge human cost. It was embarrassing for Russia to be checkmated on various fronts by the heavily outnumbered Finnish soldiers. It was a heavy blow to the reputation of the Red Army and made it look like paper tigers before Hitler. Red Army was exposed. Probably this must have emboldened his resolve to take on the USSR. The war made Finland and Germany allies and Finnish soldiers joined German forces in the 1941 war and recovered all its lost territory.

Albert Einstein Knew the Space and Time He Cherished Was Lost For Ever and Would Never Return to Germany

As luck would have it, Albert Einstein (1879–1955) was safely at California Institute of Technology, Pasadena on a visiting Professorship when Hitler was appointed Chancellor of Germany on 30th January 1933. Soon Einstein's cottage in Berlin was raided under the pretext of harbouring communist weaponry, ransacked and converted into a Hitler youth camp. His books along with those of other Jewish scientists were burned in bonfires that were becoming common in Germany. His Berlin bank account was confiscated under the pretext of being used for treason. Einstein learned that he was on the list of prominent Jews to be executed. A leading Nazi publication ran an advertisement with his photo titled *'Not yet hanged'.* Even a price of $5000 was fixed for his head. To the fury of the Nazi leadership, he pre-empted them by resigning from the Prussian Academy and renouncing his German citizenship.

By April 1933 and within four months of Hitler's ascension to power, the Reich had declared that Jews, defined as anyone with one grandparent Jewish, could not hold an office under it. Fourteen Nobel laureates in science fled. Twenty-six of the sixty scientists in theoretical physics lost their jobs. Einstein started to lobby foreign Governments to find employment for many of the Jewish scientists who were on the run. Max Planck reached out to Hitler in an attempt to temper him down but was rebuked. *'Our national policies will not be revoked or modified even for scientists'* was the terse reply from the Fuhrer. Such was his hatred for the Jews, he told Max Planck whom he held in high respect, *'If the dismissal of Jewish scientists means the annihilation of contemporary German science then we shall do without science for a few years'.* In the war that followed Germany would pay dearly for its abhorrence of Jewish scientists, as Einstein had forewarned.

Einstein was often touted as a communist for his pacifist and anti-fascist leanings. Much to the chagrin of the anti-communists he refused to subscribe to the view that drew a parallel between Stalinist purges and the Nazi Holocaust. In all probability, he must have viewed the purge of the Trotskyists under Stalin as an aberration from the norm of the Soviet ideology and attributed it to the failings of a maniac leader, as against the systematic murder of Jews on an industrial scale as a matter of policy under the Nazis. *The Holocaust was systemic to the Nazi ideology.*

During his brief stay in England during the spring of 1933 Albert Einstein was on a political mission in London. Britain never had a law on refugees. He paid a visit to the House of Commons. His mission was to get a law in England passed, which would bring succour to the Jews fleeing Germany. Looking down from the Distinguished Visitors' Gallery of the House, Albert Einstein listened to a passionate speech by a dashing, upper-class, right-wing Conservative member of Parliament,

Commander Oliver Locker-Lampson under the Parliamentary 10-minute rule proposing a motion: *'That leave be given to bring in a bill to promote and extend opportunities of citizenship for Jews resident outside the British empire'.* The Conservative MP was Einstein's host in England. He stated, *'Germany has even turned upon her most glorious citizen – Einstein'.*

The bill was never passed into law. Had England been sympathetic to the Jews who were on the run, millions would not have died in the gas chambers. They were not even permitted into the British dominions in Africa or Asia. The deliberations in the House of Commons in granting asylum even for the few highly qualified Jews meandered into nothingness. British sympathy for the Jews was just a sham. Britain, like all other European nations of significance, had a cordial relationship with Hitler. The Government gave the appearance of helping the Jews while doing nothing at all.

Attempts to grant Einstein the citizenship of England came to nothing and he set sail for America on 7th October 1933 reaching New York harbour on the 17th.

Chapter 4: Hiroshima-Nagasaki: A Message to the Soviet Union

'Nuclear bombs shocked the Japanese into surrender. Except they did not'.

– **Ward Wilson, 'The Myth of Hiroshima'**

'The Japanese were ready to surrender and it was not necessary to strike them with that awful thing'

– **President Dwight D. Eisenhower**

'The dropping of the atomic bombs was not so much the last military act of the Second World War as the first major operation in the Cold War with Russia.'

– **P.M.S Blackett, Historian**

1943 was a decisive year in WW II. It was in this year that the unquestioned eastward march of the Nazis, that began in the year 1938 with the annexation of Austria, was at last checkmated by the Red Army at Stalingrad. On the Pacific front, Japan began to face a string of defeats. By the Spring of 1945, the Japanese Navy was obliterated. The B-52 bombers which criss-crossed Japan with bombing missions were virtually unchallenged by anti-aircraft gun fire. The now legendary *kamikaze* pilots were making a successful crash, one in five, as many of them were poorly trained. With very few aircraft left, Japanese resistance was ebbing down. The aerial bombardment and naval blockade had deprived the island nation of all imports which it was heavily dependent on. The Japanese population was virtually starving. Japan signalled its willingness to surrender in February 1945. Through intercepting diplomatic messages, US intelligence knew that a severely famished Japan in spite of its military would not have had the wherewithal to hold on beyond November 1945. With the fall of Berlin in May, US intelligence was aware that Japan was on the brink of surrender. After the Potsdam Declaration in July 1945 which called for *'unconditional surrender or face prompt and utter destruction'*, Japan had been courting the Soviet Union to mediate on its behalf to a much more amicable surrender. The Japanese ambassador to the USSR was attempting to persuade the Russians to broker a peace agreement with the allies. The Soviet Union was not at war with Japan as the two countries had a neutrality pact inked in 1941 which was valid until 1946.

What Delayed the Japanese Surrender?

But what delayed the surrender was the allies' insistence on an *'unconditional surrender'*. The Japanese were averse to an unconditional surrender which would mean even the Emperor Hirohito, whom the Japanese considered to be an incarnation of the Sun God, could be put on trial and be sent to the gallows. The Japanese insisted on retaining the imperial family but the West insisted on an unconditional surrender. The allies by insisting on an unconditional surrender which they knew the Japanese would never agree to were deliberately delaying the Japanese surrender and the end of the war so that they could drop the nuclear bombs that were being developed. Japan's rejection of the Potsdam Declaration that called for an unconditional surrender came as no surprise to the allies. It was known to the US that a change in the surrender terms with amnesty granted to the Emperor, as it eventually happened, would have ensured an immediate surrender of Japan. The US harping on the unconditional surrender was to prolong the war in the Pacific and provide justification for the use of the atomic bombs. The bombs were intended to be a message to the Soviets. Japanese intransigence could be played up to rationalize the use of bombs to *'put an early end to the war and avoid further loss of American lives'* that would have been lost in the impending land invasion of Japan in November 1945. The Battle of Okinawa, fought between the Japanese and the US-led coalition forces from 1st April to 22nd June, was the bloodiest battle in the Pacific theatre, resulting in the loss of thousands of American lives. It could have been avoided had the US responded to the Japanese overtures in early 1945. In retrospect, the bombs neither brought the war to an early end nor saved American lives. Instead, the bombs prolonged the war and more American lives were lost as the war continued to ravage on. The battle of Okinawa could have been avoided had the Japanese feelers were heeded.

Why Did Not The Supreme War Council Convene In The Aftermath of Hiroshima?

In Japan during World War II, the highest decision-making authority responsible for the conduct of the war was the six-member Supreme Council for the Direction of the War. In imperial Japan, Emperor Hirohito, was the ultimate decision-maker. Whenever the Supreme Council could not come to a decision or was in a deadlock, the Emperor stepped in. As on 6th August 1945, the day of the Hiroshima bombing, the Supreme Council for the Direction of the War was comprised of Prime Minister Admiral Kantaro Suzuki, Minister of Foreign Affairs Shigenori Togo, Minister of the Army General Korechika Anami, Minister of the Navy Admiral Mitsumasa Yonai, Chief of the Army General Staff General Yoshijiro Umezu and Chief of the Navy General Staff Admiral Soemu Toyoda.

The first atomic bomb blast over Hiroshima had little impact on the Supreme Council. The Council did not convene in the wake of Hiroshima. Most Japanese cities were pulverized by the B-29 bombers and Hiroshima was just one more. The Japanese were pretty complacent as the long-term radiological effects were unknown to the world then. Japan had its own nuclear programme, and the leadership was aware of how difficult it would be to develop such a weapon. They speculated that the United States would not possess many atomic bombs, and the Japanese were correct. Although the second bombing occurred in Nagasaki on 9th August, a third bomb would not have been ready until 19th August, and a fourth bomb not until late September.

Sequence of Events

6th August: HIROSHIMA.

7th August: Soviet Union unilaterally abrogates the non-aggression pact with Japan.

9th August: Russian troops enter Manchuria.

In Japan the Emperor convenes the Supreme Council for the Direction of War to consider surrender in the wake of the Soviet attack on Manchuria. The loss of Manchuria will cut off all supplies of fuel, food, iron, steel.

As the meeting progresses the news that Nagasaki was bombed reaches the council which is in session.

The war council deliberates mostly on the Manchurian invasion and its possible fallout. The meeting is indecisive in spite of Hiroshima and Nagasaki.

Hiroshima Was Not Decisive.

Total 68 cities bombed in the summer of 1945. 26 Japanese cities had been bombed into oblivion 3 weeks prior to Hiroshima by conventional bombing. In human casualties Hiroshima was second, Tokyo was the first. In terms of square miles destroyed, Hiroshima was the 6th. In terms of percentage of square miles destroyed, Hiroshima was the 17th. City of Toyama was 99.5 percent bombed.

Fear of Soviet Invasion of Japan and the Japanese Surrender

Japan and the Soviet Union had a turbulent relationship ever since the days of the Tsar. The tension between the two countries persisted even after the communist takeover of Russia. Japan was also part of the multinational external armed aggression in the wake of the Bolshevik Revolution. Japanese troops were the last to back out from Russia. Though the US and the European troops had withdrawn from the attempted invasion by around 1922, it was not until 1925 that the last of the Japanese contingent was pushed off the Sakhalin islands.

In 1939, Japan attempted an invasion of the Soviet Union. However, the belligerent Japan suffered severe setbacks at the hands of the Red Army and peace had to be concluded on Russian terms. Japan was forced to ink a non-aggression pact with the Soviet Union in 1941 which was valid until 1946. The pact was thrust upon a belligerent Japan which suffered reverses. In the aftermath of the Pearl Harbour bombing on 7th December 1941, and the US declaration of war against Japan the next day, peace with the Soviet Union was an absolute must for Japanese prospects in the Pacific. *'The absolute maintenance of peace in our relations with the Soviet Union is one of the fundamental conditions for continuing the war'*, summarises the Japanese line of thinking. The pact inked with the USSR under duress proved to be a blessing in disguise. Adding another superpower to the war would have made the situation hopeless. Japanese leadership contended that *'Soviet entry would determine the fate of the Empire'*.

At the Yalta conference, from 4th –11th February 1945 Stalin had promised to enter in the war against Japan in the Far East within 3 months of the conclusion of the War in Europe. Germany surrendered on 8th May 1945, thus virtually ending the European theatre of war. It took exactly three months, as Stalin had calculated to transfer the Russian troops and the war machinery from the European front in the West to the Eastern Front in the Pacific. Unilaterally abrogating the non-aggression pact with Japan, the

Soviet Union entered the war against Japan on 9th August exactly three months after the German surrender. The Red Army attacked Japanese occupying forces in Manchuria. Soviet Army had a 5 to 1 superiority over the Japanese occupation army in Manchuria. Manchuria sourced all the fuel, iron, steel and coal for the Japanese war efforts. Japan, a nation poor in natural resources, was heavily dependent on Manchuria.

Soviet Entry into the War and the Urgent Session of the Supreme War Council.

> 'Since Tokyo was not directly affected by the bombing the full force of the shock was not felt... In comparison the Soviet entry into the war was a great shock when it actually came...it gave us all the more severe shock and alarm because we had been in constant fear that the Red Army forces in Europe were now being turned against us'.
>
> – **Twarashiro Kwabe, Japanese Army General Staff**

> 'The atomic bomb was a golden opportunity given by heaven for Japan to end the war. There were those who said that the Japanese armed forces were not defeated. It is in science that Japan was defeated, so the military will not bring shame on themselves by surrendering'.
>
> – **Hisatsune Sakomizu, Japanese Chief Cabinet Secretary**

The news of the Soviet offensive on 9th August midnight sent shock waves among the Japanese leadership. Peace with the Soviet Union was essential for the Japanese. An urgent session of the Supreme Council was convened on 9th August in the wake of the Soviet aggression. The council was still in session when word of the Nagasaki bomb was received.

It made no impact on the deliberations of the Supreme Council. It is to be noted that the Supreme Council was convened 72 hours after the Hiroshima bombing, and it was the Soviet Union's entry into the war that necessitated the convening of the council. The Supreme Council believed that the two nuclear bombings were no more menacing than the months of firebombing Japan had experienced and was in no haste to surrender unconditionally. The only thing that mattered was the Russian offensive. After repeated sessions on 9th August the Supreme Council dispersed without coming to a decision to surrender. The full scope of the Soviet invasion was not yet clear and so the council remained indecisive on the question of surrender. The Emperor Hirohito, knew with the Russian offensive in Manchuria that his time was up. With the Soviets marching into Manchuria it was only a question of when and not whether. As the Supreme Council was deadlocked over the question of surrender, Hirohito, expressed his willingness to surrender to the Supreme Council. It would take a couple of days before the Japanese truly came to terms with the Manchurian reality. The battle-hardy Red Army cut through the Japanese Kwantung Army like butter, stopping only when the Soviet fuel supply couldn't keep pace with the tanks crushing through the Japanese defences. In Manchuria and Sakhalin Islands the Kwantung army proved no match for the Red Army.

The Japanese were expecting 'Operation Downfall', the US invasion, could begin only by November 1945. Japanese garrisons were positioned on the southernmost island of Kyushu as it was widely believed to be the site of the American landing. US invasion 'Operation Downfall' was to be made from the Japanese island of Okinawa which the US forces occupied after one of the bloodiest fights in the Pacific theatre. Okinawa was 500 kilometres away from Kyushu. The northern and western parts of Japan were not guarded. In all probability, the Soviet Army was poised to enter Japan from the north in Hokkaido in August. It had conquered Sakhalin islands and was just 21 kilometres from Hokkaido.

With the Red Army poised to land on the Japanese mainland the Japanese leadership preferred a surrender to the US instead and made frantic efforts towards this end. They were convinced that they would be better off under the US occupation than a Soviet one. Similar to Germany, where top Nazi officials and scientists fled from the East to the West to surrender to the US-led allied forces rather than the Soviets, the Japanese leadership also preferred to surrender to the US forces. They expected the terms of surrender would be more amicable. The Emperor favoured an occupation by the US over the USSR as it offered a slim chance of retaining the Monarchy and religion which was unthinkable under a communist occupation. It was widely held that a US occupation would be less harsh on Japanese leadership than a Soviet one. But for the total surrender of Japan to the US, the Russian invasion from Hokkaido and the US invasion from Kyushu could have divided Japan into a communist North and a *'democratic'* and *'western-style'* South. Like Vietnam! Like Korea!

By 15th August, the Japanese Emperor radioed his willingness for an *'unconditional surrender'*. In his address to the nation, Hirohito announced surrender mentioning a *'new and most cruel bomb'*. It appeared to be less humiliating to surrender in the wake of a new miracle weapon that was invented during the course of the war. A scientific breakthrough, none could have predicted at the beginning of the war, seemed to absolve the Emperor of having led his country into a disastrous war. For the Japanese leadership surrender in the wake of nuclear weapons was a clever pretext as it was less embarrassing for them. It suited the US interests as well. Though the surrender was unconditional, it became apparent that behind closed doors, an agreement was reached to spare the Emperor from an impending trial, a decision that if taken earlier could have avoided the Okinawa invasion in which thousands of American soldiers perished.

American Duplicity

Why were the bombs dropped in August if the invasion was planned in November?

Because the Russians were coming…

Given the way, the negotiations over Central and Eastern Europe, which were occupied by Red Army, were progressing, Americans wanted the Soviet Union to be kept out of the Japanese question. After the bomb was tested on 16th July 1945, a day before the Potsdam conference began, Truman was in a hurry. The US wanted the Soviets to attack Japanese-occupied Manchuria in China and destabilize Japan to hasten its surrender but never wanted Stalin at the negotiation table in the event of a Japanese surrender. Towards this end, Truman insisted that Stalin should not be a signatory to the Potsdam declaration calling for unconditional surrender citing the technicality that the USSR was not at war with Japan at that point in time (Interestingly Chiang Kaishek of China was a signatory along with Truman and Prime Minister Clement Attlee). That Soviet Union was not at war with Japan was a triviality. The real compelling reason behind Truman's insistence on the hyped-up diplomatic niceties during war-time was just to ensure that the eventual Japanese surrender as a response to the Potsdam declaration before the allies would never be construed as a surrender before the Soviet Union as well. In short, Americans wanted the Red Army to pounce on Japanese-held Manchuria for that would diminish the will of the Japanese to hold on thereby accelerating its surrender, but never wanted the Soviets to have a say in post-war Japan. As things unfolded, the Soviet Union did not have a say in post-war Japan.

Conclusion

The USSR had emerged from the War thrust on itself by the capitalist powers with its prestige enhanced. The Great Depression revealed the hollowness and fragility of the capitalist system. The period also witnessed the Soviet Union making giant strides in a command economy model. The previous two decades of the Great Depression and the war had brought the entire capitalist world into a command mode with the government taking over the economic sphere of life. The people were convinced about the benefits that would usher in, had the government followed an interventionist policy in the economic realm. The capitalist countries witnessed nearly full employment for the first time, and labour gained significant influence. Britain elected a Labour Prime Minister and socialist forces were on the ascendance across Europe. America witnessed the second Red Scare. The liberation movements of the colonies were looking towards the USSR as a beacon of hope. The Soviet model provided a convincing road map for progress for these former colonies.

The Soviet Union, until then an international pariah, was calling the shots on how post-war Europe should be like. Negotiations with Stalin at the Yalta and Potsdam conferences were excruciating for the American and the British entourage. The diplomatic payoff that the bombs ushered during negotiations with the Soviet Union, post Hiroshima-Nagasaki, was incalculable. Atomic power did endow a diplomatic edge for the US. The US could elbow Stalin out from Greece, Turkey and Iran. However, this advantage enjoyed by the Americans was short-lived.

If the US and Britain had responded to the Japanese overtures for surrender as early as February 1945, the battle of Okinawa in April–June 1945 could have been avoided. Instead, the US establishment prolonged the war by insisting on unconditional surrender. US intransigence was to make a case for the use of bombs to checkmate the rising Red tide. Thousands of the US troops lost their lives in the Okinawa battle. The heavy casualty of Okinawa is often cited as the pretext to justify the use of atomic bombs on the grounds that a land invasion of Japan would have cost many more American lives. However, in reality, the very battle could have been avoided.

In retrospect the bombs did not put an early end to the war; nor did they save American lives. Hiroshima fits very well into the fabric of lies on the embodiment of American invincibility that has attained mythical status.

Chapter 5: The Soviet Union Could Have Won the War All by Itself.

It Had to Fight Nazi Germany As Well As Its 'Allies'.

'It was a question only of sleeping, eating and not being cold. That was all'.

– Jean-Paul Sartre

'... we did not suffer defeat as early as 1939 only because about 110 French and British divisions stationed in the West against 23 German divisions during our war with Poland remained absolutely idle'.

– **General Alfred Jodl, Chief of the Operations Staff of the German armed forces high command stated to the Jury at Nuremberg.**

'Field Marshall Kietel, Would the Third Reich have attacked Czechoslovakia had the western nations come to Prague's rescue'

– **asked the jury at Nuremberg.**

'Never. We were not that strong from a military perspective'

– **Kietel replied.**

---

[10] Sartre was called up into the French army and was assigned to the meteorological unit. He completed the first volume of *Chemins de la* liberte and part of *Letre et le neant* in his army meteorological station in the war front.

[11] General Alfred Jodl and Field Marshall Wilhelm Keitel were found guilty on charges of conspiracy to commit crime against peace, planning, initiating, and waging wars of aggression war crimes and crimes against humanity at the Nuremberg trials and were hanged on 16th October 1946.

Operation Pike, February 1940: Anglo-French plan to attack the Soviet Union, even while the two countries were technically at war with Germany. It had to be called off as Hitler invaded France on 10th May 1940.

Operation Dynamo: Evacuation at Dunkirk from 26th May to 4th June 1940. In the Battle of France, 350,000 British troops stationed in France promptly evacuated without offering any resistance to the invading German forces. It was the largest evacuation in military history. German forces just fifteen kilometres from Dunkirk instead of obliterating the British forces halted for days letting them evacuate.

D Day, 6th June 1944: The delayed western front at Normandy: Ground offensive in western Europe began only five years after the start of the war in 1939. By that time, German troops were in full retreat from East Europe, chased out by the Red Army. The *'allies'* of the Soviet Union wanted to prevent the liberation of France by the advancing Red Army. They also gained a slice of Germany.

Operation Unthinkable, May 1945: A plan drawn on the orders of the British Prime Minister Winston Churchill as soon as the war in Europe had ended to attack the Soviet Union while US troops were still stationed in Europe.

Britain and France Betray Poland

In March 1939, when Hitler denounced the 1934 non-aggression pact with Poland, Britain and France made declarations to safeguard Poland's sovereignty. Hitler attacked Poland on 1st September 1939. England and France declared war on Germany on 3rd September. Poland's hope for help from its western allies was in vain. The British and French forces did not attack the German garrisons. It was only on 12th September, that the Anglo-French Supreme War Council gathered for the first time at Abbeville. During this meeting, the council swiftly decided to cease any offensive actions and instead focus on a *'defensive strategy'*. The Anglo-French allies decided to defend their border in case the Germans, during the invasion of Poland turned West to fight with the combined Anglo-French forces, although it was widely known that the Germans would not pursue such a course of action. British soldiers of the Expeditionary forces that had landed in France and French soldiers were seen hanging out in the Paris cafes. RAF dropped leaflets over Germany, cautioning against the perils of war.

Opening a western front which could have potentially saved Poland from total annihilation did not happen. Such an action could have halted Hitler's advance in Poland. This marked the start of the infamous Phoney War. Britain and France blatantly betrayed Poland despite being formally obliged to come to its rescue. All that occurred in the western Front was a minor offensive that was put on hold. In the sea, there were skirmishes with the German Navy.

Hitler could afford a blitzkrieg in the East as it was a sitzkrieg in the West. During the Nuremberg trials, western complicity with German aggression was unmasked. German generals explained their quick success in the East. The former chief of the operations staff of the German armed forces high command, General Alfred Jodl's admission to the jury points to outright collaboration of the western powers. The much-decorated German General Siegfried Westphal while deposing as a witness during the Nuremberg trials stated that if the French had attacked Germany from the west in September 1939, as the Germans invaded Poland in the east, the German army *'could only have held out for one or two weeks'*. A two-front war was a sure recipe for a German military catastrophe. The *'Western Betrayal'* convinced Stalin none would come to help in the event of a German onslaught to the East. Stalin was right.

British Collusion With Nazi Germany Even After The Declaration of War

James Lonsdale Bryams, known as an English associate of the British Foreign Secretary Lord Viscount Halifax and enjoying the full backing of the Secretary, reached out to Germany on behalf of Britain to broker a separate peace treaty with Germany in early 1940. As per the proposed treaty, Hitler was to proceed with his European campaign towards the East in return for leaving the British and French colonies in Asia and Africa. It was hoped Nazism and communism would fight each other and destroy one another leaving Britain the supreme power in Europe. Though the treaty never materialised, the sitzkrieg, Dunkirk evacuation with the tacit cooperation of Germany, the ill-fated flight of Hitler's deputy Rudolf Hess to Scotland prior to the German invasion of Soviet Union, widely believed to broker peace with Britain promising her a free hand in the Empire in return of a free hand for Germany in Europe, and the much delayed western front, all point collusion of the western allies with Nazi Germany.

Operation Pike: Anglo-French Plan to Attack The Soviet Union In 1940 During WW II

During the sitzkrieg in the western front when France and Great Britain were technically at war with Germany the two nations had plans to attack the USSR. Notes by Maurice Gamelin, the French Commander in Chief during WW II which were discovered by Soviets in post-war Germany, irrefutably proved that Anglo-French allies had planned in February 1940 to invade the Soviet Union.

According to the plan, by April, the oil production centres in the Caucasian towns of Baku, Batum and Grozny were to be attacked. The air raid was to be conducted by British and French pilots from bases in Iran, Turkey and Syria. It was believed that an oil shortage would cripple the Red Army, the Soviet Air Force, and Soviet collective farm machinery, potentially leading to widespread famine. In such turbulent conditions, it was planned to incite Muslims to revolt against Moscow. The objective was to facilitate the collapse of the Soviet Union, which had successfully thwarted German aggression through the non- aggression pact. Moscow was well aware of the Anglo-French plan. However the German invasion of France in May 1940 sabotaged the plan.

The Evacuation at Dunkirk: Hitler Lets The British Escape at Dunkirk

> 'My tanks were kept halted there for three days. If I had my way the English would not have got off so lightly. But my hands were tied by direct orders from Hitler himself'.
>
> **– Gerd von Rundstedt, German Field Marshall**

> 'Churchill was quite unable to appreciate the sporting spirit of which I had given proof by refraining from creating an irreparable breach between the British and ourselves. We did, indeed refrain from annihilating them at Dunkirk'.
>
> **– Adolf Hitler in 1945 as the allies were closing in on Berlin**

Hitler sought a formal peace treaty between Germany and the Anglo-French allies to secure his western flank before further advancing eastward. Following the invasion of Poland in September, Hitler extended an olive branch to Britain and France in October 1939, which the allies promptly rejected. However, the Norwegian campaign of Hitler in April 1940 forced the Anglo-French to intervene. Norway, a neutral country held immense strategic interest to both sides, given its proximity to Sweden, whose iron ore reserves were coveted by Hitler. The northern port of Narvic in Norway held immense importance as a transportation hub for Swedish iron ore for Germany making it strategically vital in potential Atlantic conflicts. Its significance was such that it provided the German Navy with a flank to operate in the Atlantic and engage Allied ships. However, the Allied intervention on behalf of Norway ultimately proved ineffective. This intervention during Hitler's Norwegian campaign played a role in pausing his eastward advance and redirecting his focus towards the allies in the west.

1st May 1940 marked the attack on France, coinciding with Winston Churchill assuming the Prime Ministership of Great Britain. Neville Chamberlain had to resign following the debacle at the Norwegian intervention. The Anglo-French defence line in the face of the German onslaught crumbled like a house of cards. The retreating British Expeditionary forces stationed in France and numbering around 350,000 found themselves cornered in and around the French port of Dunkirk. With the invading German army in close pursuit, the entire British Expeditionary Force in France was on the brink of annihilation, a scenario that would have likely led to British capitulation to German demands.

As fate would have it, at 12:45 p.m. on 24th May, Hitler ordered the German troops just 15 miles away from the port of Dunkirk to halt. The halt endured for three days. Code named 'Operation Dynamo', 350,000 allied soldiers mostly British could evacuate marking the largest evacuation till date. German Field Marshal Gerd von Rundstedt later deemed Hitler's decision to halt at Dunkirk as an "incredible blunder" in his memoirs. Some historians suggest that the German army was too stretched thin to confront the British Expeditionary Forces at Dunkirk. Another possible explanation is that German supply lines could not keep pace with the advancing army. Additionally, some attribute the decision to Hermann Göring, head of the German air force Luftwaffe, who failed to capitalize on the opportunity at Dunkirk. However, Hitler's own statements put to rest all such rationalizations revealing the tacit understanding between the West and Germany.

The Unnecessary Battle of Britain (10th July to 31st October 1940)

Winston Churchill had been critical of German rearmament. He had strongly opposed the Munich Pact and viewed it as a sign of weakness. In the House of Commons he stated, *'With our enormous Metropolis here, the greatest target in the world ... a valuable fat cow tied up to attract the beasts of prey...we are in a position...in which no other country in the world is at the present time'.* When Paris fell Churchill emphasized England's extreme geographical vulnerability to air attack. He reasoned that while Berlin was comfortably 600 miles away from the RAF bases, London was just 100 miles from the potential enemy bases. Hitler likely regarded Churchill's appointment as Chamberlain's replacement with great concern, given Churchill's reputation as a staunch defender of England and his readiness for war. This perception may have influenced Hitler's decision to wage the Battle of Britain over the skies, seeing an invasion of England as necessary to neutralize it before advancing further eastwards.

In retrospect, Battle of Britain might not have been necessary. Hitler could have consolidated his position, ignored Britain and focussed on his invasion of Soviet Union. British would have retreated to the island regrouped their depleted forces, and deliberated on their next steps.

The Delayed Western Front

Throughout the war western powers tried to double cross Soviet Union. Following Germany's attack on the USSR on 22nd June, 1941, Stalin repeatedly called for a second front in the West. He believed that only a two-front war could alleviate the pressure on the Soviet army. For Britain, opening a western front would have been a form of revenge for the devastating air raids conducted by the German Luftwaffe during the Battle of Britain. However, the western allies did not heed to Stalin's requests, and the battle of Britain remain unavenged. The Red Army bore the full brunt of the German war machinery. In 'Operation Barbarossa', the German invasion of the Soviet Union launched on 22nd June 1941, the Germans employed around 180 divisions. It consisted of 138 German divisions and 36 more from their allies (16 Finnish, 15 Rumanian divisions, 3 Italian, and 2 Slovakian and 8 Hungarian brigades). Germans put up a daunting 2000-mile front against Russia stretching from the Arctic to the Black Sea. The Eastern Front witnessed some of the fiercest battles of World War II. The battles of Stalingrad, Leningrad, Kursk, Warsaw and Berlin were unmatched by any other theatre of the war:

80 percent of the German casualties occurred in the East. US and Britain put together contributed close to 180 divisions, while the Soviet Union committed around 400 divisions, more than twice the number of divisions than the rest of the allies put together. Though Franklin D. Roosevelt did everything within his ambit to cause the Japanese to attack its Pacific fleet at its Naval base at Pearl Harbor (7th December 1941) and cry victim, a perfect pretext to enter the war on behalf of Britain, the European theatre of war had to wait till June 1944. While the fiercest battles were fought in East Europe, Britain and US troops were engaged in minor skirmishes with Rommel in the North African Desert to guard British oil supplies from the Mediterranean. The western allies established a western front in Normandy only as late as 6th June 1944 by which time the Germans were on the run chased out of Europe by the Red Army.

Operation Unthinkable: 1945 Plan to Invade The Soviet Union

In May as the war in Europe drew to close, the British Chief of Staffs Committee, acting on the orders of Prime Minister Winston Churchill, devised a plan to launch a surprise attack on the Red Army stationed in the newly liberated territories of Europe. The intention was to impose the will of the western allies on the Soviet Union regarding the type of government liberated countries would adopt. However the planners concluded that even with substantial assistance from the US, Britain stood no chance against the battle-hardy Red Army. The assessment signed by the Chief of Staff on 9th June 1945, stated, *'It would be beyond our power to win a quick but limited success and we would be committed to a protracted war against heavy odds'.* The Soviet leadership soon became aware of the plan and was put on high alert and made it known to Britain that it was privy to such a plan to wade away any pre-emptive strike on it.

Conclusion

President Harry S Truman's statement while he was still a Senator from Missouri on the floor of the Congress on 23rd June 1941, a day after Nazi Germany launched an attack on the Soviet Union, that the US should help the losing side with the aim of prolonging the conflict between the two and causing both to bleed to death, sums up the West's approach towards the war. During the war, the alliance forged between the western powers and Soviet Union was more rhetorical and clumsy than anything operational. The western allies, despite having a joint command among themselves, never established one with the Soviets. At times one would even wonder whether it was truly a world war. The Pearl Harbour bombing on 7th December 1941, which the US desperately was eyeing for and did everything within its capacity towards it to have a pretext to enter the war, was followed by the German declaration of war on the US on 11th December 1941. Instead of taking Nazi Germany head-on in Europe, the US preferred to play cat and mouse with the German troops elsewhere. In clear violation of the 'Trading with the enemy act of 1917' US Inc collusion with the Nazi Germany continued unabated. This unholy alliance of the US Inc with Nazi Germany which greatly augmented its firepower, continued even after American soldiers began fighting the Germans.

While the allies were keen on double-crossing the Soviet Union, it must be acknowledged the Soviet Union fully met its obligations to its allies and always offered assistance when the allies reached out. On 6th June 1944, as the Allied troops landed in Normandy, Stalin launched 'Operation Bagration' in Belarus. By carrying out a simultaneous large-scale operation a new front was opened relieving the Allied troops from facing the full brunt of the German war machinery in the West. This should be viewed in the context of West's adamance in not opening a western front in spite of appeals from Stalin for the same since 1941. Later as the European theatre of war drew to a close, Stalin in full accordance with the Yalta agreements, declared war on Japan on 7th August 1945 despite the non-aggression pact inked between two countries in 1941.

> 'By the middle of 1944, the enemy was expelled from virtually all of the Soviet territory. However, the enemy had to be finished off in its lair. And so the Red Army started its liberation mission in Europe. It saved entire nations from destruction and enslavement, and from the horror of the Holocaust. They were saved at the cost of hundreds of thousands of lives of Soviet soldiers'.
> **– Vladimir Putin In his article titled 'The Real Lessons of the 75th Anniversary of World War II'.**

PART 3

CONCESSIONS BY CAPITAL TO LABOUR

Warding off the Red Scare

'Dear Mr. President,

You have made yourself the Trustee for those in every country who seek to mend the evils of our condition by reasoned experiment within the framework of the existing social system. If you fail, rational change will be gravely prejudiced throughout the world, leaving orthodoxy and revolution to fight it out'.

– John Maynard Keynes in an open letter to President-elect Franklin D Roosevelt.

Chapter 6: Attempts of a Welfare State in the Capitalist West

'The Treaty includes no provision for the economic rehabilitation of Europe, – nothing to make the defeated Central Empires into good neighbours, nothing to stabilise the new States of Europe, nothing to reclaim Russia; nor does it promote in any way a compact of economic solidarity amongst the allies themselves; no arrangement was reached at Paris for restoring the disordered finances of France and Italy, or to adjust the systems of the Old World and the New'.

– John Maynard Keynes,
'The Economic Consequences of Peace'

'I have the gun in my hand. I kill Kings and Presidents first and next all capitalists'.

– Giuseppe Zangara during the trial of his assassination attempt on the President-elect Franklin D Roosevelt

What should have taken place at the Versailles Conference was a sincere effort to address the inherent contradictions of the capitalist system, which fuelled inter-imperialist rivalries leading to a devastating war, rather than solely focusing on punishing Germany as the defeated nation. Restoring Germany to its material prosperity would have been to Europe's advantage. However the provisions of the treaty were yet another manifestation of the greed of the capitalist powers finding material expression and legal sanctity. When the Great Depression set in during the late 1920s, individual countries failed to grapple with its implications or address the causative factors. Wresting out of the Great Depression required nations to come together under a cooperative framework. Isolationism was the recipe for a catastrophe. No country can sustain itself being an island in the economic sphere. It was essential to advocate for government spending to offset the austerity measures adopted by private capital. However, these calls for effective intervention fell to deaf ears, resulting in missed opportunities for meaningful action.

Until the Great Depression, the capitalist world largely adhered to the principles of Social Darwinism, believing that economic downturns were nature's way of weeding out inefficient and unfit firms leaving the arena to strong parent companies able to beget powerful offspring that were fit to survive competition. However the 1930s saw even powerful companies facing existential threat. The initial reaction was to resort to financial austerity. Italy and Germany witnessed the rise of fascist ideology. Under Hitler, Germany pursued aggressive rearmament, blatantly violating the Treaty of Versailles. Similarly, Japan adopted militarism as a strategy to overcome the economic crisis. Heavy government spending on militarization enabled Germany and Japan to emerge from the depression faster than other nations, achieving near full employment.

It was only in 1933 under Franklin D Roosevelt that a genuine attempt was made to address the issue in the US. Referred to the *'New Deal'*, Roosevelt enacted a slew of legislations establishing government agencies aimed at revitalising the economy. The government took up the development of infrastructure on a mammoth scale to put people back to work. In April 1933 Roosevelt took the US off the gold standard so that he could print sufficient currency to finance the giant infrastructure projects under New Deal. But by 1937, the Congress which had initially stood by the President started to get belligerent. The Press became increasingly sceptical of the New Deal legislations. The US Supreme Court struck down many of the New Deal legislations terming them unconstitutional. It was, one must admit, the high spending by the government in its resolve to be the *'arsenal for democracy'* in the wake of WW II that got the American economy moving. It was only during WW II that the capitalist nations registered near full employment since the onset of the depression. The infrastructure developed during the New Deal built the solid economic-industrial foundation for the United States in the years to come. In England and France however expansionary policies to tide over the depression had to be rolled back as those were severely resented by Capital. The two economies remained in deep depression until wartime production jumpstarted the economy.

Welfare State in the West

From the 1930s Capitalism was in disarray. The depression had bared it all. The greatest depression the capitalist world plunged into was premeditated and tailored. Unfortunately, it resulted in misfortune for many while benefiting a select few. The squalor and destitution that the capitalist world witnessed despite presiding over the loot of its colonies made it imperative that the system was fundamentally flawed and was in need of an overhaul. The capitalist system which was considered to be benign did not cater to the *'Wealth of Nations'*. This was writ large. In the US production was down by 25 percent, investment by 50 percent and unemployment was up by 20 percent. One in every five Americans was unemployed. In Germany, the desperate situation threw the men into Hitler's arms. Hitler who got only 2 percent of the votes in 1929 had by 1933 polled 33 percent of votes. Even in the US, anti-Semitism gained currency. The Ku Klux Klan menace peaked. There were *'Hail Hitler'* marches in America.

From October 1929 until March 1933 the US economy was in a downward spiral. President Herbert Hoover (1929–1933) made half-hearted attempts to stem the crisis. Hoover opposed any intervention from the federal government in the US economy. He sought to avoid direct federal intervention, believing that the best way to bolster the economy was through the strengthening of businesses such as banks and railroads. It was axiomatic in those days to believe that *'In the long run'* the market will correct itself. Hoover found a convenient scapegoat in the migrant population for the Depression. He instituted policies of *repatriation and deportation of the migrants to Mexico*. President Hoover's actions did not measure up to the dimensions of the crisis. His remark in 1931, '*My greatest ambition is to see the overthrow of Bolshevism in Russia*' summarises his apathy towards the financial crisis his nation and her people were suffering from. But then it was characteristic of his class.

In the 1932 Presidential election, the Democratic candidate Franklin D Roosevelt secured a landslide victory over the incumbent Hoover. On 15th February 1933, President-elect, Roosevelt, narrowly escaped an assassination attempt, while making a speech in Miami. The assailant, a deranged unemployed bricklayer who later confessed to the attempt, expressed his hatred for *"all officials and everybody who is rich"* during questioning.

While the capitalist world reeled under the Great Depression with soup kitchens becoming the norm, the young Soviet Republic was making steady progress in every aspect of human endeavour. The inherent merits of a planned economy became increasingly evident and palpable for even to the critics of the Soviet system. This recognition gave rise to a sense of urgency for government intervention, even within capitalist countries, as they sought to address the pressing challenges and replicate the achievements showcased by the Soviet model.

New Deal Under FDR

'A civilised nation is possible only in a well-run economy'.

The prevailing approach up to that point, whenever a nation's economy exhibited signs of recession, typically involved relying on monetary measures, such as implementing spending cuts and raising taxes. However Roosevelt was convinced that imposing too much austerity during a global recession would be self-defeating. Households may tend to save during distress. But if nations too resort to austerity it could be catastrophic. *'Beggar thy neighbour'* will never get the nations out of depression as one country's imports are another country's exports. He firmly believed that businesses would bloom and mass production resume only if the masses were given the capacity to buy these goods and services through a mass transfer of huge wages, an encapsulation of a kind of economic thought advocated by the British economist John Maynard Keynes which has since then come to be known as *Keynesian Economics*. A series of measures by Roosevelt to restore the buying power of the working class came to be referred to as the New Deal.

The New Deal which saw government intervention in the economy on behalf of the common man marked the first attempt to build a Welfare State in the US. Unlike the sops offered to labour in the post-war period which witnessed the return of 4 million soldiers from the front and 9 million laid off workers of war factories, New Deal was not a temporary inoculation against the Bolshevik infection to ward off the communist challenge. Though the measures contemplated were informed by the learnings of the Soviet experiment and to an extend in response to the rising Red tide, New Deal was the outcome of a paradigm shift in the very perception of how the government of the day should function. The government was no longer to remain mere mediators and arbitrators in business conflicts but to be the motors for social change encompassing the entire spectrum of civic life.

In his first 100 days in office, Roosevelt enacted a multitude of initiatives that prioritized the welfare of the common man, marking a significant shift in the focus of the US government. The voice of the common man echoed in the inner councils of the government for the first time since 1776. The core objective of the New Deal was to facilitate employment opportunities and restore economic stability. In essence, the emphasis was on providing jobs. The immediate societal value of the tasks at hand was not a primary consideration. The key aim was to re-establish the people's ability to earn and spend, reviving the economy and improving their overall well-being.

The programme focused on what historians refer to as the '3 Rs':

- relief for the unemployed and for the poor
- recovery of the economy back to normal levels
- reform of the financial system to prevent a repeat depression

The New Deal created the basis for the new world. It instituted social welfare, old age pension, unemployment benefits, minimum wage and outlawed child labour for the first time in the capitalist world. Women and Blacks were not to be discriminated for matters related to employment. Worker Unions were brought under a legal framework.

It brought together manufacturing and construction under social welfare schemes. The construction of roads, highways, bridges, schools, hospitals, dams to control floods and generate electricity provided employment to millions and ensured the welfare of the people by augmenting the infrastructure The decision to take the nation off the gold standard in April 1933 made available more paper money to provide loans to trigger the economy and create jobs in their millions. By early 1937, the economy was back to the pre-depression levels of 1929.

Capital Resents an Interventionist Government

An interventionist government that employs people, sets minimum wages, working hours, abolishes child labour and punishes discrimination based on gender or colour and ensures the welfare of the people, is never to the liking of big business. The initiatives on behalf of the working class impact the profitability of big business which considers the government as its mere appendage facilitating its own enhancement. For it, any intervention by the government in the economy should be on its own behalf. Roosevelt was even accused of legislating hatred. The President, the privileged class accused, fused corporatism, fascism, nationalism, xenophobia into a potent pill and administered to the masses to hoodwink them into willing submission. 'FDR's New Deal is a disguise for a totalitarian state' cried his predecessor, Herbert Hoover. And Roosevelt who himself had an aristocratic background was branded a *'traitor to his class'.*

A Republican-controlled Supreme Court led the attack against the New Deal. It struck down one New Deal legislation after another terming them unconstitutional. The Supreme Court had turned itself into an agent of the Business and Capital. On 20th January 1937, during his second inauguration when the Chief Justice, while administering the oath of office to the new President, came to the words *'to preserve protect and defend the constitution'* Roosevelt later said he felt like saying *'not the kind of constitution your court has raised up as a barrier to progress and democracy'*. During his second tenure, Roosevelt fearful of the Supreme Court that it would strike down the Social Security Act, the law that gave the unions the right to collective bargaining, was determined to tame it. He wanted a Court that would rule favourably on legislations. Under the pretext to alleviate the workload on the Supreme Court, Roosevelt proposed the Judiciary Reorganization Bill of 1937, which aimed to grant him the authority to appoint additional judges. However, this move faced resistance and opposition from various quarters. Even Democrat senators took exception to Roosevelt's urge. In the words of Democrat Representative from Indiana, Samuel B Pettengill, *'This is more power that a good man should want, or a bad man should have'.* The bill did not see through the Congress.

The Supreme Court and Congress successfully curbed Roosevelt's power, forcing him to yield to the combined influence of business interests, the Judiciary, and Congress. Despite initially granting Roosevelt dictatorial powers, Congress began to reclaim its authority, leading to a decline in the momentum of the New Deal. Even though the economy had showed signs of partial recovery there were still millions out of work. The economy snapped. The stock market crashed. Businesses failed. By December 1937, 2 million people had lost their jobs. The government spending started to dwindle paving the way for another depression. The business class had got their act together. They could get the Congress and the Supreme Court to rally behind them if not toe their line.

It was only with the start of WW II that the US economy registered near full employment. It was the pump priming and rearmament to be the 'arsenal of democracy' as Roosevelt put it, that got the economy ticking and ensured full employment in the entire history of capitalism. Keynes never subscribed to the view that New Deal under Roosevelt ended the Great Depression: It was military spending or *Military Keynesianism* as it has come to be known since then that ended the depression.

The New Deal and the government intervention in every aspect of the economy during the war was a great learning for the Americans. The command economy during the war had ensured near-full employment for the first time in the history of capitalism. The working class had become resurgent. Post-war they never wanted to relapse into destitution as was the norm during the depression years. The thought that the government of the day should step into the economic sphere of life rather than let the market take the calling had gained traction.

The inadequacy of political rights alone for the *'pursuit of happiness'* was being felt during the Great Depression, thus, paving the way for the Welfare State in America. President Roosevelt could not see it through the Economic Bill of Rights he championed towards the end of the war. But the momentum that Roosevelt had impacted on the system was such that even a Republican President Richard Nixon (1969–1974) remarked: *'We are all Keynesians now'*. Seven successive Presidents, Democrat or Republican continued the legacy of Roosevelt until President Ronald Reagan toppled the entire edifice of the flourishing Welfare State.

Welfare State in Britain

'No society can legitimately call itself civilized if a sick person is denied medical aid because of lack of means'.
  – Aneurin Bevan, Minister for Health in Clement Attlee's Labour Government who spearheaded NHS in Britain

Although Britain had a Labour Prime Minister Ramsay Mc Donald as the Great Depression unravelled, following the first election with universal adult franchise, his coalition government was dominated by the Conservatives and would not let him embrace Keynesianism. It was only after WW II that Britain took concrete steps towards the establishment of a Welfare State.

Winston Churchill's Landslide Defeat and The Inauguration of The Welfare State in Britain

There are no two views about Winston Churchill as a war leader. With the German surrender, the European theatre of war had come to an end in May 1945. His approval ratings stood at 83 percent, an all-time high for any British Prime Minister up to the point. But, when Churchill raised his hat and raised his two fingers with the now familiar Victory 'V' sign at the British Army's victory parade in Germany, the troops were calling not his name but that of Clement Attlee, his deputy in the Cabinet and the Leader of the Labour Party who had been in his entourage as an observer during the Potsdam conference. It was a sign of things to come.

Barely two months after the defeat of Germany, Churchill was to face the most humiliating blow of his life. He suffered *'an extraordinary gesture of ill gratitude'* at the hands of the British electorate. Yes, the British electorate did approve of his conduct of the war, but, it had its fears about how he would run the post-war economy and manoeuvre the nation in the coming years.

The 5th July 1945 election saw a high turnout with 72.8 percent of the electorate voting. With almost 12 million votes polled, Labour won 393 seats while the conservatives could only manage to win 197 seats. The 12.0 percent national swing from the Conservatives to Labour, remains the largest ever achieved in a British general election. Labour for the first time in history had won an outright majority in the Parliament. It was a landslide.

In the election Churchill stood from the Woodford constituency. As a mark of respect for their war-time leader, his seat was left uncontested by the Labour Party. The electorate felt let down and disenfranchised. After all, this was the first general election since 1935 as in Britain no general elections were held during the World War II until allied victory was assured; hence the 1935 House sat until 1945. The only person willing to stand against Churchill was a local farmer, Alexander Hancock. He described himself as a *'Philosophical Communist'*. Churchill polled a disappointing 27,688 votes while Hancock, a novice to electoral politics with no backing from any of the registered political parties polled 10,488 votes. Churchill barely made it to Parliament.

But Why The Turn Towards Left

During the war, the British economy was virtually run by the government. The Britons had at last experienced what it was like, if the government stepped in from being on the fringes of economic affairs and ran the entire economy in a command mode. Winston Churchill's daughter Sarah Churchill's remark summarizes the British attitude: *'Socialism as practised in the war, did no one any harm and quite a lot of people good. The children of this country have never been so well-fed or healthy. What milk there was, was shared equally. The rich didn't die because their meat ration was no larger than the poor, and there is no doubt that this common sharing and feeling of sacrifice was one of the strongest bonds that unified us. So why, they say, cannot this common feeling of sacrifice be made to work as effectively in peace'?*

Churchill's attack on socialism contemplated by the Labour, the fruits of which the British population had started to enjoy, backfired. His remark that national control of the economy would be a fallback on *Gestapo* did not go well with the electorate. The general sentiment was *'If you can plan for war why can't you plan for the well-being of people during peacetime'?* It appeared that the British people were well off in a war economy that was managed by the government than in a peace time laissez faire!

The British electorate had also been sensitised by the very concept of a Welfare State. In 1942 William Beveridge, an economist, published a Report titled *'Social Insurance and Allied Services'*. Known as the Beveridge Report, it proposed a kind of government that would take care of every citizen from the *'cradle to the grave'*. The report outlined the five giants that prevented Britain from becoming a modern society.

- WANT
- IGNORANCE
- DISEASE
- SQUALOR
- IDLENESS

The Labour Party endorsed the report and promised to transform Britain into a Welfare State. While Churchill was preoccupied with the War, the Labour Ministers had done a splendid job with the wartime economy. Clement Attlee, the leader of the Labour Party, who had been Deputy Prime Minister since 1942 had been overseeing the domestic affairs. The Labour Party leaders in the War Cabinet had won the confidence of the people. Although all major parties committed themselves to fulfilling the aims outlined in the Report, Attlee's Labour Party had gained the much-needed legitimacy of the British public through their astute management of the economy while being a part of the coalition government headed by

Winston Churchill. The British were convinced that the Labour Party alone would put its heart and soul into implementing the Report if returned to power.

The Labour government of 1945 radically changed the British society. It also embarked on decolonisation. Clement Attlee presided over the dissolution of the British Empire, and the creation of a new, progressive, social and economic consensus back home that embraced every citizen. Clement Attlee proclaimed, *'Aim of socialism is to give greater freedom to the individual'*. The **N**ational **H**ealth **S**ervice continues to be its crowning glory. The Health Minister Aneurin Bevan instrumental in the establishment of the system based on clinical need and not on the ability to pay stated that *'It is a piece of real socialism. It is a piece of real Christianity'*. Even though Churchill did make a comeback in October 1951, he chose not to dismantle the NHS until his resignation in April 1955. As fate would have it, the NHS, the pride of Britain, too fell victim to the wave of neoliberalism that was to engulf Britain in the 1980s.

Post-War Consensus

Though Franklin Delano Roosevelt was often dubbed as a traitor to his class his greatest achievement was to restore the faith of millions of Americans in American Capitalism. But for the New Deal, many would have embraced communism or fascism. He made capitalism humane. Through his fireside chats the President for the first time in the history of the US reached out to every family and struck a chord with every American. With the capitalist world witnessing high levels of employment during the war with the economy in command mode, there arose a consensus that there should be a greater involvement of the government in the economy aimed at securing the economic well-being of the people even after the war.

Post-war the tide of history was in favour of labour. In the tussle between Capital and labour it appeared labour had won. The financial class was alarmed at the growing importance of the government in the running of the economy. When President Harry S. Truman (1945–1953) proposed a National Health Care Policy the American Medical Association resented it stating *'Socialized medicine: White House was following the Moscow party line'.* Across the Atlantic, the British Medical Association (BMA) despised the NHS and in the *British Medical Journal* described Aneurin Bevan as *'a complete and uncontrolled dictator'.*

The concerns of the financial class found material expression in the *'Mont Pelerin Society'* an international organization composed of economists, philosophers, historians, intellectuals, and business leaders founded in 1947. The Society perceived the very welfare measures that brought succour to the millions in the capitalist world as *'dangers faced by civilization'.* In the post-war euphoria, the Mont Pelerin Society preferred to remain in the side-lines bidding its time. It gathered sufficient experimental data in its experiments in the despotic regimes of Latin America, which it viewed as its laboratory. Soon it was to engulf the capitalist world and then the entire spectrum of civilization towards the turn of the millennium. Neoliberalism unleashed by the MPS is the most vicious onslaught of Capital over the gains of labour. The territory Capital had to concede to the population and its democratically elected governments was soon retaken.

It is a matter of irony that Heads of Governments in the US and Britain, with middle-class background whose families stood to gain by the welfare measures in their own respective countries during their youth, were to preside over its very dismemberment in less than four decades. Ronald Reagan who came of age during the New Deal described himself to be an *'ardent New Dealer'* having his family finances saved by the New Deal was to systematically dismantle the welfare measures of Roosevelt. Reagan learning from Roosevelt the importance of speaking to the common man marshalled his skills in communication and persuaded the population to embrace a path that eventually led to their own disenfranchisement from the parental embrace of the State. In the era of TV the great communicator, as fondly remembered by the Americans, accomplished the rollback of welfare schemes that had outlived seven US Presidents. Together with Margaret Thatcher, he took the baton of neoliberalism to such lengths that neither Bill Clinton nor Tony Blair, much to the bewilderment of the very constituencies that got them elected to high offices, did not reclaim lost ground but instead dismembered what was left of the Welfare State.

Chapter 7: John Maynard Keynes: The Man Who Saved Capitalism from the Capitalists

> 'Capitalism is the astounding belief that the wickedest of men will do the wickedest of things for the greatest good of everyone.'

> 'His radical idea that governments should spend money they don't have may have saved capitalism.' — **TIME 1999**

> '...use fiscal measures to stimulate domestic demand to rapid effect, as appropriate, while maintaining a policy framework conducive to fiscal sustainability.'
> — **Leaders of G 20 countries at G 20 Summit in Washington DC Nov 2008**

'*In the long run we are all dead*' quipped Keynes sarcastically at the classical economists who held that the free market will put everyone back into employment in the long run. The entrenched view at the time of the Great Depression was that the workers were temporarily unemployed as they moved between jobs or it could be that they preferred to remain idle as they were on welfare. It could also be that the wage rate the workers demanded was more than the investor could afford. But the high figures of unemployment, of up to 3 million in Britain and 15 million in the US, could not be explained away by such reasoning. Unemployment at such a scale was unprecedented. As years rolled by, contrary to the widely held belief, there was no sign of an equilibrium in the demand for labour and its supply. Demand for labour made no sign of picking up and the unemployment crisis continued to worsen.

There was a broad consensus that the primary issue afflicting the world economy was the lack of demand. The high rates of unemployment had rendered a vast proportion of the population with no disposable income. This curtailed the purchasing power of individuals. The lack of demand for goods was driving out businesses which resulted in further unemployment that accentuated the depression. The economy was in a downward spiral.

Traditionally government intervention in the economy was focused on monetary measures on the side of supply. It was limited to some measures like slashing interest rates and effecting cuts on government spending. The rationale was that by slashing interest rates businesses would invest more, thus, providing for more employment opportunities. If the workers were also flexible in their wages, it was argued, it would stimulate businesses to make investments that would create jobs and, thus, check unemployment *in the long run*. By this logic, the classical economists held that as wages and labour demands equalized, more people would get employed. With the new-found income, demand will be restored, and the economy will kick start all by itself.

Keynes took issue with the widely held notions of classical theory which stressed monetary measures as a pill for every economic ill. The cardinal aspect of the Keynesian rationale was a change in theory concerning the factors determining employment levels in an economy. The Keynesian revolution replaced the classical understanding of employment with Keynes's view that employment is a function of demand and not supply. He cautioned that an economy in a downward spiral would never reinvigorate itself by mere monetary measures alone. Cuts on spending by the government could be catastrophic. Keynes reasoned that the economy would remain sunk for an indefinite period if the businesses, individuals and government too stopped to spend money. The austerity at the level of the individual and business is quite understandable. But, cuts on spending by a national government could ring the death bell for every initiative in the economy.

At the national level, he insisted on pursuing a policy that was contrary to the prevailing logic of the times. Keynes stood for an activist role for the national government rather than relying on the market to correct itself. It should step in and start to spend money in the economy to bridge the gap left by the measures of austerity by the business. It is only with such government expenditure on grand projects with huge employment potential will the laid-off workers get back to work. Keynes stood for fiscal measures from the government to stem the crisis and power the economy back to its vibrant state. It was a break from the classical thinking of the monetarists that advocated market would kick start on its own as the wage rate and labour requirements match in a climate of very low-interest rates. Keynes felt that even if the interest rates were slashed the business would not invest in new opportunities, given the doomed state of the economy. In the prevailing climate of pessimism, the *'animal spirits'* were lacking. In a state of despondency slashing of interest rates would not translate into higher investments by the business fraught with scepticism. Keynes was right. He stood for government intervention on the Demand side. The workers laid off by the private sector should be absorbed into the workforce by the government. He stood for decisive government intervention to provide employment to offset the loss of jobs in the private sector by stepping up government spending to make good the loss of private spending. When Keynes said *'Government should hire people to demolish the city of London and rebuild it'* he was making his point clear. To put people back to work the government should embark on massive construction projects which had huge employment potential. If need be, the government should run a budget deficit to finance its projects that ensure the unemployed are absorbed back into the workforce. In short, the government should spend money it did not have, to fund massive construction projects to generate employment which would put money back into the hands of the common man to drive up his demand, thus, jump-starting the economy. As more people get employed government saves money on unemployment benefits which the government has to spend anyway if they remain unemployed. The extra spending by the newly employed will pay for itself through higher tax revenues. In a radio broadcast he advised, *'Activity and enterprise individually and national must be the cure'.* In less than a decade from 1936 to 1946, Keynes effected a paradigm shift in thinking in economics. The tide of history was in favour of Keynes.

As irony would have it, around the world Keynes' ideas became axiomatic and served as the guiding principle in the decades to come, except in his homeland Britain. Despite having a Labour Prime Minister, Ramsay MacDonald, the Cabinet was predominantly composed of conservatives, which limited his ability to fully implement Keynesian policies. As a result, Britain did not fully capitalize on the potential benefits that could have been derived from Keynesian economics during the Great Depression.

Keynes' view that demand, and not supply, was the driving factor, determining levels of employment was as much a revolt against the prevailing logic in economics as Einstein's in physics. The Economist's statement that *'the difficulty lies, not in the new ideas, but in escaping from the old ones, which ramify, for those brought up as most of us have been, into every corner of our minds'* did resonate with that of the great physicist's, *'Problems cannot be solved with the same mind-set that created them'.* During the great depression, Keynes wrote in an essay *'The increase of technical efficiency has been taking place faster than we can deal with the problem of labour absorption'*. Einstein who happened to be in America at the height of the depression and never made it to Germany with the rise of Hitler is said to have remarked that the economic depression especially in America seemed to be caused mainly by technological advances that *'decreased the need for human labour'* and there-by caused a decline in consumer purchasing power.

John Maynard Keynes was no socialist. He did not approve of socialism as an economic doctrine. He even despised the Soviet Union. Keynes believed in capitalism. As explicitly stated in his open letter to the President-elect Franklin D Roosevelt his sole aim was to stave off a socialist revolution. But his was no advocacy for the unfettered free market either. Keynes was convinced that left to its own devices in the absence of a regulatory framework the system could go seriously wrong. He believed governments have it in their power to regulate the capitalist economy through the injection of money and regulation to even out the peaks and troughs of the economy. In a way, he was saving capitalism from the capitalists! He stood for social investment not necessarily welfare policies. It was not passion for social justice that formed the bedrock of his economic theory. His inclination was to jump-start the economy and get the capitalist system working.

Keynes always had the capacity to envision the unimaginable. He was clairvoyant. At times he could even be prophetic. In 1919 he resigned in disgust from the British delegation to Versailles. He was deeply disturbed at the harsh terms being imposed upon the defeated Germany. The treaty demanded Germany to foot the bill for everyone's war expenses. In his 'Economic Consequences of Peace' authored in 1920 he termed the treaty as immoral and impractical and even stupid, given the enormity of the reparations that were imposed on a war-torn Germany. Keynes advocated for leniency towards Germany. The continent was a single economic unit tied together not just through geography and a common history but also through a very vibrant trade system. He insisted that Germany should be spared of economic ruin for the good of all. Germany should never be economically crippled and rendered an international pariah but be allowed to rebuild and rejoin the international community. He insisted that a heavily industrialized Germany was to Europe's advantage. He reasoned that disrupting this ecosystem by insisting on high reparations made no economic sense and could be counterproductive. Keynes was accused of being sympathetic towards Germany, the aggressor. He even cautioned Germany would seek revenge on Europe for the crippling effect that the treaty provided for. In his book, he stated, *'If we aim deliberately at the impoverishment of Central Europe, vengeance, I dare predict, will not limp. Nothing can then delay for very long that final civil war between the forces of reaction and the despairing convulsions of Revolution, before which the horrors of the late German war will fade into nothing, and which will destroy, whoever is victor, the civilisation and the progress of our generation'*. Germany did seek revenge. Fanning the flames of national indignation a man of no consequence, a watercolour painter turned dispatch runner who spent most of his time in regimental headquarters far away from the front politicking to win awards of *'bravery'*, could rise to the Chancellorship of Germany in no time. The victors were to pay dearly for their arrogance. In a sense, one can say John Maynard Keynes was a forerunner of behavioural economics.

Keynes' understanding of economics was not bound by dogmas hitherto considered infallible. He could interpret axiomatic beliefs in the wake of ground reality and, if need be, discard them. He is said to have famously answered when someone drew his attention to his change of stand on certain critical issues, *'If the facts change I alter my conclusions. What do you do, Sir'*.

Keynes could visualise a vast macro-economic architecture. He had a deep conviction that Capital should remain national. Its jurisdiction should coincide with that of the Nation-State. Only then will a national government be able to pursue domestic economic policies that ensure full employment. If the Capital refuses to remain national and graduates to a realm in which the writ of the national government does not prevail on it, the government's efforts in taming the business cycles will fail, as is the case in the neoliberal era. To prevent the flight of Capital across nations and the formation of International Capital he sought to impose strict control over the movement of Capital across nations. Keynes led the British delegation at the Bretton Woods in the US in which the intelligentsia of the allied countries cerebrated and hammered out the post-war economic policy which came to be known as the *'post-war consensus'*. Barriers to the flight of Capital across nations were one of the cardinal contributions of Keynes. Bretton Woods agreement which the world nations subscribed to was an encapsulation of his ideas. The two Bretton Woods institutions IMF and World Bank were his brainchildren.

An activist state is never to the liking of Capital. The welfare policies by the government that ensure near-full employment unshackle the labour from the dictates of the Capital. In such a scenario trade unions get to be powerful. The high inflation and high employment witnessed in the late 1960s and early 1970s provided the perfect opportunity for the **M**ont **P**elerin **S**ociety waiting in the wings to pounce upon Keynesianism. Stagflation the phenomenon of inflation and high unemployment was unprecedented. The burgeoning war bills of the US on account of the Vietnam War and its ever-increasing current deficit since the 1960s and the oil shock of the 1970s were the causative factors of high inflation. But these were conveniently carpeted and glossed over. Instead of addressing the real causative factors of inflation within the framework of Keynesian welfare economics, Keynesianism in its entirety was discredited and held accountable for the high rates of inflation. As events turned out, Keynes untimely death in 1946 was to have a disastrous effect on the world economy.

In the 1980s with Thatcher and Reagan at the helm of affairs, Keynesianism was administered a quiet burial. Mont Pelerin think tank asserted its influence on the course of economic planning. Thus, was born the neoliberal era with stress on cut in welfare measures, a rollback of government from every sphere of life and deregulating the financial sector. In the neoliberal era with such barriers of Capital to cross borders being razed down the government of the day is finding it difficult to pursue policies that tame Capital for the benefit of labour. Capital resents an activist government. Always in search of speculative gain, Capital flies to that country, the government of which agrees to bow before it. The very Bretton Woods institutions of IMF and World Bank were turned into mercenaries of Capital implementing what has since come to be known as the *'Washington Consensus'*. Keynes's brainchildren were being employed to dismember Keynesianism.

But in 2008, when the global economy spiralled into decline and plummeted to new low levels Keynesianism was resorted to get the economy back on track. Once the first line of defence of monetary measures appeared to be quixotic given the scale of the downturn rather than wait for the market to correct itself as the neoliberals always advocated, G-20 nations announced an economic stimulus package of around two percent of GDP to stimulate growth.

As John Donne, a metaphysical poet and a contemporary of Shakespeare. wrote

'No man is an island entire of itself;

every man is a piece of the continent, a part of the main;

if a clod is washed away by the sea,

Europe is the less, as well as if a promontory were,

as well as any manner of thy friends or of thine

own were; any man's death diminishes me,

because I am involved in mankind.

And therefore, never send to know for whom

the bell tolls; it tolls for thee'.

PART 4

COLD WAR

The Context of the Cold War: Capital In Action
Pre-emptive Strikes on the Welfare States

'From Stettin in the Baltic to Trieste in the Adriatic an Iron Curtain has descended across the Continent.'
— **Winston Churchill**

'The Cold War was North-South… West versus East… fought to protect the resources of the East and South from the natives.'
— **Noam Chomsky**

'The United States should respect the right of the people to develop the economy the way it should be and they want it to be.'
— **Salvador Allende**
President of Chile (1970–1973)

---

[12] Turning a much loved 'Uncle Joe' of the American public into a dictator to be feared was a Cold War PR which was inaugurated by Churchill's 'Iron curtain' speech made at the behest of the US President Harry S. Truman at Fulton Missouri, on 5th March 1946. Churchill, consigned to political wilderness by the British electorate, must have basked in the limelight that followed.

> 'We viewed these conflicts (Vietnam, Burma, Indonesia, Malaya, and the Philippines during the 1950s) not as nationalistic movements—as they largely appear in hindsight—but as signs of a unified communist drive for hegemony in Asia'.
> **– Robert Mc Namara, US Secretary of Defence (1961–1968)**

Chapter 8: The Context of the Cold War

'The fear today in England and other capitalist countries is not so much of Soviet armies, as of something more intangible and yet more powerful and dangerous, of Soviet ideas…

… It is obvious that there can be no really friendly relations between the Soviets and the imperialist powers. The differences between them are fundamental. The victors and the vanquished in the world war may come together, but not the communists and the capitalists. Peace between the latter two can only be temporary; it is but a truce.'

— **Jawaharlal Nehru**

'They were still using horse-drawn wagons, cavalry pieces, horse-drawn artillery… We couldn't imagine how they could have advanced against the might of the Germans with such primitive weaponry… The soldiers were on horseback. It was like the medieval times meeting the American times.'

— **Noted a PFC in the US Army on the Red Army units as the two armies met at the Elbe river near Torgau in Germany on 25th April 1945**

'Rumours of war are being put about extremely intensively by our enemies. The English and Americans are using their agents to spread rumours to scare the people of those countries whose politics they don't like. Neither we nor the Anglo-Americans can presently start a war. Everyone is fed up with war. Moreover, there are no war aims. We are not getting ready to attack England and America. And they are not risking it either. No war is possible for at least the next 20 years.'

— **Joseph Stalin**

'Uncle Joe'

Stalin during the war years was the TIME Man of Year twice, in 1939 and 1942. LIFE magazine on 29th March 1943 came up with a special issue on USSR. Starting from Mission to Moscow (1943) which was made in response to a request by President Roosevelt, Hollywood churned out pro-Soviet Union movies like

The North Star (1943)

Song of Russia (1944)

Three Russian Girls (1943)

Columbia's The Boy from Stalingrad (1943)

Counter-Attack (1945)

These movies took an extremely solicitous view of not just the Soviet system but of Joseph Stalin as well. For Americans, Stalin was 'Uncle Joe'. All this was to change with the cessation of hostilities in Europe. With the dawn of the Cold War, Hollywood came out with a slew of anti-Soviet movies very much critical of the Soviet Union and Stalin. Uncle Joe was to be turned to a monstrous dictator with such propagandistic films like

Bells of Coronado (1950)

Face to Face with Communism (1951)

Arctic flight (1952)

Assignment Paris (1952).

The Soviet 'invasion' of Afghanistan triggered the Rambo series beginning in 1982.

'We have not had a single day of tranquillity since October' echoed by any Russian during the Cold War is emblematic of the existential threat the first worker's welfare republic had to face under a constant capitalist siege, boycott and sabotage. The compulsion to take on Soviet Union had its origins in the class struggle within the capitalist countries. Any alternative to the then-established capitalist-imperialist model gaining traction in its bid to extricate millions from abominable living circumstances had an aura of convincing propaganda. The domestic working class in the capitalist countries was getting belligerent. The recalcitrant domestic working class had to me tamed if not maimed. The foreign policy of every capitalist country had a singular focus- contain the Soviet experiment. After all the foreign policy is nothing but domestic policy by other means.

The external armed aggression of the Soviet Republic, bankrolling Hitler into the Chancellorship of Germany and letting him rearm to obscene levels in violation of the Treaty at Versailles were consistent with the western scheme of things to dismember the Union of Soviet Socialist Republic. The Munich Pact, one among the last pacts that the western powers signed with Nazi Germany, had convinced Moscow what the western powers were up to. The Anglo-French sitzkrieg or the phoney war in the western front during the initial months of WW II convinced the Soviet leadership of the western resolve to dismember their Republic. The 1940 Winter War with Finland necessitated by its refusal to swap territories with the Soviet Union which was in search of a strategic depth in the event of a German attack resulted in its summary suspension from the League of Nations. 'Operation Pike' the Anglo-French plan drawn up in April 1940 to attack the Soviet Union, the delayed western front at Normandy cemented the Soviet belief beyond doubt that the western capitalist powers considered the Republic of Workers to be a far greater threat than Nazi Germany. 'Operation Unthinkable', the plan to take on Soviet Union as WW II was drawing to a close is a reflection of how much the West abhorred the Soviet cause.

No sooner had the world war came to a close, the deep fault lines between the Soviet Union and the West started to become the new zones of conflict. Contrary to what was expected at the start of the war, Soviet Union despite the initial reverses expanded into a commanding presence in the Eastern and Central Europe. With Germany decimated, Kremlin was convinced that the West, especially the US which had come out strong after the war *'would seize any opportunity, embrace any enemy and employ any means'* to wipe out the Soviet Union from the map. In his famous 'Iron curtain' speech Winston Churchill had lamented that *"Behind that line lie all the capitals of the ancient states of Central and Eastern Europe. Warsaw, Prague, Budapest, Belgrade, Bucharest and Sofia; all these famous cities and the populations around them lie in what I must call the Soviet sphere, and all are subject, in one form or another, not only to Soviet influence but to a very high and in some cases increasing measure of control from Moscow'.*

Kremlin's fears were confirmed when Truman pledged to the Congress on 12th March 1947 to contain the communist uprisings in Greece and Turkey. The day of his speech to the Congress is regarded as the formal inauguration of the Cold War. Soon it was very much a matter of US foreign policy to commit material resources and support to a nation to prevent its slide towards the Soviet camp. Soon this commitment was viewed as a doctrine. The 'Truman Doctrine' as it came to be referred to was to guide US foreign policy all throughout the Cold War.

The western powers were obsessed with Soviet Union. The defence establishment was aware that the Soviet threat did not even exist. World War II had thoroughly decimated the nation. The war-torn nation was recuperating. The heavy losses in men and material was colossal. The trumped-up threat rationalized the huge spending on military. The pretext of fighting an enemy was a necessity for the capitalist countries. Soviet Union and the Cold War legitimized the military-industrial complex. To make matters worse Soviet Union's principled stand to reach out to the newly independent nations of the Third World infuriated the former colonial powers as it interfered with their scheme of things for their former colonies in the post war era. The irony of the Cold War era was that while the capitalist nations had started institutionalizing welfare measures and slowly turning themselves into welfare states within the context of capitalism, they viewed Soviet Union, a mammoth welfare state as a threat. Though the standoff between capitalist bloc and the Soviet bloc never reached a flash point in the temperate world, it was the Third World tropics that bore the entire brunt. Every Third World country, without an exception, that sought to institutionalize welfare measures for its citizens with Soviet help was perceived as a potential threat by the capitalist nations.

Soviet Union's Spectacular March of Success

The Soviet Union which lost 27 million of its people in the War and saved the world from Hitler had a great standing in the minds of the people the world over, especially the newly independent former colonies of the Third World. The World War (1939–1945) was fought primarily on the Eastern front. Until the Normandy landing on 6th June 1944, it was the Red Army that took on the fascists almost single-handedly. Even after the Red Army had expelled Nazis virtually from all of the Soviet territory by mid-1944, it pursued the Nazis and chased them out of Europe and wiped them off from its nerve centre. The Red Army liberated Europe from the clutches of Nazis and saved entire nations from wanton destruction and enslavement. It put an end to the holocaust. Millions were saved at the cost of Soviet soldiers.

Though the US had tested the Atom bomb in 1945, the Soviet Union quickly caught up with it without much delay. In the pursuit of conquest of space, the Soviet Union edged the Americans out. A series of unparalleled achievements starting with the first artificial satellite, the first living being in space, the first human being in space, the first woman in space, the first spacewalk, and the first mission to Venus to say a few cemented the Soviet

Union's unique position as a pioneer in science and technology. The first socialist experiment was being viewed with much enthusiasm the world over. The paternalistic role of the government was something unheard of in the western capitalist democracies. The social contract any Soviet citizen could fall back on minimized, if not eliminated, the vulnerabilities that an ordinary American citizen considered routine. This was widely viewed to be worthy of emulation. The protective embrace of the State moved many Americans. In the Manhattan Project, many scientists readily collaborated with Russian intelligence and smuggled confidential information on the design of the Atom bomb. Even Oppenheimer was suspected of being a Soviet spy.

The newly independent Afro-Asian nations looked up to the Soviet Union as a model to emulate. The universalization of education, health care and housing were identified as the primary reason for the Soviet success in surpassing the capitalist colonial powers in so little time. Khrushchev's boastful statement that the Soviet Union would conquer the whole world in the classroom should be viewed in the light of Soviet realism and its unwavering obsession with education. As Americans would later lament following the spectacular success of the Soviets in space, *'We lost out in the classrooms'.*

The labour class of the US and the West European countries looked towards the East. Joseph Stalin was fondly referred to as *'Uncle Joe'* by the Americans. To wean away the US and the West European labour class from espousing any pro-Soviet sentiments, systematic attempt to discredit the Soviet Union and its leader was made. It was pictured as a police State and workers were told it was no workers' paradise. The American psyche was planted with fear of everything Soviet. The mandatory Civil Défense drills in schools and offices in response to the perceived threat of a nuclear attack by the Soviet Union was nothing short of an anti-Soviet propaganda. Hollywood too stepped in to demonise Joseph Stalin who was very popular among the American public.

'We Will Bury You' [13]

While addressing the western states at a reception at the Polish embassy in Moscow on 18th November 1956 at the height of the Cold War, the temperamental and moribund Soviet General Secretary Nikita Khrushchev said: *'About the capitalist states, it doesn't depend on you whether or not we exist. If you don't like us, don't accept our invitations, and don't invite us to come to see you. Whether you like it or not, history is on our side. We will bury you'!* He was just paraphrasing the Marxian statement *'The proletariat is the undertaker of capitalism'*. The word *'undertaker'* is translated as a *'gravedigger'* in Russian. In his memoirs, Khrushchev stated that *'enemy propaganda picked up the slogan and blew it all out of proportion'*.

Those were the days when the capitalist world was convinced that in the battle for the hearts and minds of the newly independent former colonies, the developing world, the Soviets were winning. When Kennedy met Khrushchev at the Vienna Summit in June 1961 he admitted that the Bay of Pigs invasion, the attempt to overthrow Fidel Castro had been a mistake. The Soviet leader turned the knife in the wound by insisting that wars of national liberation would now be won by communists and that the United States was on the wrong side of history. The West was losing the Cold War.

By the end of 1962, the year in which the two superpowers took things to a nuclear flash point in what is known as the Cuban missile crisis, a million US soldiers were stationed in more than two hundred foreign military bases. The military bases stretched from Greenland to Turkey, from Portugal to the Philippines. There were listening posts and USAF facilities in Iran, Pakistan, and an electronic monitoring station in a distant Ethiopia.

---

[13] *'This is what America is capable of, and how long has she existed? 300 years? 150 years of independence and you have got only this far. We have been independent only for 42 years. And in 7 years we will be at the same level as you. And we will keep on moving. When we pass you, we will just wave.'* said the Soviet General Secretary Khrushchev to the US Vice President Richard Nixon during a series of impromptu exchanges through interpreters in what would be known as the 'kitchen debate' at the opening of the American National Exhibition at Sokolniki Park in Moscow on 24th July 1959.

As much as three and a half million troops belonging to America's allies were garrisoned around the Soviet Union's borders ready to pounce on it at short notice. There were American nuclear warheads in Italy, the United Kingdom, and Turkey. Despite Khrushchev's rhetoric about building missiles '*like sausages*', he knew that the missile balance was stacked against their budding Worker Republic and that his long-range missiles were limited in their capability in thwarting the capitalist challenge.

Imperialistic Underpinnings of Cold War

Imperialism refers to the economic dominance of one spatial entity over the other. Colonialism, a special case of imperialism in which dominance is achieved by the institution of an apparatus of governance on the subjugated territory by the subjugating territory to serve its imperialistic purposes is the most visible and discussed form of imperialism.

The end of World War II marked a paradigm shift in the international arena. Colonialism the way it existed for centuries was put to an end. The colonies were granted political independence. But, even after political decolonization that was pursued with vigour, economic decolonization was still a far cry. Through indirect means, the newly independent nation-states, despite all the pretensions of sovereignty, continued to be subjugated. French garrisons remain in West Africa and for all economic purposes the region is still a colony of the French.

The post-war period was marked by a concession from Capital to labour. Keynesianism came to be accepted to be the norm the world over. Decolonisation and the institution of the universal adult suffrage by the capitalist colonial countries in response to the Soviet threat marked a new epoch in world affairs. It is to be borne in mind that it was as late as in 1945 that France and in 1946 the US implemented universal adult franchise. With decolonisation and the institution of democratic governments in the erstwhile colonies the Third World started to witness unprecedented social progress. For the first time, the people of the tropics were empowered and in charge of the material endowments of nature and were steering towards a destiny of their choice. The white man was to remain confined to the temperate after a long time marauding through the tropics. The Third World countries organised a kind of government along Soviet lines. With technical know-how which the Soviet Union was more than ready to share these nations embarked on the path of national reconstruction. The wealth of the tropics came to be harnessed for the material well-being of its inhabitants. The natives were at last protagonists of their own destiny.

Banana Republics of the Self-Sufficient Tropics

> 'In political science, the term banana republic describes a politically unstable country with an economy dependent upon the export of natural resources.'

The temperate West since the hey days of colonialism is dependent on the wealth of the South. In fact, it was its deficiency in meeting its domestic demand that propelled its colonial conquests in the first place. Even to this day, it continues to be so. The dependence is not confined to the vast amount of minerals and hydrocarbons. It extends to the agricultural produce of the tropical land mass. After all, it was pepper that brought the Portuguese to India.

During the summer the tropical and subtropical lands produce a basket of agricultural products uniquely endemic to it, like rice. During the winter when the temperate lands are frozen and agriculture stands arrested, the tropic-subtropic region can produce a basket of agricultural products which are usually grown in the summer growing season in the temperate lands. This asymmetry that exists between the temperate and tropical lands in its growing season dictated by the climatic regime, economists Utsa Patnaik and Prabhat Patnaik theorize to be a major underpinning of imperialism. The tropical-subtropical belt can produce all the agricultural products which the temperate regions are in need of. Hence, the latter will never ease its grip over the former. The round-the-year growing season which should stand the tropics in good stead ironically proves to be its curse. The temperate land mass cannot exist without the tropics. But for the tropics catering to its needs in the winter, the temperate population will starve to death. Post-decolonisation when the native became the master of his resources, imperialism took a new form to ensure that the West continued to secure to itself its share at a price which was at its bidding.

At the start of colonialism, a major chunk of Latin America was colonised by Spain and Portugal. It was home to very rich colonies with Haiti being the richest colony that had ever existed. Armed revolts in Latin America against colonial suppressors found early success. Latin America shrugged off its colonial yoke in the nineteenth century. However, the presence of the United States of America to its north had a detrimental effect on the native government's effort to tap the productive energies of its people for their own betterment which persists even to this day.

The monoculture of banana in many Latin American countries on the dictates of its master quite a few miles to the north at the cost of the native population's genuine need for a highly variegated agriculture is emblematic of imperialism. Such a monoculture of bananas resulted in starvation, malnutrition and diseases in these tropical countries. The institutions in the social sectors like education and hospitals were ill-equipped and fell short of the demands of the population. The infant mortality rate, maternal mortality rate, life expectancy, left much to be desired. The literacy ratio was one among the lowest in the world. A genuine demand to practise agriculture that catered to the wholesome need of the population was seldom heeded. Latin American population in those days had only two classes of population: either the super-rich owners of the land, usually the officials of the US Inc. and the poor landless tillers who lived in abject poverty in abominable living conditions. The middle class was simply missing.

Any attempt by the native government to provide for a wholesome diet for its population met with opposition from Washington. And in the extreme event of the nation shrugging off the Yankee yoke in its humanitarian attempt to bring under the plough arable land for cereals and vegetables, it was deemed time for a regime change by Washington. A puppet government that shall toe the line dictated by the masters in the temperate world would be propped up and the status quo restored. The term "Banana Republic" should be seen in the broader context of the Third World tropical land masses and its people being exploited for its resources by the privileged few in the temperate zones, the seat of western Capital.

The Domino Theory

'Finally, you have broader considerations that might follow what you would call the "falling domino" principle. You have a row of dominoes set up, you knock over the first one, and what will happen to the last one is the certainty that it will go over very quickly. So you could have a beginning of a disintegration that would have the most profound influences'.

– President Dwight D. Eisenhower

Though it was first mentioned by President Truman in the context of increasing Soviet influence in Europe, the domino theory had come to be known after President Eisenhower following his aforesaid statement in the context of Indochina. China turning communist alarmed Washington prompting the question, *'Who lost China'*? The rapid growth of China since the communist takeover had a great demonstrative power in the Indochina region. The revolutionary social change brought about in the newly independent former colonies by their responsible national governments always had a contagion effect. Much like the Soviet Union which was in search of a strategic depth against the capitalist powers in Europe, China, it was feared, would resort to create a buffer to its east and south for fear of an existential threat. Like a pack of dominos, it was feared that the entire region would be subsumed by communism with governments owing allegiance to Kremlin and Beijing. Adherents of the theory cautioned about the *'World Revolution'* that Lenin had called for. North Korea having been liberated by the Red Army had turned into a communist bastion. Eisenhower feared, left to themselves, countries like Laos, Cambodia, Thailand, Indonesia, Malaysia, Burma and even India would turn communist. Even Japan and the Philippines very much under the US sphere of influence were feared to be lost to the communists. The French withdrawal from North Vietnam following the abject surrender of its troops at Dien Bin Phu in 1954 was to be compensated by the US in such circumstances for a void would soon be filled by a communist regime.

Conclusion

'The clear goal has been to relativize the unique crimes of Nazism, bury those of colonialism, and feed the idea that any attempt at radical social change will always lead to suffering, killing and failure.'

– Seumas Patrick Charles Milne , Journalist

The political decolonization that was witnessed post-war was conducted amid much alacrity. As long as the free flow of resources from the newly independent former colonies to their former masters at prices fixed by the latter continued, the exploitative terms of trade that had come into being during the colonial days would continue. Hence political decolonization posed no threat to the capitalist countries. As the newly independent Third-World countries of the tropics vied against each other in selling the same basket of products to the West to earn the much-needed foreign exchange, the former masters faced no threat of increasing prices of the raw materials and commodities from the East and South as the former colonies could easily be pitted against each other. As the Third-World nations took upon themselves the task of national reconstruction which the Soviet Union came to its help for, there was a perceptible shift in the price of the commodities that were being exported from them to their former masters. As the Keynesian demand management system came to be widely subscribed to by the Third World countries in their attempt to extricate themselves from the squalor, deprivation and unemployment, the living standards of the population too improved. With high levels of disposable income that is concomitant with such high standard of living, domestic consumption of these resources in the Third World too peaked. Such a steep rise in the domestic demand for these products resulted in the rise of prices of such commodities globally. A rise in the procurement price of raw materials from the East and South is to the chagrin of western Capital. In short, economic decolonization in the absence of which political decolonization would be rendered meaningless, was fraught with danger to the very capitalist system.

Across the former colonies, the US at the behest of western Capital actively started to pursue a policy of sabotage either by covert or overt means, if necessary against governments which by their domestic policies of resource management eyeing on human development disturbed the delicate price mechanism that was erected since the colonial days. And that explains the Cold War.

US Presidents from Eisenhower (1953–1961) to Ronald Reagan (1981–1989) consistently reading a Soviet threat into every nationalist upsurge in the Third World was to hoodwink the US public into believing that their Government was fighting the Soviet menace on their behalf, while in reality, it was wiping out an alternative socio-politico-economic model that their people would come to subscribe if not nipped in the bud. The farcical bomb drills very much a part of the curriculum in schools instilled in the children a fear of anything that was Soviet. Even social medicine!

Chapter 9: Iran's Tryst with Democracy Comes to an End

'The Eisenhower administration believed that its actions were justified for strategic reasons. But the coup was clearly a setback for Iran's political development'.

– Maldeine Albright, Secretary of State

'We had some involvement with the overthrow of a democratically elected regime in Iran'.

– President Barack Obama

In the years after World War II, the currents of nationalism and anti-colonialism that surged across Asia, Africa, and Latin America were culminating in nationalist governments. Nationalism in the context of the newly independent former colonies meant a claim over its resources for its own development. Latin American countries, despite throwing off the Spanish-Portuguese colonisers, were no different from those in Asia and Africa as they had been effectively yoked under the US business interests for most part of the nineteenth and early twentieth centuries.

In Iran Mohammad Mossadegh became the Prime Minister in 1951. The new Prime Minister proceeded to do what Britain had done under the Labour government of Clement Attlee with their coal and iron industries. Nationalisation! Both houses of the Iranian Parliament voted unanimously to nationalise the Anglo-Persian Oil Company, the forerunner of British Petroleum. It was a defining moment not just for Iran, but for the entire Third World. The native was claiming back his resources which until the other day, had been deprived of by his coloniser. Iranian Parliament did not snatch the oil industry from the British. As per the law passed by the Parliament, Iran agreed to compensate Britain for the investments they had made in Iran, notwithstanding the fact the investments made were just a tiny fraction of the profits that were siphoned off from Iran in the preceding decades.

The nationalisation of the Anglo-Persian oil company brought Mossadegh into conflict with the British government. The British government had a majority stake in the Anglo-Persian Oil Company. The entire British fleet was dependent on Iranian oil during WW I and WW II. Britain was determined to maintain it.

Churchill, voted back to power in October 1951, feared that if the Prime Minister's move, whom he nicknamed *'Mussy Duck'*, went unchecked, it would be setting an unwarranted precedence that would undermine British imperial power across the globe in the days to come. Britain was thoroughly devastated after the war and could never invade Iran. The Truman Administration rejected the idea of a full-fledged invasion of Iran. The presence of the Red Army in Central Asia served as a deterrent for the US Administration. In those days of Cold War, any attempt of a military takeover of the sovereign nation Iran, was feared to land the Iranians in the Russian bloc. Moreover, Truman contended that a military crackdown of a democratically elected government led by a Prime Minister, who in no time had come to be liked by the world over, by the two self-proclaimed apostles of democracy would not go down well in the international forums.

With Eisenhower elected to the Presidency of the United States in 1953 things were to change. He was a military man and a Republican. He was hawkish. The new President appointed John Foster Dulles as the Secretary of State. His younger brother Allen Dulles was to head the CIA. Thus, for the first and only time in American history, two siblings were to run the overt and covert arms of foreign policy. The two brothers literally set the tone and character of the US approach which went on to be its cornerstone of foreign policy during the Cold War. The CIA founded in 1947 had not until then undertaken a regime change. The organization was preoccupied with funding anti-communist parties in Europe. The Dulles brothers convinced the President that Iran was on its way to join the Soviet block and cautioned that with the Soviet Union gaining a foothold in the Middle East what was at stake was 60 percent of the world's then-known oil resources. Eisenhower approved the plan of the Dulles brothers to oust Mossadegh. The Prime Minister was to be removed constitutionally. The operation was code-named Operation AJAX.

To discredit a popular leader, a smear campaign against Mohammad Mossadegh was unleashed. He was depicted as a tyrant cast in the mould of Hitler and Stalin. He was branded an atheist planning to present Iran to the Soviet Union on a platter. In an extremely religious society like Iran, it was worse than blasphemy. There was a communist party in Iran, known as Tudeh. It was a modest affair. The Tudeh party, like any other party, had supported the oil nationalization project. Mossadegh, a Democrat, took a principled stand and allowed Tudeh to function freely. But, he did not embrace its principles. The Prime Minister did not include even a single communist in his government.

In a pre-emptive move, Mossadegh called for a national referendum on a proposition that would allow him to dissolve Parliament and call for new elections. The result was overwhelmingly favourable for the Prime Minister. As the Parliament ceased to exist, the CIA move to topple him democratically was stalled. Now that the *'parliamentary means'* had been exhausted CIA and MI6 unleashed a campaign of disinformation. *Agents provocateurs* orchestrated a series of riots across the country. High-ranking military and police officers were won over. The ouster of the most popular political figure in Iran was staged as a popular uprising in August 1953 by the CIA and MI6. Paid demonstrators ran amok in the streets of Teheran projecting themselves to be the supporters of the symbolic Monarch of Iran. The mayhem in the streets of Iran was enacted with theatrical precision. In a strange turn-around of events, the most erudite Iranian of his day was unseated and put on trial and sentenced. Till his death in 1967, he was under house arrest. He was denied a public burial but was interned in his own house.

CIA had thus unseated a democratically elected government. The Monarchy which was until then symbolic was restored with full powers. The United States got rid of a government that was not to its liking and imposed one that it did which would perform as bidden. It embittered a generation of Iranians who had long considered the US as a beacon of democracy and liberty. Mohammad Reza Shah, the restored ruler, warmly welcomed Gulf, Standard Oil of New Jersey, Texaco, and Mobil to Iran and granted unbridled freedom of operation. A grateful Shah lavished money on the Presidential campaigns in the US. Once returned to the Peacock throne, the Shah unleashed a tyrannical reign of terror. The fate of the people of Iran was sealed. Iran was stripped of its democratic institutions. Every dissenting voice, be it the supporters of the ousted leader or communists or the socialists was silenced. In Shah the US found an important ally as Iran had a 1000-mile-long border with the Soviet Union. With the fall of Mossadegh the Soviet Union lost the much-needed strategic depth in Central Asia. It had now an American ally ruled by a Monarch who owed his throne to the US sharing its borders. In 1975 Gerald Ford and Kissinger received the Shah in the White House. Two years later, Jimmy Carter who had announced human rights as a cornerstone of US foreign policy and had officially designated every US ambassador on earth to be his personal human rights representative went one step further. *'If ever there was a country which has blossomed forth under enlightened leadership',* Carter said in his banquet toast to the Shah Reza Pahlavi, *'it would be the ancient empire of Persia'.*

The only forum where people could ventilate their grievances was the Mosque. Thus, was sown the seeds of the Islamic revolution. The clerics through their uncompromising resistance to the Shah, won the popular support of the people. When the revolution broke out, Islamic clerics would lead. The clerics obviously detested the West. The West in turn labelled them medieval. The Islamic revolution in 1979 finally put an end to the twenty-six-year rule of the despotic Shah. Ever since Iran has been under US sanctions. The US was to find a new ally in neighbouring Iraq as the communist government of Kassem was overthrown by the nationalist Ba'ath Party. On assuming the reins of power Saddam Hussein launched a military campaign against Iran at the bidding of the US.

---

[14] The exiled leader Ayatollah Khomeini returned to Iran on 1st February 1979 following the Islamic Revolution ending 2500 years of dynasty rule. It was the first religious revolution in modern history and the first televised revolution. He described the US as the 'Great Satan' and the Soviet Union as 'Lesser Satan'.

Chapter 10: Guatemala Follows Suit

> 'I was incapable of disobedience. And those employers exploited my obedience. They took advantage of my innocence.'

> 'My mother said that when a woman sees her son tortured, burnt alive, she is incapable of forgiving, incapable of getting rid of her hate.'

> 'My father said: "Some have to give their blood and some have to give their strength; so while we can, we'll give our strength".'

> What hurts Indians most is that our costumes are considered beautiful, but it's as if the person wearing it didn't exist.'
>
> **– Rigoberta Menchú**

The October Revolution of Guatemala

Latin America shrugged off her colonial yoke more than a century before Africa and Asia. But, it was relegated to be a backyard of the US. The United Fruit Company, the forerunner of the present-day Chiquita headquartered in Boston, owned acres of land and a major chunk of infrastructure in many of the Latin American countries. Banana was cultivated in large quantities in these vast acres of agricultural land known as Latifundios. The companies pioneered Industrial Agriculture. For the United Fruit Company. Guatemala was just an estate to grow bananas. UFC was called the octopus, for the way it held Guatemala in its grip. It owned the roads and rails. The only port opening to the Atlantic was owned by it.

During the 1930s and 1940s, the United Fruit Company thrived in Guatemala under the patronage of Jorge Ubico, a puppet of the US. The life of the Guatemalans was harsh and pathetic under Ubico. Ubico branded everyone who harboured economic and political ideologies that were more progressive than his own as a communist. The peasant worked for 50 cents a day while UFC declared profits of $65 million, twice the income of Guatemala. People rose in revolt against the misrule of Ubico and in October 1944 Young military officers toppled the tyrannical puppet regime in what is known as Guatemala's own *'October Revolution'*.

A few months later in March 1945 Guatemalans went to the polls and elected Juan José Arévalo Bermejo a Professor of Philosophy to be their President. In his inaugural address, on 15th March 1945, the new President Arévalo cited Roosevelt as his inspiration. As President, he enacted a slew of legislations aimed at social reforms. This included an increase in the minimum wage, regularization of working hours, providing adequate medical care, literacy programmes and measures to ensure the social inclusion of the native population. He also oversaw the drafting of a new constitution in 1945. President Arévalo laid the solid foundation for a pluralistic democracy in Guatemala. During his six-year term from 1945 to 1951, the country's first social security system was established, trade unions were brought within the legal framework and fixed a forty-eight-hour work-week. The land-owning class was brought within the ambit of taxation.

Guatemala was turning itself into a Welfare State. The progressive measures of minimum wages and regularisation of work hours started to eat into the profits of UFC. The welfare measures that emancipated the Guatemalans from squalor were not to the liking of the UFC Inc. In his six-year Presidency, he survived no less than 25 coup attempts. The new popular government of Guatemala was never a military threat to the US. But, its welfare measures were a threat to the United Fruit Company. At the end of his first term Arevalo, though just 47 years of age and at the zenith of his popularity, did not wish to get re-elected for a second term. Instead, he chose to hand over power to Jacobo Árbenz who was his Defence Minister in his Cabinet and was instrumental in the October Revolution and had a pivotal role in putting down many of the coup attempts that marked his six-year Presidency. Arbenz won the election by a margin of more than 50 percent votes over his immediate rival. It was the first time a peaceful transfer of power had taken place in the history of this country. As fate would have it, it would take decades for the Guatemalans to witness yet another peaceful transfer of power from one democratic head of government to another.

Accepting the baton of governance from Arevalo and building on the foundations built by him, Jacobo Arbenz embarked on an ambitious programme to transform Guatemala even further into a Welfare State within the capitalist framework. Like Arevalo he too admired Roosevelt and believed a Welfare State was possible within capitalism provided the government stepped in on behalf of the people. Distributing the nation's misallocated resources was something Arbenz's predecessor was not successful with, a shortcoming that Arevalo did lament in his farewell speech. The US Inc owned and operated all major infrastructure. A government-owned deep water port accessible to all was constructed under Arbenz. As the government stepped in each sector, be it the construction of an Electric company or rail roads, the entrenched vested interests started viewing Arbenz with caution.

Arbenz's crowning achievement was the passage of The Agrarian Reform Law, by the National Assembly on 17th June 1952. As per the law, the Guatemalan government could seize and redistribute all uncultivated land on estates in excess of 672 acres. Provisions of the law enacted stipulated that the owners of the confiscated lands be compensated by an amount they themselves had declared as the value of their land holdings for taxation purposes. In a country in which the majority of the citizens were starving, to let large tracts of land remain fallow was inhuman. The government started buying fallow land. In return, it offered the landowners the value they themselves had declared for taxation purposes. This was an affront to United Fruit, which owned more than 550,000 acres, nearly one-fifth of the country's arable land. UFC cultivated less than 15 percent of the 550,000 acres it owned

Sam Zemurray, the visionary *'Banana Man'* under whom UFC had steadily risen to its mammoth size, was irked by the developments in Guatemala. With the dawn of democracy in Guatemala, he knew unless the movement towards democracy was rolled back UFC would be in a perilous situation. He commissioned a public relations expert Edward Bernays, a nephew of Sigmund Freud to sway public opinion in the US against the new Guatemalan government. Bernays is one of the pioneers of modern mass psychology as we know it today. He was quite right when he described himself as the *'father of public relations'*. Indeed, he was. His focus was what he referred to as *'the conscious and intelligent manipulation of the organized habits and opinions of the masses'*. On his suggestion, United Fruit launched a campaign to discredit the Guatemala's government before the US public. In 1951 far across in distant Asia, Iran under Mohammad Mossadegh, had nationalised the Anglo--Iranian Oil Company. It was feared Guatemala might follow suit. In the Cold War era every Third-World country was perceived as a domino. Newspapers and magazines in the US ran stories of Guatemala falling to the Soviet camp and an imminent takeover of the entire Latin America by the REDS. The US public was administered heavy doses of highly indoctrinating material on the subservience of the Guatemalan leadership to the Kremlin. Members of the Congress too echoed such 'fears' and a consensus for the ouster of the Guatemalan government was carefully crafted. This rhetoric reached a new peak after the Agrarian Reform Law was passed. Any radical measure, even the confiscation of the fallow land, ran the risk of being deliberately misconstrued to be undertaken at the behest of the Kremlin. Guatemala did not have any diplomatic relationship with the Soviet Union at that point of time. No delegation from Guatemala had ever visited the Soviet Union until then. Guatemalan Communist Party had a very miniscule presence in the National assembly. The party was well organized but in no way had the strength to bring its influence to bear. The communist movement was very much indigenous to Guatemala and was never under the tutelage of Moscow. But, like all other parties, it welcomed the reallocation of land resources and such other radical measures.

The welfare measures of the Guatemalan government were eating into the profit of the UFC. The US Secretary of State John Foster Dulles was a former attorney of UFC. His brother Allan Dulles who ran the CIA was on the board of UFC. The ease with which Operation AJAX, the operation to remove Mohammad Mossadegh, was accomplished in Iran had bolstered the Dulles brothers' confidence in pulling down democratically elected governments and replacing them with US puppets.

Eisenhower approved the CIA operation to oust Arbenz. Code named 'Operation PB Success'. It was operational by August 1953. The Catholic Church in Guatemala was hand in glove with the propertied class. The Church was lavished with wealth by the aristocracy. The time had come for the Church to show its gratitude. The Church reached out to its believers in pastoral letters and radio broadcasts. From disgruntled exiles, mercenaries were organized and trained. They were provided with superior arms and telecommunication devices that could jam the government communication lines. The Guatemalan army was thoroughly ill-equipped to take on the heavily armed mercenaries with state-of-art technology. CIA pilots dropped propagandist leaflets that exhorted the Guatemalans to *'Fight for God, Fatherland, Freedom, Work, Truth and Justice and to fight against Communist atheism, Communist interventionism, Communist oppression, Communist poverty, Communist lies, and Communist police'*. The US which had been the main supplier of weaponry to Guatemala stopped arms trade with Guatemala and blocked every attempt by the Guatemalan government to procure arms from elsewhere. However, Jacobo Arbenz did manage to procure arms from Czechoslovakia. On 15th

---

[15] Guatemala in 1954 did not have a Soviet Embassy or any diplomatic ties with the Soviet Union.

May 1954, a Polish ship docked in Guatemala with two thousand tons of small arms and ammunition made in Czechoslovakia. It was the first time a Latin American country had bought arms from the Eastern bloc. Secretary of State, John Foster Dulles grabbed this opportunity. Acquiring arms from a Soviet bloc country was played up as a Soviet presence in Latin America and made a perfect case for the overthrow of the Arbenz government. CIA trained rebels and mercenaries armed to the teeth raided from Honduras. A clandestine radio station *Voice of Liberation* started to spread rumours and false reports about an impending civil war. The radio broadcasts claimed that the rebels had almost taken over the country and were inching towards the Presidential palace which was hardly the case. It started to report on mutiny by certain divisions of the military which were untrue. Such propaganda did yield results. The soldiers were demoralised. Its rank and file refused to fight as they perceived they were up against a formidable enemy. The army that was loyal to Arbenz and had refused to be won over by the CIA started to crack. The psychological warfare employed found success. In the mayhem and confusion that prevailed Jacobo Arbenz had to resign. Thus, the Guatemalan revolution that began in October 1944 had at last come to an end by June 1954.

A puppet government working under the dictates of Washington was put in the place of a widely popular democratic government. Guatemala's tryst with democracy, thus, came to a sudden end. With it all the aspirations of turning Guatemala into a modern Welfare State were administered a quiet burial. The new regime under orders from Washington abolished the banana workers' federation, revoked the Agrarian Reform Law, and banned all political parties and peasant groups. Farmlands apportioned to the peasants were taken back and the previous land owners were restored. Monoculture of bananas resumed. Labour reforms that had heralded adequate wages and humane working conditions were rolled back. Peasant cooperatives were dissolved, health, housing and literacy programmes grounded to a halt. The puppet government under directions from Washington ordered the arrest of thousands of suspected leftists. The country soon plunged into civil war. The civil war that ensued from 1960 continued unabated until the peace accords of 1996.

Rigoberto Menchu in her touching autobiographical sketch *'My Name is Rigoberta Menchú, and this is how my Awareness was Born'* in graphic details reflects on the years of wanton savagery of the military that secured Washington's imperial interests. The world press reported in the 1980s on the systematic violence of the Guatemalan army on its citizens, especially the natives, the descendants of the great Mayan civilization. General Ríos Montt, the then leader of the military junta that brutalized the people was a great friend of the US President Ronald Reagan. He reassured President Reagan that the Guatemalan government's counter-insurgency strategy was not one of *'scorched earth'* but rather of *'scorched communists'*. Reagan was dismissive of reports of his pathetic human rights record and was in full praise of him.

Cold War | 123

Chapter 11: 'North Vietnam Attacks US'. US Had to Retaliate!

'It is because of the criminal war unleashed by the U.S. government that hundreds of thousands of young Americans have been drafted and sent to a useless death far from their homeland, on the Vietnamese battlefield. In hundreds of thousands of American families, parents have lost their sons, and wives their husbands'.

– **Ho Chi Minh's appeal to the American people**

'Half a million US soldiers with 700,000 Vietnamese allies, with total command of the air, with total command of the sea, backed by huge resources of modern weapons we are unable to secure a single city from the acts of the enemy whose total strength is about 250,000'.

– **Robert F Kennedy after the 1968 Tet Offensive**

'The image of the Vietnamese getting into their PT boats and coming across the Pacific and taking California is an insult to the US Navy'.

– **Walter Lippman**

'All men are created equal. They are endowed by their Creator with certain inalienable rights, among them are Life, Liberty, and the Pursuit of Happiness'.

Does that ring any bell?

Thus stated the Vietnamese leader Ho Chi Minh on 2nd September 1945, on the day of the Japanese surrender in WW II, as he proclaimed the independent Democratic Republic of Vietnam at Hanoi's Ba Dinh square. By those words, reminiscent of the American Declaration of Independence in 1776, he was making an overture towards the US to intervene on behalf of his country on the French question. He wrote to President Truman soliciting his support. The US did intervene. But not as expected of that great country that professed to cherish *'Life, Liberty, and the Pursuit of Happiness'.*

Vietnam under Ho Chi Minh would have never been anti-American. He had a warm feeling for America. He had a lifelong admiration for its people. He cherished its very founding principles. With weapons supplied by America, Viet Minh, a nationalist organization under his leadership, had fought the Japanese during WW II who had come to occupy their country following the French fiasco. Ho's declaration of independence on 2nd September 1945, the very day the Japanese surrendered to the allies was symbolic. Vietnam was to be a free country thereafter. France never wanting to part with its colonial possessions refused to recognize his new government. He expected the US to intervene on Vietnam's behalf, as he had no other allies. Communist leaders in China and the Soviet Union were sceptical of his nationalism. It was only logical for him to turn to the US for help. Definitely, Ho Chi Minh would not have let the US Inc run amok in his country. Neither would have he aligned himself with the US. Instead, he would have steered his country into an independent foreign policy not aligned with any blocs very much like Tito of Yugoslavia. Perhaps Vietnam could even have been a bulwark against Chinese expansionism. For historical reasons, the two countries shared a not-so-cordial relationship. When the People's Republic of China under Mao Tse Tung rolled the red carpet for the US President Richard Nixon in February 1972, for his week-long visit, the first ever by a US President, the US troops were fighting Vietnamese close by.

The war in Vietnam is often cited as the epitome of American cruelty meted out on a newly independent infant nation attempting to exert its sovereignty. The plight of the hapless American soldiers, most of them who had just turned sixteen and who were butchered or maimed in the war in their thousands for a cause that they found hard to connect, is often missed.

America and the Quagmire of Vietnam

Vietnam was a French colony. With the capitulation of the French to the Germans very early in the war, French colonial possessions in Indochina came under Imperial Japan. With the Japanese surrender to the allies on 2nd September 1945, Vietnamese nationalist leader Ho Chi Minh proclaimed independence. However, the French government wanted to retain its former colony (The French had a strong presence in the southern parts of Vietnam). President Harry S Truman (1945–1953) and his successor Eisenhower (1953–1961) were keen on helping the French reclaim its colony. Both the Presidents subscribed to the 'Domino theory' which provided a convenient way of framing the geopolitics in the context of the Cold War. To start with, US involvement was however limited to the supply of arms, ammunition and finance.

The French, in spite of the US support, were convincingly defeated. Under the leadership of Ho Chi Minh and General Vo Nguyan Giap, Vietnamese army ousted the French from North Vietnam. The bitter guerrilla war ended with the surrender of 12,000 French soldiers at Dien Bien Phu in 1954. Peace was ushered in by the UN-brokered talks in Geneva and the country was to be sliced into two halves at the 17th parallel. Democratic Republic of Vietnam to the North and the Republic of Vietnam to the South were to be separated by a demilitarized zone. Elections were to be conducted on matters related to the unification of the two Republics in two years as per the Geneva accord. North Vietnam embraced a socialist pattern of economy under Ho Chi Minh. South Vietnam, now a de facto ally of the West, the US to be precise, under a puppet government embraced the free market economy.

The US Secretary of State Dulles, had represented the US in the talks in Geneva and was very much apprehensive of the developments. He did everything he could to prevent the French from leaving their posts in Vietnam. But, the French had it enough. The Vietnamese had resolved to be independent. They had seen the French troops meekly surrender before an Asian country, Japan. With no sign of victory in sight, the French were determined to leave once and after all. That did not mean, however, that Dulles would recede and resign himself to Vietnam as a lost cause. There was no question of him letting the Vietnamese voters elect a communist to lead their reunified country. Instead, he would leave no stone unturned to prevent the reunification of the country. Even if, it meant a sabotage of the accord inked at Geneva.

The government of South Vietnam at the dictates of the US balked at the very idea of unification. North and South Vietnam were to remain as two different countries. The Head of State of South Vietnam, Ngo Dinh Diem, a devout Catholic systematically marginalised the population believing in Buddhism, Confucianism and Taoism from positions of authority. Catholics were preferred and patronized much to the chagrin of the rest of the population. With American support, his was a reign of terror. Soon forces within South Vietnam wanting a unification of the two provinces and to put an end to American involvement in the running of the administration of their motherland took up armed insurgency. They organized themselves into Viet Cong and launched a guerrilla war against the puppet government of South Vietnam. Assuming the responsibility of South Vietnam, the US pumped as much as $7 billion in economic and military aid into South Vietnam from 1955 to 1961.

President Kennedy Wanted to Exit from Vietnam

> 'In the final analysis, it is their war. They are the ones who have to win it or lose it. We can help them… give them equipment…We can send our men as advisors. but they have to win it… We are prepared to continue to assist them. But I don't think the war can be won unless the people support the effort.'
> — Kennedy in an interview to CBS TV

> 'But today I feel differently. Having reviewed the record in detail, and with the advantage of hindsight, I think it highly probable that, had President Kennedy lived, he would have pulled us out of Vietnam. He would have concluded that the South Vietnamese were incapable of defending themselves, and that Saigon's grave political weaknesses made it unwise to try to offset the limitations of South Vietnamese forces by sending U.S. combat troops on a large scale. I think he would have come to that conclusion, even if he reasoned, as I believe he would have, that South Vietnam and, ultimately, Southeast Asia would then be lost to communism.'
> — Mc Namara, Secretary of Defence

Kennedy did subscribe to Eisenhower's prediction in 1954 that if Indochina fell, the rest of Southeast Asia would 'go over very quickly' like a 'row of dominoes'. In a highly publicised speech in 1956, Senator Kennedy had referred to Vietnam as: 'It is our offspring. We cannot abandon it, we cannot ignore its needs'. However, President Kennedy was determined that the US should never commit ground troops in Vietnam.

Very early in his Presidency, he confided to his Cabinet 'We are not going to bungle into war'. On ascending to the Presidency he increased the American presence from a meagre 865 to 17,000 military personnel.

But, these were mostly military advisors, technicians, pilots, supply and administrative personnel. They were airlifted and pressed into service to help train the South Vietnamese to defend themselves and South Vietnam against the threat from North. Kennedy was very particular that America should limit its role to providing training and logistical support to the South Vietnamese as it was *'their war'*. He abhorred the very idea of US marines battling in the jungles of Vietnam and insisted under no circumstances should an American boy be thrown into the midst of war between the two Vietnams. Though in his inaugural address, he had urged the nation *'to pay any price, bear any burden, meet any hardship, support any friend, oppose any foe to assure the survival and the success of liberty'* Vietnam was a price he never intended to pay as the South Vietnamese leadership did not deserve it. Neither Truman nor Eisenhower, even while conceding that a fall of Indochina would signal the fall of entire South East Asia and even East Asia, including India, were reluctant to commit combat troops to South Vietnam. A *'transition from advice to partnership'* was resented by Washington. The reasoning was that if there had been a sincere and strong South Vietnamese effort to contain the threat from the North, the need for US troops did not even arise… and in its absence, the US combat forces operating from the midst of a hostile population, would be sitting ducks for the Viet Cong guerrillas (as it eventually turned out to be). Kennedy flatly refused to send combat troops to South Vietnam though he was consistently being cautioned and prodded to do the same. Kennedy at no point of time appeared to be ambivalent. He was categorical. The US shall not intervene in a war 10,000 miles away to help a native army of 200,000 fight a handful of 16,000 guerrillas. Unlike in the Korean context, there was no invading army that came from the North. The Viet Cong Nationalists were native to the South and waging a struggle to unify with the North. The raison d'etre for US involvement did not exist. The situation was delicate.

Very much in line with what was the prevailing logic, a phased withdrawal of the US troops from Vietnam was recommended by Mc Namara the Secretary of State for Defence on 2nd October 1963. Kennedy in receipt of the recommendation announced that he expected the US training mission to be completed by 1965 and that he would begin withdrawing U.S. training forces within ninety days i.e. by 31st December 1963. On 11th October 1963, the White House issued National Security Action Memorandum (NSAM) 263, which called for the withdrawal of 1,000 U.S. military personnel by the end of 1963 and 1000 US troops did return to the US to have their Christmas with their family. This act infuriated the war mongers. In the context of the Cold War, it was projected as Kennedy buckling under the *'Soviet threat'*. As 1964 was an election year he could not afford to be viewed as being soft on communism. The President was effecting a balancing act with utmost care. However, President Kennedy had no intention in engaging a full-scale combat in Vietnam. In his second term, Kennedy would have pulled out from the South in its entirety.

On 1st November in a coup Diem was killed. Though Washington was shocked at the developments in Saigon, Kennedy did not vacillate in his resolve to bring the boys back home. On 14th November 1963 in a news conference, a week before his assassination, answering the question *'Would you give us your appraisal of the situation in South Vietnam now, since the coup, and the purposes for the Honolulu conference'?* he replied: *'The purpose of the meeting at Honolulu…is to attempt to assess the situation: what American policy should be, and what our aid policy should be, how we can intensify the struggle, how we can bring Americans out of there. Now, that is our object, to bring Americans home, permit the South Vietnamese to maintain themselves as a free and independent country'*. President Kennedy during the course of the news conference asked rhetorically *'Are we going to give up in South Vietnam'?* He answered the question by saying, *'The most important program, of course, is our national security, but I don't want the United States to have to put troops there'*. Those were the President's last public remarks on Vietnam before he was killed 8 days later on 22nd November in Dallas.

Kennedy's assassination cleared the deck for full-scale American involvement in the Vietnam War. Lyndon B Johnson, though convinced that US Army would find it difficult to fight a highly unconventional enemy in the jungles half a world away, had an inclination towards the war mongers in Pentagon. The decision to fight a war so distant from the mainland of America, which possessed neither strategic significance nor any material resource to offset the war expense, was hardly contested among the powers that be.

On 26th November a day after Kennedy was buried the new President Lyndon B Johnson signed NSAM 273, which called for increased US commitment and in it lay the seeds of the disastrous Vietnam War. It effectively reversed NSAM 263. Though the draft of NSAM 273 was in the making following the coup in South Vietnam, while Kennedy was still alive, given his public posturing against any further involvement in Vietnam, he would never have approved it. Had Kennedy been alive the very draft of NSAM 273 would have read something different. Lyndon Johnson, right from his first visit to Saigon as the Vice President in May 1961, was harping on increased US involvement. During his visit to Saigon Lyndon B Johnson had assured the South Vietnamese President Ngo Dinh Diem full support in combating the Viet Cong battling for the unification of Vietnam. He even referred to the US surrogate as the *'Churchill of Asia'*. Back home he warned the domino theorists that South Vietnam was close to being taken over in total by the Viet Cong and that soon the US would have to fight the Vietnamese *'on the shores of Waikiki'* and eventually *'on our own shores'*.

Gulf of Tonkin Resolution: 7th August 1964

On 2nd August 1964 destroyer USS Maddox during patrolling operations in the Gulf of Tonkin fired at North Vietnamese torpedo boats. The fire was promptly returned. In the ensuing skirmish, a couple of North Vietnamese boats were sunk and Vietnamese Navy suffered casualties. An aircraft on USS Maddox was damaged but there was no American casualty.

On 4th August 1964, the US Navy alleged that the North Vietnamese launched an attack on the destroyer. To substantiate the claim of being attacked a RADAR image was produced and exhibited before the Congress. The RADAR image that was produced to make a case of a North Vietnamese attack was not clear. Speculation was rife that the whole incident of US vessels coming under attack was conspiratorial and the RADAR image doctored. President Johnson and the Secretary of Defence Mc Namara convinced the Congress that the US Navy had come under attack by a belligerent North Vietnam. The Congress was coerced into adopting the *'Gulf of Tonkin Resolution'* which authorised the President and conferred upon him sweeping powers to commit the US troops to the South East. 1964 was an election year and hence Jhonson though being conferred sweeping powers, did not escalate the war. On 8th March 1965, barely two months after his second inauguration 3,500 Marines of the 9th Marine Expeditionary Brigade arrived in Da Nang, South Vietnam. These marines were the first U.S. combat troops to enter the war. That was how US Marines started to get involved in the Vietnam War. A war that Kennedy never wanted to fight. Over the years the US presence would increase to 5,50,000 combat-ready marines.

The war was tightly fought. The Viet Cong cadres with perfect knowledge of the terrain and camouflaged by the thick tropical forests could successfully checkmate the Americans with superior firepower and weaponry. The *Cu chi* network of tunnels helped the Viet Cong in this war. Under the iconic leadership of Gen. Giap the Vietnamese replicated the strategy of Sun Tsu and Mao Tse Tung. Napalm bombs, Agent Orange and defoliants that were pumped into Vietnam were no match for the revolutionary spirit of the Vietnamese. It was in this war that helicopters were pressed into massive use. It was also the first televised war. Americans back home could watch their boys being airlifted and dropped into the lush green tropical forests to be butchered by the unseen enemies hiding behind the jungles. Many soldiers fell prey to the tigers and lions in the forests. Many of them died of snake bites.

Republican Candidate Richard Nixon Torpedoes Peace Talks to Prolong The War

The war reached a stalemate by 1968 with heavy casualties on both sides. There was no chance of an American win. The 'Tet Offensive' in January 1968 by the Viet Cong and the North Vietnamese was decisive in turning the American public opinion against the war. The offensive was a well-coordinated massive attack on more than 100 towns and cities, 36 of the 44 provincial capitals, 5 of the 6 autonomous cities, 72 of the 245 district towns, and the southern capital of Saigon. Almost South Vietnam in its entirety was under the Viet Cong guerrillas. Even the US embassy in South Vietnam came close to being ransacked. The offensive was the largest military operation conducted by either side up to that point in the war. It took months for the US army to completely retard the guerrillas. Though technically the US could repulse the communist guerrillas, it was a big political victory for the Viet Cong. It convinced the US public that they were being lied to by their political and military leadership.

Americans started to question the rationale behind the war. With 27,000 American casualties until then and no sign of an American victory, Americans wanted their kids back home. The domino theory found no takers. An American withdrawal, even if it be a sign of weakness, seemed imminent. 1968 being an election year the public mood against the war could no longer be ignored. President Johnson made earnest efforts to bring peace in Vietnam and bring back the American boys. The UN-brokered peace talks between North and South Vietnam in Paris were heading for an amicable solution. By around October 1968, barely months before the election the fighting had almost stopped.

With long-term peace around the corner chances of American boys getting back home seemed real. Lyndon B Johnson's Vice President Hubert H. Humphrey, who was the Democrat nominee for the Presidency, seemed all poised to win the 1968 election (President Lyndon Johnson disgraced by the war had refused to run for a second term in office). The Republican candidate for Presidency was Richard Nixon. His campaign team sensing defeat swung into action. They secretly colluded with the South Vietnamese government. He secretly insisted South Vietnam to withdraw from the Paris peace talks by promising a better deal for South Vietnam than under a Democratic President (Interestingly his campaign slogan was *'Peace with Honour'*). This was effected through the embassy of South Vietnam in Washington. Throughout the campaign, the Nixon campaign team maintained a secret channel to the South Vietnamese.

The Nixon campaign's clandestine effort to thwart President Johnson's peace initiative by reaching out to the South Vietnamese government through its embassy in Washington no doubt crossed all limits of political jockeying even by the American standards. It amounted to treason. South Vietnam's withdrawal at Nixon's insistence derailed the peace process. After the lull, the war resumed. All prospects for peace vanished. The tide of the election changed. The unsuspecting electorate disgusted with the renewed hostilities and aggravated war switched sides to favour Republican Richard Nixon who in effect had caused the war to escalate and prolong!

Upon entering the White House, the new Republican President Richard Nixon dragged on his promise. He expanded the war into Laos and Cambodia. The war continued for four more years. And more than 30,000 soldiers were to die in those four years. Nixon wanted to win the election and he won. Once in power, he rewarded his sponsors.

It is very clear that US Presidents after Kennedy refused to view Vietnam as a political question, and this was not without a reason. A political answer to Vietnam would be to let the bifurcated Vietnam unite under communist rule. The giant leaps in the social development of a united people under communist rule would have had a great demonstrative effect. The power of an example was simply too great for the capitalist world to contain. A comparative analysis of the development of the two Vietnams was not that encouraging for the US. An intelligence estimate in May 1959 held that development in South would lag behind that in the North, and South Vietnam would continue to rely on US non-military aid to close the gap between resources and requirements. The focus of North Vietnam was on overall national development.

In Retrospect

> 'When it came to Vietnam, we found ourselves setting policy for a region that was terra incognita'
>
> – Mc Namara

No sooner had WW II ended that 16 nations led by the US under the aegis of the UN were at war with North Korea. An attempt to unite Korea, which came to be divided into North and South at the 38th parallel following its liberation from Japanese occupation by the Red Army from the North and US army from the South, was hotly contested by the West. The Korean War (1950–1953) was indecisive. The two forces fought themselves to a stalemate. By then Japan, a sworn enemy of the US had turned itself into a bastion of capitalism and an ally of the US in Asia with huge investments from US Inc. The only purpose the war served was to galvanise the Japanese economy and help the investors reap handsome profits. Korea remains divided even to this day.

The next phase of the war was to be in Vietnam. Vietnam, a French colony had witnessed the surrender of its French garrisons to the Japanese during the war. With the surrender of Japan in the war the French wanted to retain its possession in Indochina. The French located in the southern parts of Vietnam with US help did cling on until the disastrous defeat in Dien Bien Phu in 1954. Following the UN mediation, the country came to be divided into two at the 17th parallel. The Soviet Union stood solidly behind the North Vietnamese. President Kennedy was averse to sending ground troops to Vietnam. Kennedy himself being a war hero of the World War II was acutely aware of the futility of another Trans-Pacific War. Unlike the Korean War, the US could not count upon any of its allies this time. He limited the US involvement to sending arms and military advisors to aid the puppet government of South Vietnam in its war efforts. A stand that would cost the President his life. His successor reversed the US policy on Vietnam. From 8th March 1965 till 29th March 1973, when the last of the US military units left, the Americans were trapped in Vietnam for a cause they failed to connect..

What was the US plan to win the war? It turned out, there was none. The plan was to stay within it hoping the enemy would finally give up. *'To wear the enemy out'* as the military pundits put it is no plan at all. Jhonson's successor Richard Nixon (1969–1974) who won the election on the promise of *'Peace with honour'* committed more troops to Vietnam. It is no longer a secret that Richard Nixon during the Presidential campaign supported the peace process in public but derailed it in secrecy by promising the South Vietnamese a better deal under his Presidency.

The burgeoning expense of the war and the huge current account deficit the US had to bear took a heavy toll on its economy. The oil price hike in the 1970s made matters worse. The primary cause of stagflation that the US and Europe experienced was primarily due to the Vietnam War. Under the pretext of tackling inflation which was blamed on the welfare measures, Ronald Reagan (1981–1989) and Margaret Thatcher (1979–1990) systematically rolled back the welfare measures inaugurated during the Great Depression and continued in the post-war period. Ronald Reagan cut down on welfare measures to pursue his Strategic Defence Initiative which sought to nuclearize outer space. Going one step further he announced the largest tax cut in US history which incapacitated the government's ability to administer basic welfare schemes which the citizens of his *'evil empire'* and many of the Third World nations took for granted.

Chapter 12: In POL POT US Seeks Revenge!

> 'All the foreigners involved have to be called to court, and there will be no exceptions... Madeleine Albright, Margaret Thatcher, Henry Kissinger, Jimmy Carter, Ronald Reagan and George Bush ... we are going to invite them to tell the world why they supported the Khmer Rouge'.
>
> **– The Cambodian lawyer defending Ta Mok, the Khmer Rouge military leader stated during the trial.**

> 'The US government insisted that the Khmer Rouge be fed. The US preferred that the Khmer Rouge operation benefit from the credibility of an internationally known relief operation'.
>
> **– US relief aid workers, Linda Mason and Roger Brown write in 'Rice, rivalry and Relief: Managing Cambodian relief'.**

> 'He [Pol Pot] was the enemy of their enemy: Vietnam, whose liberation of Cambodia could never be recognised because it had come from the wrong side of the Cold War. For the Americans, now backing Beijing against Moscow, there was also a score to be settled for their humiliation on the rooftops of Saigon'.
>
> **– John Pilger, Journalist**

Pol Pot was no communist. He was, instead a stooge of the US and Britain. In Pol Pot US found a convenient ally to avenge the humiliating retreat from Saigon. He never subscribed to dialectical materialism, an article of faith that underlines Marxism and Leninism. His *'experiments'* were borne out of his perverted views rooted in superstition. After coming to power in 1975, the genocide he orchestrated is often wrongly attributed to his purported belief in Marxism. The US fully aware of the genocidal nature of the regime turned a blind eye towards it.

It was the Republic of Vietnam that unseated Pol Pot. Vietnamese communist forces launched an attack on 25th December 1978 against the Khmer Rouge. After a 17-day war the Vietnamese troops liberated Cambodia from the clutches of Khmer Rouge and chased its cadres into the jungles. A responsible government was constituted in Cambodia on 8th January 1979 by the Republic of Vietnam. Vietnamese troops stationed in Cambodia to repel any attempt from the Khmer Rouge, which had the backing of western powers, to stage a return. Vietnam brought to light for the first time the genocide committed by the ousted regime.

According to American political scientist Michael Haas, the U.S. despite publicly condemning the Khmer Rouge following its ouster, offered military support to the organization and was instrumental in preventing UN recognition of the Vietnam-aligned government of Cambodia. The US directly armed the Khmer Rouge in order to weaken the influence of Vietnam and the Soviet Union in Southeast Asia. The US joined hands with China, Vietnam's arch-rival and Pol Pot's underwriter in its attempt to destabilize Cambodia. US slapped sanctions on Vietnam and blocked loans from IMF which the war-ravaged country was badly in need of. Though the Khmer Rouge was ousted from Cambodia, the United States, self-proclaimed apostle of democracy and freedom and the ASEAN countries voted for the Khmer Rouge and the Khmer Rouge-dominated Coalition government of Democratic Kampuchea (CGDK) in exile to retain Cambodia's seat in United Nations (UN) until as late as 1993. The flag of the Khmer Rouge flew over the UN premises until then. Anti-Vietnam fervour of those in US military grew into a cancer afflicting the body politic of the US.

The Rise and Fall of Pol Pot

Until 1969, the Khmer Rouge was a minor insurgency located in the jungles of Cambodia close to the Vietnamese border. Khmer Rouge's potent combination of a perverted interpretation of Maoism and medievalism had no popular base. It was the Vietnam War that propped Pol Pot and Khmer Rouge into power. By dropping the equivalent of five Hiroshimas on a peasant society during the illegal bombing of a neutral Cambodia from 1969 to 1973, Nixon and Kissinger killed an estimated half a million people. It was the indiscriminate bombing as well as a US backed coup in Cambodia in 1970, that toppled the Cambodian Chief of State Prince Norodom Sihanouk, that paved the way for Khmer Rouge to become a national threat. Eventually, it started to wield formal power from 1975. Throughout the Khmer Rouge's reign, until its ouster in December 1978, the United States denied that a genocide was taking place.

The US support for the Khmer Rouge began during the Carter Presidency (1977-1981) and continued long after it was ousted and its genocide stood well documented and was public. As a cover for its secret war against Cambodia, the US set up the Kampuchean Emergency Group (KEG) in the US embassy in Bangkok. President Carter's national security adviser, Zbigniew Brzezinski, said, *'I encouraged the Chinese to support Pol Pot'*. The US, he added, *'winked publicly'* as China sent arms to the Khmer Rouge through Thailand. In 1980, under US pressure, the World Food Programme handed over food worth $12 million to the Thai army to pass on to the Khmer Rouge. According to former Assistant Secretary of State Richard Holbrooke, 20,000 to 40,000 Pol Pot guerrillas benefited. This aid helped restore the Khmer Rouge to a fighting force to reckon with. Based in Thailand it continued to destabilise Cambodia. With Ronald Reagan assuming the Presidency in 1981 the dividing line between the international relief operation and the US war blurred. It did not take much time for the two, relief operations and the US war to blend. In a correspondence between Congressional lawyer Jonathan Winer and the

Vietnam Veterans of America Foundation, it was revealed that close to $85 million was pumped into the Khmer Rouge militia from 1980 to 1986. Winer said the debilitating information had come from the Congressional Research Service (CRS). Weapons from West Germany, Sweden and the US were being channelled into the Khmer Rouge cadres through Singapore as a conduit, thus making the country the arms capital of Asia.

The British Connection

Until 1989 when it erupted, the British involvement in Cambodia was a heavily guarded secret. On 25th June 1991, after about two years of vehement denials, the British government finally admitted that the British Special Air Service (SAS) had been secretly training the Khmer Rouge cadres since 1983. And since 1986, the training became an exclusively British operation after the *'Iran-gate'* arms-for-hostages scandal broke in Washington in 1986. The scandal had put President Reagan on the defensive. President Reagan could no longer afford another fiasco and Thatcher took the entire responsibility of the Khmer Rouge training. *'Asia Watch'* furnished the details: The SAS taught *'the use of improvised explosive devices, booby traps and the manufacture and use of time-delay devices'.* Rae McGrath who authored the report, (who shared a joint Nobel Peace Prize for the international campaign on landmines), wrote in the Guardian that *'the SAS training was a criminally irresponsible and cynical policy'.*

Cambodia is the most heavily mined country in the world. Estimates say there could still be as much as 10 million unexploded mines and ordnance in the country rendering agriculture the mainstay of its economy extremely difficult. It has close to 50,000 amputees, a significant figure for its population. Unbridled assistance from Washington flowed to the Khmer Rouge, which often conducted raids into Vietnam and clashed with its forces. Meanwhile the United Nations was often the means of the western powers to suffocate the government of Cambodia. Cambodia was the only country, in all its history of the world body, it withheld development aid from. The US denied religious groups export licenses for books and toys for orphans in Cambodia. 'Trading with the Enemy Act,' a law dating from the First World War was applied to Cambodia and Vietnam. Neither the recalcitrant Cuba nor its arch-rival Soviet Union had faced a total ban from the US with no humanitarian or cultural exceptions.

In the UN, the term 'Khmer Rouge' hardly found any mention since the 1990s. It was rebranded as *'Representatives of Democratic Campaign'*. The word genocide too disappeared from UN reports on Cambodia. By insisting on the involvement of the Khmer Rouge in any peace settlement, tantamount to including Hitler in the denazification of Germany, Pol Pot was being whitewashed and his organization was being bestowed legitimacy. Until his death in April 1998, Pol Pot operated with impunity and was never brought to justice.

Hun Sen, Prime Minister of Cambodia, paying tribute to the Republic of Vietnam in 2014 stated:*'Only Vietnam, under the leadership of the Communist Party of Vietnam, voluntarily sent her children and loved ones to help liberate and save the lives of the Cambodian people in times of great danger when Cambodia begged to the whole world to come and save us. The Vietnamese volunteers' help given by their own blood and bones, was the humane and righteous aid. This support should have been the main obligation of the international community in helping a people in need because of the Pol Pot regime's policy of institutionalised, top-down, organised genocide'.*

Chapter 13: 9/11 Chile: The Neo-Liberal Laboratory
'Shock Therapy' Began Here

> 'The elections in Chile are much too important to be left to the Chileans alone'.
>
> — **Henry Kissinger**

> 'We are the victims of a new form of imperialism, one that is more subtle, more cunning and, for that reason, more terrifyingly effective. . . . External pressure has tried to cut us off from the world, to strangle our economy. . . . We find ourselves facing forces operating in the twilight, without a flag, with powerful weapons'.
>
> — **Salvador Allende,**
> **President of Chile, in his address to**
> **the United Nations, 4th December 1972**

> 'Soldiers… Look around… Only thing you will find to fear about is poetry'.
>
> — **Pablo Neruda**

'A dagger pointed at Antarctica' remarked the US National Security Advisor Henry Kissinger in 1969 at the height of the Cold War. Kissinger was referring to the South American Republic of Chile sandwiched between the Andes and the Pacific with a desert in the North and glaciers in the south. By that dismissive statement, Kissinger meant Chile did not measure up to be a strategic interest for the US. With the US establishment preoccupied with the war in Vietnam, Chile was never a priority. It seemed Chile was safe. Chile had a tradition of democratic governments coming to power through general elections for about four decades. It had the longest history of a stable democratic government in the entire

Latin America. Blessed with the largest deposits of Copper in the world it had a very vibrant economy. The two American-owned companies, Kennecott and Anaconda, operating in Chile were the titans of the world copper business. Besides mining and consumer-products companies, International Telephone and Telegraph (ITT), played a major role in Chile.

In the early 1960s, Marxist guerrillas were fighting US-backed governments in Guatemala, Venezuela, Colombia, Peru and the Dominican Republic. But in 1970 Chile put up a different challenge which the US establishment found difficult to grapple. In September 1970, Dr Salvador Allende won the Presidential election in a closely contested three-way race. Allende was a socialist to the core. He was a Marxist-Leninist. He stood for social investment. An ardent admirer of Castro he stood for the nationalisation of the country's copper mines to better the living conditions of the Chileans. A socialist coming to power on a plank of nationalization in Latin America, not by the barrel of the gun, but by the ballot had a great psychological effect on many countries in the western hemisphere. A population's socialist aspirations finding material expression through general elections was unprecedented. Unlike in Guatemala or Iran, where the incumbent took measures like nationalization not to the liking of western Capital after coming to power, Allende's inclinations were known to western capitalists for decades. He had run for the Presidency in 1952, 1958, and 1964 though unsuccessfully. CIA had funded his opponents in all the Presidential races. It had unleashed propaganda against him since 1952. The American companies showered millions on the campaign of his political opponent Eduardo Frei, leader of the left Christian Democratic Party in the 1964 Presidential election. In April 1970 during the run-up to the elections, ITT Chairman Harold Geneen publicly stated *'Willing to assist financially any government plan to help protect private American investments in Chile'*.

At the height of the Cold War Allende's victory was a vindication for the socialist movement across the world. Chile had the potential of becoming the rallying point of all democratic movements in securing to its people a government based on socialist ideals. Unlike Fidel Castro, on whom aspersions of high-handedness could be cast, Dr Salvador Allende was even by western standards, blemishless. That made the socialist win more appealing and hence more emulative.

Allende was very much like Franklin D. Roosevelt. He was born into the privileges of the Chilean aristocratic class. He vigorously campaigned for radical social change. And, like Roosevelt, he was branded a traitor to his class. As a nation, Chile was the most prosperous in South America. It had high literacy and a buoyant economy. The middle class was well off. But millions of Chileans lived in squalor. The native Indians were excluded from the social fabric of Chilean life. Himself a physician, he was appalled at the high rates of infant mortality and maternal mortality. The high mortality rates among the under-privileged were shocking. The deaths that could have been prevented by the diversion of a miniscule amount towards welfare through appropriate taxation of foreign companies that were making vulgar profits, did hurt him.

During the late 1960s and 1970s, until the 'invasion' of Afghanistan by the Red Army, the US-Soviet relation was marked by a remarkable cooling off of all hostilities. Détente marked the beginning of personal rapport between Richard Nixon and his Soviet counterpart, Leonid Brezhnev. In 1972 Richard Nixon paid a week-long visit from 21st to 28th February to the People's Republic of China marking the cessation of hostilities. The US never had any diplomatic relations with the communist state since its inception twenty-five years ago. But, the President harboured a visceral hatred for Allende and his commitment to welfare in his home country. He did not endorse Kennedy's programme of *'Alliance for Progress'* which involved substantial US aid to the Latin American countries to retain them in the US orbit. He preferred to associate with the right-wing constituents in the political landscape of Latin America. Nixon openly favoured the business elite and military and leaned on them to keep their country glued to the US.

The Pre-emptive Strike

Barely a week after Allende's election on 3rd September 1970 and 6 weeks prior to being inaugurated, National Security Advisor Henry Kissinger and the CIA Director Richard Helmes walked into the Oval office to meet Richard Nixon. Declassified documents suggest that it was decided in this meeting to see to it that Salvador Allende was not to be inaugurated. Track I was to prevent the President-elect's inauguration through Parliamentary trickery. Track II was to involve the Chilean military to oust him in case Track I was to fail.

The Abortive Coup

In the 1970 elections, Salvador Allende representing the Popular Unity alliance won a narrow plurality. He polled 36 percent votes. As he had not won the mandatory absolute majority of 50 percent of the votes polled, his election had to be certified by the Chilean Congress. CIA tried its level best to manipulate the Chilean Congress. The convention in Chile was to elect the candidate who had garnered the maximum number of votes. As the days went by, it became clear the Chilean Congress could not be won over by the CIA. Allende in all probability would be certified by the Congress to be their President.

Soon Track II was set into motion. A section of the Chilean army hatched a military coup to prevent Allende's inauguration. But, the biggest stumbling block towards this end was the Chilean Commander-in-Chief Rene Schneider. He was a staunch constitutionalist and would have nothing to do with disrupting Chile's decades of civilian government. CIA came to the conclusion that he should be *'neutralised'*. Coup plotters decided to abduct him and leverage the confusion that would ensue to stage a coup and pre-emptively prevent the inauguration of Allende. But, the attempt to abduct the General was botched up and in the pandemonium an attempt was made on his life that severely injured him. This created much resentment among the public resulting in country-wide protests.

Chileans responded to such an outrageous act with a rare display of solidarity. Chilean Congress met on 24th October and by a vote of 153 to 24, certified Allende's election. Such a certification by the Congress by a landslide was a reflection of the Chileans resolve to align with Allende. General Schneider succumbed to his wounds in the subsequent days. The state of Chile mourned the death of this great General. Dr Salvador Allende took office on 3rd November 1970.

Assuming office against the backdrop of a *'coup climate',* Salvador Allende embarked on national reconstruction. Aged 62 Allende epitomised practical wisdom. He was in the thick of electoral politics and was tutored by the circumstances of his young nation for four decades. With a Republican President none other than Richard Nixon in the White House, being advised by Kissinger on National Security, Allende knew he was treading a narrow line.

His administration continues to be unparalleled in that it delivered so much in so little a time against all odds. In three years this democratically elected Marxist-Leninist government implemented, among other things, universal health care and education, land reforms, nationalised copper and silver mines, effected price control, ensured milk to new-born and lactating and expectant mothers, free nutritious lunch in schools for poor children, constructed and distributed houses for the houseless, put a check on inflation, raised the minimum wages, provided electricity in the remotest villages, awarded scholarship to the native Mapuche population, thus ushering a complete integration with the white population.

The Soviet Union was sceptical about Allende's success and survival. He, as they put it, *'was too kind and benevolent and the use of force even in extreme cases was not acceptable to him'.* The fact that his opponents had no qualm in resorting to violence could not alter his convictions. Castro too tried to convince Allende that the situation called for a radical approach. Allende was unperturbed.

American companies operating in the US, ITT, Dow Chemical, Kennecott, Anaconda, Bethlehem Steel, Charles Pfizer, Bank of America, Ralston Purina, Firestone Tire & Rubber, and W. R. Grace in unison started to work with officials in Washington who were tasked by Nixon and Kissinger to *'handle the Chilean problem'*. CIA's newly formed Chilean Task Force was required to use economic, political and psychological warfare against Allende to harass the Chilean economy into submission. Many of Chile's high-ranking military officers were trained by the US in its military bases. Such was the US involvement in Chilean affairs that Edward Korry, the US ambassador to Chile in 1967, asserted that his government had a *'fiduciary responsibility'* for Chile. Chile until the ascendance of Salvador Allende had been the recipient of American aid under *'Alliance for Progress'* programme. The US funding abruptly stopped. The US started vetoing any attempt by Allende to avail loans from the IMF. Two important US agencies, the Export-Import Bank and the Agency for International Development, announced that they would no longer approve *'any new commitments'* of U.S. bilateral assistance to Chile. The US representative at the Inter-American Development Bank was instructed by Washington to block all loans to Chile. When its President protested, as Chile was exceptionally prompt with the loan repayments, he was shown the door. The new President reduced Chile's credit rating from B to D. Private banks followed suit. All loans started to dry up. The intention was to *'Make the economy scream'*.

Washington was successful in triggering the union of truck owners into a nationwide strike, thus, resulting in a severe shortage of essential items. The resulting pandemonium was to be leveraged to the fullest extent. By September 1973, CIA was finding some luck with the Chilean military officers. General Pinochet, who stood by Allende in the abortive coup on the eve of his inauguration had switched sides and placed himself on the CIA payroll. A successful coup replacing a democratically elected government was staged on 9/11, 1973. As military jets started pounding the Presidential palace Allende addressed the nation. He refused to surrender and declined the safe passage out of the country. He pledged to die fighting. True to his word Allende died fighting holding an AK 47 which was gifted to him by Castro.

'The Brick' by the Chicago Boys

Chilean economists educated at the Department of Economics of the University of Chicago under Milton Friedman had prepared a 189-page 'Program for Economic Development' titled *El ladrillo*, meaning 'The Brick'. It was a blueprint to implement neoliberal principles in the running of the Chilean economy. The West was yet to embrace neoliberalism. After Augusto Pinochet came to power, it became the basis of the new regime's economic policy. The foundation of neoliberalism was to be laid *'brick by brick'* in Chile.

Shock Therapy

Chile was chosen to be the laboratory of neoliberal economics. While the West still ran its economy in the Keynesian mode, under the leadership of the Chicago boys neoliberalism was practiced on the Chileans to collect experimental data. In Chile the disciples of Milton Friedman seized upon an opportunity. The policies followed by the Chicago boys are referred to as shock therapy as they could hurt the economy and the people in the short run due to the rollback of welfare measures and employment, but in the long run prove to be beneficial. As it turned out, wherever it was applied it was all shock and no therapy.

As the key economic advisors of the Pinochet dictatorship, the Chicago Boys were steering the economic policies of that government. They championed the rollback of the state from the pursuit of welfare. They stood for a decrease in national spending. They promoted a policy of strict austerity, and cut government expenditures substantially. Free trade agreements and the breakdown of barriers to trade decimated the native industry. Privatisation was taken up on a scale unheard of in Latin America

International Influence

The success of the Chicago Boys in securing huge return for the financial class was a critical part in bolstering the Pinochet regime abroad. The Chilean miracle as it was called, attracted a lot of necessary positive attention for the Pinochet government and allowed Pinochet to exercise political repression without condemnation by economic allies. New policies, such as structural adjustment, free trade and tax cuts, became incredibly popular with Conservative political groups throughout the western world. Chile was one of the first countries to embrace these policies and soon the two Bretton Woods institutions, the IMF and World Bank were to endorse such policies.[16, 17]

---

[16] The minutes of the meeting of President Richard Nixon, National Security Advisor Henry Kissinger and CIA Director Richard Helmes plotting the coup against Allende is in public domain.

[17] *1 in 10 chance perhaps, but save Chile! Worth spending; Not concerned; no involvement of embassy; $10,000,000 available, more if necessary; full-time job-best men we have; game plan; make the economy scream; 48 hours for plan of action.*

Chapter 14: Nicaragua: A Government is Democratically Overthrown!

> 'Contras are not the solution to the problem in Latin America. Contras are the problem.'

The Chilean socialist experiment had been closed with the ouster of the democratically elected Allende government. In 1976 Argentina too had fallen. By the late 1970s, almost all of Latin America with the exception of Cuba had right-wing military junta in power owing allegiance to Washington. The neoliberal experiment had begun right in the backyard of the western Capital. The Sandinista Revolution in Nicaragua in 1979 was the last gasp of armed socialist resurrection. The fall of the Nicaraguan domino irked the western Capital.

The Sandinistas of Nicaragua stood out. The country witnessed the unique confluence of Liberation theology of Latin America, Christianity, Nationalism and Marxism aimed at nation-building. Unlike the Marxist-Leninist movements across the world which denounced religion and the very institution of the Church, the Sandinista movement had a tolerant view of it. The movement led by Sandinistas was not centred around a narrowly defined class of people, say the proletariat. It was an all-encompassing one. It was truly nationalist. The acceptability of the socialist movement cut across every conceivable barricade that divided the peoples of nations until then and, to an extent, even to this day, be it ethnicity, religion, or social class. The movement stood for mass literacy, universal health care, and distribution of agricultural lands to the farmer-owned cooperatives.

Nicaragua in the 1980s represented an ideological challenge before the Reagan-Administration which it found hard to grasp. President Reagan had right from the inaugural address made no attempt to hide his resolve to roll back the Welfare State that seven Presidents before him had presided over. In fact, he was very vocal in his commitment to restore the interests of the financial capital. Sandinistas establishing a Welfare State so close to the US borders did not sit well with the vision Washington sought to further!

The Context of Nicaragua

Nicaragua had been ruled by the Somoza family since 1936. The Somoza family enjoyed the blessings of successive US Presidents. The family contributed handsomely to the Republican and Democrat candidates for the Presidency. The family even ran a blood factory where the starving Nicaraguans used to donate blood for bread coupons. The blood was sold in the US for a high price. Somoza family was protected by the National Guards, a private army. The US recruited, trained and equipped the National Guards. They tortured and killed almost like a sport. One of their favourite delights was to drop opponents of the family from helicopters into live volcanoes. It must be said that the Somoza family's brutalizing of the Nicaraguan population since 1936 had a unifying effect on the people. In those days in Nicaragua, it was a crime to be young!

The Sandinista Movement

Sandinista **N**ational **L**iberation **F**ront (FSLN) was formed in the year 1961 to fight the atrocities of the Somoza family, the virtual rulers of Nicaragua. It took its name from the national hero Augustinho Sandino who fought against US imperialism in Nicaragua. Sandinistas were very much influenced by FLN movement of Algeria. After a protracted armed struggle, the Somoza family was overthrown and the Sandinistas established a socialist rule in 1979. Though the leaders were devoutly Marxist-Leninist, the coalition they formed was ideologically pluralistic. It was a fusion of socialism with liberal democratic principles. And the leadership was virtually packed with intellectuals, poets and such men nurtured in the socialist effervescence in Latin America. Many of the leaders had not even turned 30! Three Catholic priests were members of Cabinet: Miguel d'Escoto Brockmann as Minister of Foreign Affairs, Fernando Cardenal as Minister of Education, and his brother, Ernesto Cardenal, as Minister of Culture.

Sandinistas in Power (1979–1990)

Political pluralism, non-Alignment and mixed economy were the guiding principles of the Sandinista government. Revolutionary councils that come into being after a successful revolution targeting the abettors of the previous regime are more a norm than an exception the world over. But, the Sandinista regime that took power in 1979 was the most generous of all revolutionary governments. The first major legislation of the Sandinistas pertained to the abolition of the capital punishment. The maximum incarceration duration was limited to 30 years. Many of the officials and the rank and file of the notorious National Guards of the Somoza family were pardoned as they were merely following orders. None were punished solely for being a member of the infamous National Guards. Those who were found guilty after an impeccable and transparent trial were awarded sentences. But, none received a sentence of more than 30 years which was the maximum term stipulated by the new law. Jails were centres of reformation. Reconciliation and nation-building were what the Sandinistas focussed on. The Nicaraguan leaders learning from the mistakes of the previous socialist regimes elsewhere preferred local cooperatives to organise the ownership of farms and practice of agriculture and animal husbandry (the concept of state-owned farms did not find any taker among the Nicaraguan socialists). A person was allowed to own as much as land he could till. Access to health and education was made universal. To reorganize agriculture and animal husbandry along modern lines Soviet machinery and Cuban expertise were put into effective use. Like Allende of Chile, the Sandinista government of Nicaragua too was in a hurry. Poverty, illiteracy, malnutrition, high infant and maternal mortality rate due to unassisted delivery, homelessness and such other social issues that plagued the small country were addressed on a war footing. The contribution of Cuban doctors in this endeavour can never be brushed aside even by the worst Castro critics. The improvements in the social sector were phenomenal even by the most pessimistic account.

Sandinistas' efforts in participatory democracy won the world's attention. Its attempts in *'outlawing poverty'* was widely appreciated by the UN and Oxfam. In spite of the civil war and the earth quakes the country was prone to, the mortality rate of the population almost halved with the Sandinistas in power. Such a dramatic improvement in living conditions was perceived as a threat by Washington: The threat of an example of what could be done for the people if the government chose to. The poorer and impoverished the country be, the greater would be its demonstrative power.

The Generosity of the Nicaraguans

During the time when Nicaragua was run by the Somoza family as its estate (1936–1979) International financial institutions had loaned the country millions of dollars in aid. The money was hardly spent for the benefit of the Nicaraguans. With it, the Somoza family acquired large amounts of assets across the continent. On being overthrown the Somoza family nearly emptied the national coffers while fleeing. In such situations, a country is not liable to pay back a debt that its deposed dictators have embezzled. The Bolsheviks after coming to power had repudiated the debts of the Tsarist government and had declared that *'Governments and systems that spring from revolutions are not bound to respect the obligations of fallen Governments'*. But, the new Sandinista regime made it a point to return the debt by their nimble means. But such generosity was not reciprocated when Nicaraguans approached the financial institutions for more aid. Washington did see to it that Nicaragua was not loaned a penny. But still, the Sandinistas continued to service the loans. Nicaraguans! They are a great people.

Reagan Administration and The Sandinistas

President Reagan had a visceral hatred for Daniel Ortega, the leader of the revolution of 1979 and President of Nicaragua. Obviously, the Sandinistas had put an end to the reign of the Somoza family, and embarked on a reconstruction of the impoverished nation. A new competing social order was evolving. The 1983 US storming of the Grenada and the change of regime were widely considered to be a dress rehearsal for the imminent attack on Nicaragua.

Nicaragua, an impoverished country, inheriting the legacy of despots and unending civil strife in no way posed a threat to the US. A rationale for attacking Nicaragua did not exist. It was to be carefully synthesized. Nicaragua with an army of 22,000 soldiers with virtually no naval or air power was projected as a threat to America. The story that a country with 86 percent of its population living in abject poverty taking on the mighty US was hard to sell even to the most gullible among American audience. An urgent need was felt to condition the citizenry of an imminent attack by this tiny nation. Reagan repeatedly through his speeches to the Joint Sessions of the Congress and in his address to the nation projected the fall of Nicaragua to the Sandinistas as a grave danger for freedom and democracy in the US. To substantiate his claim Reagan took resort to Libya's Col Qadhafi's rather innocuous statement on the victory of the Sandinistas: *'Nicaragua means a great thing. It means fighting America at its borders... fighting America at its door step'.*

CIA-Backed Contra Rebels

A sizeable chunk of the National Guards of the Somoza family which the Sandinista regime pardoned relocated to Honduras. The CIA started to train them into a militia known as the Contra rebels in 1981. The Congress passed the *'Boland Amendment'* in 1982 that effectively tied Reagan's hands from funding the Contras. The amendment outlawed any further US assistance to the Contras in over throwing the Nicaraguan government. But the President would not be deterred by such legislations. Reagan through overt means that even risked his Presidency, in what has come to be known as the Iran-Contra affair, funded the Contras through the proceeds from an arms sale with Ayatollah's Iran which at that time was subject to an embargo by the US. Funding for the Contras also came from the cocaine trade. Ironic, as it would seem back home Reagan had launched a war on drugs that saw high rates of incarceration. Reagan was determined to scuttle the welfare revolution.

The Contra rebels armed to the teeth waged a war against the Sandinistas. From Honduras and neighbouring Costa Rica the Contra rebels were pushed into Nicaragua. Sporadic violence and acts of terrorism were projected as Civil war to denigrate the Sandinista government. The young nation once again slipped into violence and bloodshed. The influential Catholic Church threw its weight around the Contras. When the Pope visited Nicaragua, he refused to bless the nation, as it was customary, though Sandinistas had three priests in their Cabinet.

The Contra death squads ransacked schools, hospital clinics, vaccination centres, cooperatives, medical shops and food distribution centres: the welfare initiatives that most exemplified the improvements that had been brought about by the revolution. Intellectuals, doctors, Midwives and engineers building infrastructure were gunned down. Immunization campaigns were targeted. To combat the Contra rebels conscription was introduced in Nicaragua. Teenagers had to be forcefully taken from schools to be trained to take on the Contra mercenaries. This move backfired as the populace resisted their boys being taken away by the army. To fight the Contras Soviet help was sought. This gave Reagan the much-needed pretext of the US *'fighting the Soviets at its doorstep'*. Like Cuba, yet another nationalist government which stood for non-alignment was driven to the 'Soviet camp'.

The 1990 Nicaraguan Elections

The 1990 Nicaraguan election was the perfect play field for Washington to bring its influence to bear. Violetta Chamorra, widow of a writer and publisher Pedro Joaquín Chamorro Cardenal who was gunned down by assailants, an act that precipitated the 1979 Sandinista revolution, led a coalition of 14 parties ranging from the Conservatives to the Liberals against the Sandinistas. Initially a member of the cabinet of the Sandinista government, she was won over by the CIA. Her campaign was well-funded. In fact, it was much more well-funded than Bush's Presidential campaign the previous year. Bush who had succeeded Reagan shared with his predecessor a bitterness for Ortega and had referred him as a *'skunk in a garden party'*. Washington made it clear that Violetta Chamorro was their choice for the Presidency and promised to end the Contra war, if she was elected. On her visit to the White House in November 1989, the US pledged to maintain the excruciating embargo against Nicaragua, unless Violeta Chamorro won. The Contras repeatedly struck across Nicaragua during the course of the campaign killing many of the Sandinista Parliamentarians.

The social welfare schemes fuelled by the reforms in agriculture with the inauguration of cooperatives were yielding rich dividends. The achievements in the social sector, be it reduction in infant mortality rate or maternal mortality rate, the steep climb in literacy thanks to the thousands of hospitals and schools that were opened stood the Sandinistas in good stead. Riding on a plank of real and tangible improvement in the lives of the people, Daniel Ortega was all set to win if not sweep, the 1990 elections. Opinion polls indicated a landslide victory for FSLN led by Ortega.

With the Sandinistas preparing for a victory rally, Washington was preparing to bite the bullet. But the outcome of the 1990 Nicaraguan elections shocked everyone. The leader of the 14-member coalition Chamorra won with Ortega trailing behind. It is widely held by social scientists and political analysts that the electorate though appreciative of the achievements of

FSLN wanted peace at all costs. The violence unleashed by the Contras convinced the voters to vote for the opposition that enjoyed the support of Washington. Elections being rigged or elections being annulled by powers that be are common. The electorate being coerced into casting vote against their free will on the promise of cessation of terrorism in a free and fair election is unprecedented till date.

The Nicaraguan experience offers great learning material. In spite of all the graciousness that the Sandinistas had bestowed bordering on magnanimity, the socialist government and its people continued to be harassed by its neighbour. The slaughter houses that the Contras were running and the rape that was institutionalized during the civil war were used to bully the very population into submission.

Gracious in defeat the transfer of power to the new incumbent was smooth putting to shame even the worst critics of the Sandinistas. Ortega declared he shall '*work from below*' with the people. FSLN returned to power only in 2007. It took Ortega and FSLN 17 long years to be back in power after being in political wilderness.

> *It's a wonderful feeling to work in a country where the government's first concern is for its people, for all of its people'.*
>
> **– Benjamin Linder**

On 28th April 1987, Benjamin Linder, a 27-year-old mechanical engineer from the US and two Nicaraguans were killed in a Contra ambush while traveling through the forest to scout out a construction site for a new dam for the nearby village of San José de Bocay. The autopsy showed that Linder had been tortured and shot at point-blank range in the head. Linder was inspired by the Sandinista revolution and had volunteered. In El Cuá, a village in the Nicaraguan war zone, Linder had helped form a team to build a hydroelectric plant to bring electricity to the local population. President Ortega himself read the eulogy for Ben at his funeral.

During the Congressional hearing in May 1987, the Republican Congressman from Florida Connie Mack accused Elisabeth Linder, who had just given emotional testimony about her son's work and motivations, of using her grief '*to politicize this situation*', adding, '*I don't want to be tough on you, but I really feel you have asked for it*'.

Chapter 15: The Cold War: A Fact File

'...They may not themselves have been communists... But they had been subjected to the inflammatory influence of communism which avowedly uses extreme nationalism as one of its tools'...

– John Foster Dulles, Secretary of State

'National independence and revolutionary social change, if successful, may very well be contagious.'

– Noam Chomsky

The dependence of the temperate capitalist world on the tropical Third World is permanent. A government of the Third World, be it dictatorial, nationalist, socialist, or communist, which embraces an independent path towards the establishment of a Welfare State presents a challenge to western Capital. It is in the interests of western Capital to maintain the Third World tropical countries in an archaic and unjust socio-economic structure. High levels of inequality and poverty in the tropics and its concomitant low levels of demand for domestic resources ensure that the resources of the tropics are available in plenty to the temperate consumer. When the nations of the tropics vie against each other in exporting the same basket of products, it makes the export market of the former colonies of the tropics a buyer's market. Impoverished tropic is to the temperate world's advantage.

Post-war with the emergence of the Soviet Union as a major force to reckon with, the US could no longer effect a regime change by overt means. Operation AJAX marked the beginning of regime change by the US through covert means. With the disintegration of the Soviet Union, it is common knowledge that the US at the behest of Capital relies more on overt means to secure its objectives in the Third World.

Contrary to what had been widely circulated, in the run-up to the coups that toppled the nationalist regimes in Iran, Guatemala and Chile no evidence has ever emerged to support the American conviction that these governments were under Moscow's sway. All the three countries had their own communist parties demanding a radical change and were mostly at loggerheads with their governments for being too slow in effecting social change. These radical elements were in political wilderness in their countries and had no chance of coming to power in the foreseeable future. Washington knew it. In the real politik of the Cold War, the Third World nations were perceived not as geographic entities with populations harbouring their own dreams of a better tomorrow but as mere dominos waiting to fall into the Soviet bloc. All that mattered was that the dominos should not fall into the Soviet orbit. Even nationalism was viewed as a *'trojan horse for communism'*. The nationalist movements in Asia, Africa, and Latin America which were hell-bent on correcting gross historical wrongs of colonialism ran the risk of being perceived as a Soviet ally.

There is a remarkable parallel between the CIA-orchestrated coups in Iran, Guatemala and Chile. These countries were well endowed with natural resources. As a legacy of a bygone era, the ownership of these resources which were in high demand in the West continued to be with western Capital even after political independence. The democratically elected responsible governments under nationalist leaders on behalf of the people laid claim on them. The *'captains of industry'* in the West petitioned their governments to act on their behalf. Their governments heeded to their call. The response was swift and severe. Colonization as it had come to be understood had come to an end by the end of the Second World War. But, the Third World was far from being sovereign nations in charting their domestic economic policy. Imperialism had entered a new phase with decolonization. Though the 1970s witnessed a thaw in the US-Soviet relations and a warming up of the US towards China with a week-long visit of Nixon to China in February 1972, the US was consistent in its stand against smaller nations of the Third World resisting to toe the US line.

The abortive attempts to build a Welfare State in Iran and Guatemala had a great influence on the Cuban revolutionaries. In the early 1950s, Che Guevara was in Guatemala at the time of the CIA-orchestrated coup. Che had come under the scanner and had a narrow escape as he had got entangled in the socialist experiment. He reached Mexico where he met the revolutionary Castro brothers. The lessons learned from a close scrutiny of how a nationalist government embarking on a transformation of the nation to a Welfare State could easily be up-seated by a disgruntled group of officers, propertied class and mercenaries remote-controlled by Washington had a bearing on the future course of Cuban revolution. It set the tone of all subsequent leftist movements in Latin America. Operation AJAX and Operation PB SUCCESS convinced the Latin American Left that democratic nationalism could easily be toppled by the CIA. A near permanent bureaucracy, military, police, state personnel and most importantly organized religion with their deeply entrenched institutions could scuttle any move that challenged the prevalent socio-economic structure. When the Cuban revolutionaries took power every remnant of the deposed Batista Administration was wiped off in its entirety. CIA-sponsored Bay of Pigs invasion could be thwarted solely because of the fundamental radical nature of the Republic. *'Cuba is not Guatemala'*! Castro shouted following the Bay of Pigs fiasco. The Cubans contended that a government that is radical in approach with a monolithic political structure alone had any chance of surviving the attempts of sabotage and in hindsight, it appears they were right. In the tiny Caribbean island Dominican Republic, Juan Bosch won a landslide victory in the first election after three decades of brutal dictatorship and was sworn in as the country's President in February 1963. He was his country's first democratically elected President. On assuming power Juan Bosch embarked on sweeping changes to rebuild his nation. The new constitution which was promulgated, granted the people freedom they had never known. The new constitution declared labour rights, institutionalised trade unions and made welfare provisions for expectant mothers, homeless people, farmers, and for illegitimate children. Next, he enacted laws to break up large tracts of farms and distribute the same to the farmers. That was it. The Church hand in glove with the land-owning propertied class decreed he was a communist. In September 1963, in less than 7 months the democratically elected President was deposed and a military junta took power. It promptly reversed many of Juan Bosch's initiatives. In April 1965 young officers of the army fed up with the corruption and lawlessness rose in revolt of the military junta demanding the restoration of Juan Bosch, their democratically elected leader who was in exile. When it became apparent that the army faction fighting on behalf of Juan Bosch could be successful in restoring their elected leader back to power the United States launched *'Operation Power Pack'* to block his return. The US dispatched 42,000 heavily armed troops to the island Republic in support of the anti-Bosch forces. The rebellion was crushed. On 1st May 1965 Lyndon B Johnson proudly declared *'The American nation cannot... must not and will not permit the establishment of another communist government in the western hemisphere'*. Jhonson could not afford to have another Cuba in the Caribbean lake! A popular joke those days was the US marines must have had a real tough time to locate this tiny island on the map. It was not the sheer size of the experiment that threatened Washington. Any alternative model irrespective of its scale or swath of area had the potential of destabilizing the capitalist apparatus. The more impoverished the nation, the greater was its demonstrative power.

The socialist experiment in Chile under Allende is a telling example that confirms and underscores the point that a radical and monolithic political apparatus alone can survive. In Chile democratically elected Salvador Allende's approach was severely resented by the radical left who were frustrated at the slow pace of reforms and demanded the use of stern measures, if necessary. Those were the hey days of the Soviet Union. Though it was a federation of Republics, it had a near monolithic political structure under a singular party and a centralized command and had ensued a highly radical policy. The Soviet and the Cuban leadership were sceptical of the survival of Allende's government right from the beginning for the sole reason he was an out-right constitutionalist insisting on dialogue and consensus, while his opponents in the payroll of CIA harboured no such pretensions. The Secretary of State Colin Powell would later remark. *'It is not a part of American history that we are proud of'*.

Ronald Reagan Unilaterally Upping The Ante

Ronald Reagan's inauguration in 1981 was against the backdrop of a wave of leftist militancy finding success in the Caribbean and high inflation in the capitalist West with the US itself in recession. In Nicaragua, Marxist Sandinistas had ousted the US puppet Somoza. In El Salvador and Guatemala Marxists were fighting the US-backed government troops. Jamaica, Guyana, and Surinam witnessed the rise to power of anti-imperialists by the ballot. In Iran, the clergy had ousted the Shah an ally of the US and even held the US diplomats hostages for a record 444 days, as a much-delayed revenge to Operation AJAX. The oil price hike and the Vietnam War which forced on the US a high current account deficit had begun to take its toll. The capitalist West experienced high rates of inflation. Baby boomers were also coming of age and in the absence of sufficient opportunities swelled the pool of the unemployed. A state of high unemployment with high inflation hitherto unknown to the capitalist world prevailed.

Western Capital viewed the Soviet Union as a stumbling block in its attempt to lay hands on the resource of the tropics. The Soviet system, in spite of its shortcomings was a huge welfare system ever built. It was built on sound principles. The Soviet economy, though it was in stagnation in the 1980s, had never witnessed a recession let alone a depression, in its entire history and was a beacon for the Third World. The Soviet Union had been in the vanguard in providing the much-needed technical know-how to the Third World in developing its infrastructure. By the 1980s the erstwhile colonies had chartered an enviable growth and were no longer available on a short leash for their former colonisers. An activist State administering welfare schemes and furthering the interests of the people and steering an independent path, presents a challenge to Capital as its resource wealth will no longer be available to the West at its bidding. An affluent domestic population makes a demand on its own resources, thus, upping the price at which the western Capital could procure the same. This has an inflationary effect on the capitalist countries which are invariably dependent on their former colonies. In short, the Soviet system was a menace to the value of money in the West.

The Soviet Union, ever since Leonid Brezhnev replaced Khrushchev as the General Secretary, had been warming up towards the West in normalising its relations. Kremlin sincerely wanted a thaw as the Cold War was a financial strain it could do well without. Brezhnev adhered to the principle of peaceful co-existence or détente. Though Cubans had a theory of *'Let us have a 100 Vietnams'* and had been fighting the US-backed forces across the continents, Brezhnev preferred a relaxation of international tensions without conceding territory to the West.

Yuri Andropov who replaced Brezhnev in November 1982 called for arms reductions. He offered to cut back SS-20s in Europe and proposed an East-West Summit to ease tension. Andropov even went on to suggest nuclear-free zones in parts of Europe and the Mediterranean and a ban on the sale of arms to the developing world. At a Warsaw Pact meeting in January 1983, the Soviet leader proposed a non-aggression undertaking in which NATO and the Warsaw Pact would agree not to use force against each other, or against member nations of their own bloc. His adviser Georgi Arbatov described this gesture as *'a crucial breakthrough'*. It was also a break with the *'Brezhnev Doctrine'* articulated in 1968 calling on the Soviet Union to intervene, including militarily, in countries in its bloc where socialist rule was under threat.

Within days of Andropov's offering his olive branch, Reagan on 8th March 1983 responded with his famous speech calling the Soviet Union an *'evil empire'* and the Soviet leaders *'the focus of evil in the modern world'* in an address to the to the National Association of Evangelicals. Two weeks later, on 23rd March 1983, in a speech calling for support of the defence budget, Reagan rejected the whole concept of mutual deterrence that had prevented nuclear war for more than three decades. Referring to the doctrine of 'Mutually Assured Destruction' that had really worked during the Cold War era as a suicide pact, he initiated the Strategic Defence Initiative (SDI). SDI, which called for a system of missile defence based in space to spot incoming missiles and neutralise them, put the US in an advantageous position, thus, effectively nullifying the deterrence built on mutual destruction. Now the Soviet Union was rendered vulnerable. American Physical Society contended that it would take at least a decade of research to ascertain whether such a space-based nuclear shield would even be technically feasible. Star Wars as SDI was referred to was initiated solely to outspend the USSR in defence expenditure and bleed it. Though he advocated and was instrumental for a complete rollback of welfare measures citing huge fiscal deficit, he took the US deficit to astronomical proportions with such initiatives. Reagan added more to the national debt than all the Presidents of the US put together, peacetime and wartime.

The implosion of the Soviet Union and cessation of the Cold War thereupon marked the triumph of western Capital. From then on, it was all Capital.

PART 5

NEOLIBERALISM: THE BEGINNING OF THE END OF THE WELFARE STATE

Capital Regains its Lost Ground. Thirty-four Golden Years of Controlled Capitalism Come to an End.

> 'Only a crisis real or perceived produces real change. When that crisis occurs the actions that are taken depend on the ideas that are lying around… The role of people is to keep ideas alive until a crisis occurs'.
>
> **– Milton Friedman**

> 'The nine most terrifying words of the English language are, "I am from the Government and I am here to help"'.
>
> **– President Ronald Reagan**

> 'There is no alternative'.... 'You turn if you want to – this Lady is not for turning...There is no such thing as a society... only individual men and women...and their families'.
> — **Prime Minister Margaret Thatcher**

> 'The era of big Government is over'
> — **President Bill Clinton**

> 'We live in a post-ideological society'
> — **Prime Minister Tony Blair**

Chapter 16: From Post-War Consensus to Washington Consensus

Concessions by Capital Ends...

'Over large stretches of the Earth's surface, the essential conditions of human dignity and freedom have already disappeared. In others, they are under constant menace from the development of current tendencies of policy. The position of the individual and the voluntary group are progressively undermined by extensions of arbitrary power. Even that most precious possession of western Man, freedom of thought and expression, is threatened by the spread of creeds which, claiming the privilege of tolerance when in the position of a minority, seek only to establish a position of power in which they can suppress and obliterate all views but their own'.

– 'Statement of Aims' of the Mont Pelerin Society dated 8th April 1947.

As governments around the world embraced Keynesianism in pursuit of transforming their nations into welfare states, a group of economists, historians, philosophers and such members of the scholarly community from Europe and the United States met at Mont Pelerin, Switzerland, from 1st to 10th April 1947 to deliberate on what they called *'crisis of our times'.* It was conceived to be the coming together of that segment of the intelligentsia that harboured a visceral hatred for any form of collectivism, be it Marxian or Keynesian or even Gandhian. The huddle was financed by the Business. They were apprehensive of how the wartime planning and the association of their governments with the Soviet Union would play out. They detested the *'Post-War Consensus'* of highly interventionist

---
[18] John Maynard Keynes's (1883–1946) untimely death and the long lives of Hayek (1899–1992) and Milton Friedman (1912–2006) that spanned almost the entire 20th century had a profound effect on world economy.

State and championed the case of unfettered free-market capitalism. Founded by Frederick Von Hayek, Austrian political thinker, Mount Pelerin Society (MPS) as the think tank came to be known as was to remain in the wilderness for much of the late 1940s and 1950s. The highly articulate, if not proselyting Professor of the Chicago School of Economics, Milton Friedman had an unparalleled pioneering role in handholding the society's economic doctrine from the margins of economic thought subscribed to a tiny elite to its being subscribed by world leaders and their advisors. The whispers of a few were to be the rhetoric of the majority in a few decades. By the 1990s it wiped out Keynesianism and supplanted itself to be the ruling economic orthodoxy. It was so subtle, yet hypnotic, that it could hoodwink millions across the world into their own dismemberment from the economic and later socio-political life. It was so pulverizing that there was no going back to the Keynesian days even when it became clear that neoliberalism had not just delivered, but it was never designed to.

Raison d'etre of Capitalist Concessions

The Soviet Union had emerged from the World War with its prestige immensely enhanced. It had faced the brunt of the Nazi war machinery in its entirety all by itself. The second front in the West against Germany by the allies for which Stalin had virtually been pleading before Roosevelt and Churchill since 1941 which would have taken the pressure off the Red Army never materialised. By the time the allies finally landed at Normandy on 6th June 1944, the Nazi army was on its humiliating retreat. The liberation of East and Central Europe by the Red Army, the enormous sacrifices the Soviet population endured in defeating the forces of fascism, the sacrifices made by the communists in the anti-fascist struggle all over Europe, and the second Red Scare in America and Europe jolted the decision makers in accommodating the welfare of the population too in their scheme of things. In Italy, Greece and Turkey, Capital found it really hard to arrest the Red Tide. To ward off the communist threat certain concessions had to be made. '...*leaving orthodoxy and revolution to fight it out*' was in the post-war context unsafe for western Capital. To continue to hold ground, Capital found it to be wise to yield some ground to labour. China too turning communist cemented the case for a Welfare State within the capitalist framework.

On the domestic economic front, highly interventionist state with a Keynesian demand management system aimed at maintaining high employment, came to be adopted as the mainstay of economic policy. During the Great Depression, John Maynard Keynes had challenged the neo-classical view that markets in the short to medium term would automatically provide full employment, if the workers were flexible enough in their wage demands. Keynes held that government intervention was necessary to put people back to work. During a downturn of the economy, business would be sceptical of making investments. Keynes contended that the government of the day should bridge this shortfall in investments. The government he argued, by borrowing from the Central Bank of the country, i.e., by running a fiscal deficit, should undertake projects of infrastructure augmentation, like the construction of dams, schools, public housing and hydro-electric plants aimed at putting labour to work. As employment rates soared, Keynes reasoned that people with disposable income would spend money that would drive the aggregate demand in the economy, thus, jumpstarting it into vibrancy. With businesses too pitching in as their confidence stands restored the economy would be restored to its pristine state. Right lessons were learned from the rise of Hitler and Mussolini and the institutionalization of fascist tendencies across Europe during the depression years. It became imperative that an interventionist government that dampened the cycles of business and ensured the welfare of the common man was in the interests of world peace and domestic tranquillity.

On the political front, these capitalist countries also witnessed the institution of democracy based on universal adult franchise for the first time. In France universal adult franchise was implemented in 1945 while in the US it became a reality by 1946. It is to be borne in mind it was only as late as 1932 that Britain had its first election based on a universal adult franchise.

As part of the post-war consensus decolonisation was pursued. Though countries like France, Belgium and Portugal were reluctant to give up their colonial possessions, it must however, be said that decolonization came to be widely subscribed by the capitalist countries in the West. Around the world, it came to be widely believed that with adequate government intervention the capitalist system was malleable enough to be rendered humane. It was widely held that Capital could be reined in by national governments. Such was the acceptance of Keynesian demand management system across the political spectrum that very much against their class instincts the Republican President Eisenhower (1953–1961) and Conservative Prime Minister Winston Churchill in his second innings (1951–1955) dared not tamper it. It was genuinely felt that world peace and tranquillity within the capitalist framework was possible and had at last been achieved. Marx and Lenin appeared to be obsolete.

It is ironic to say that while the western capitalist governments accommodated welfare policies at home much to the dislike of domestic Capital, they unleashed the Cold War to contain the *'Soviet menace'* as per the dictates of the domestic Capital. President Richard Nixon who had come to subscribe to Keynesianian welfare policies, overthrew the democratically elected Marxist-Leninist government of Salvador Allende in Chile and prised open the country to be a laboratory for neoliberal policies that halted and rolled back its welfare measures. President Richard Nixon's act was emblematic of the double standards of Washington all throughout the Cold War.

The virtual annihilation of the victors and the vanquished, and the division of Germany and the demilitarization of Japan under the aegis of the occupying US forces greatly enhanced the likelihood of peace to prevail for an extended period of time. With decolonisation, the potential for any inter-imperialist rivalry over the question of colonies too did subside. The 16-nation invasion of Korea (1950–1953) and the prolonged conflicts in Vietnam (1945–1975) and the numerous proxy wars in the context of the Cold War were episodic and were confined to geographically limited specific theatres. It never engulfed the globe in its entirety.

The newly independent developing nations that had shrugged off the colonial yoke had a daunting task ahead, that of nation-building. These nations had to rapidly industrialize to be self-reliant. With Soviet technology, these nations developed an industrial base in the public sector which turned their raw materials into value-added articles of exchange to earn the much-needed forex. The three decades following the world war were in general a prosperous time for much of Europe, America and the newly independent Afro-Asian nations. Unemployment fell to very low levels. In Britain, in spite of losing its entire colonial empire, official unemployment stood at just 2 percent. It was as low as 4 percent in the US. The capitalist world had never known such low levels of unemployment during peacetime. As in the Soviet Union and many socialist countries, the job market had turned into a seller's market. With very low levels of unemployment, the workers could wrest out better wages and working conditions. Rising labour productivity translated to rising wages. The living conditions of the workers improved.

Bretton Woods Conference

The groundwork for the prosperity that was witnessed in the decades following the war was laid even before the war had come to an end in Europe. Seven-hundred and thirty delegates from 44 allied nations came together and deliberated from 1st to 22nd July 1944 at the Mount Washington Hotel in Bretton Woods, New Hampshire, US on the blueprint of an economic system for the future. Thus, was born the Bretton Woods Agreement which instituted a system of rules, institutions and procedures to regulate the international monetary system. The conference established IMF and IBRD or the World Bank as it is widely known today. At the conference, the US insisted the Bretton Woods system should rest on both gold and US dollar. The Soviet delegates had attended the conference, but refused to ratify the accord as they felt it to be *'branches of Wall Street'*. Events in the later decades proved the Soviets were clairvoyant.

The Inflation of the 1960s… Emergence of International Finance Capital…

> *'Lenin is said to have declared that the best way to destroy the capitalistic system was to debauch the currency… And Lenin was right. There is no subtler, no surer means of overturning the existing base of society than to debauch the currency'.*
>
> *'……….above all, let finance be primarily national'.*
>
> **– John Maynard Keynes**

Every capitalist economy needs a stable medium of holding wealth. This need of a capitalist economy is served by money. Wealth is stored in money and money equivalents. In addition to serving as a stable medium of holding wealth, it also serves as a medium of circulation. Money will cease to be a medium of circulation the moment it ceases to be a storehouse of wealth. Inflation for the common man is rising prices. Definitely, this is the case. But, there is a greater malaise associated with inflation. Rising prices mean that a greater amount of money is required to procure the same amount of goods than a while ago, which means the value of money has depreciated. Such depreciating currency creates panic. Depreciating currency loses its trust and ceases to be a medium of holding wealth. It ceases to be in circulation. In such a scenario people tend to hold commodities. This further erodes the value of money and causes a further rise in the price of commodities. Inflation or the loss of value of money undercuts the very functioning of capitalism which relies on the value of money as an article of faith. The loss of value of money is something a capitalist system can tolerate only at its peril.

Towards the late 1960s and all through the 1970s developed economies witnessed high rates of inflation due to a variety of reasons. Keynesian measures of demand management that ensured high employment rates placed high disposable income in the hands of the working class. The surge in demands for goods and services in the capitalist world started to drive cost-push inflation in the economy. Added to this was the huge demand for consumer goods that was under-served during the war years, as the entire industry was pre-occupied with war production. To make matters worse, the oil shock of the 1970s that saw a quadrupling of oil prices and the US war with Vietnam necessitating a high current account deficit exacerbated the inflation. Baby boomers too were coming of age. With employment opportunities not keeping pace with the swelling demands for jobs, the capitalist world witnessed an unprecedented scenario of stagflation: that of high inflation and unemployment.

Inflation had to be brought down at any cost for the capitalist system to survive. It became imperative that for the survival of the capitalist system, inflation, i.e., loss of value of the money, had to be curtailed. Though the causative factors of inflation were many, the very idea of the government spending money, it did not have to ensure high rates of employment and welfare started to come under the scanner. Keynesian demand management which did achieve its goal of high rates of employment, in fact the highest the capitalist world had known during peacetime, was being viewed with suspicion. Economic think tanks were soon obsessed with the need to rein in inflation. If the retreat of government from demand management, employment generation and welfare was necessary, so be it. There was a school of thought, advocated by the socialist camp, to curb inflation within the existing Keynesian framework without jeopardizing the working class and the Welfare State that was built over the decades. It found no taker.

The Bretton Woods conference on the insistence of Keynes had imposed tight controls on the speculative flight of Capital across borders. The sovereignty of the national government over Capital could be enforced only if the Capital remains national. Capital migration was deliberately made difficult for the sole reason of ensuring its subservience to the national government. Only then would the national governments be able to undertake demand management to boost the aggregate demand in their respective national economies and ensure near full employment, a basic pre-requisite for the maintenance of domestic tranquillity. All this changed starting from the 1960s.

The United States had traditionally been a current account surplus country. In the post-war conjuncture in preparation for meeting the Soviet challenge, a challenge Pentagon knew did not even exist, the defence spending of the US burgeoned. The military bases the US built across the world to checkmate the *'belligerent Soviet Union bent on world domination'* was a strain on the US. The current account surplus country that the US was, soon became a current account deficit country from the 1950s. The US could afford to be a current account deficit country by virtue of the unique position of the dollar, thanks to the Bretton Woods system. Under the Bretton Woods system, the dollar was a reserve currency convertible to gold at the rate of $35 per ounce of gold. The system that held the dollar to be *'as good as gold'* enabled American firms to buy up European firms with dollars printed in the US. Leveraging this role of the dollar, the United States could afford to run huge current account deficits for maintaining its military bases across the world. The 1960s saw the US engaged in a never-ending war with Vietnam. As the scale of the war with Vietnam touched new heights, there was a torrential outpour of dollars from the US to the Metropolitan banks. The oil shocks of 1973 and 1980 further swelled the Metropolitan banks with Petrodollars. These Metropolitan banks with the slush of dollars were in search of investment opportunities across the world. The precautionary measures like tight control over the speculative flight of Capital across nations instituted by Bretton Woods Agreement and agreed upon by the national governments of the day were coming in the way of huge chunks of Capital that were accumulating in Metropolitan banks that were in search of investment opportunities. The time had come for these Keynesian measures of Capital control to be dismantled, facilitating its migratory, often speculative flights to suitable destinations in search of profitable investments. Thus, began the systematic undoing of the provisions of the Bretton Woods conference. Such dismantling of the barriers to Capital flow across the nations at the instance of the Metropolitan banks marked the beginning of globalisation of finance or the formation of international finance. Small chunks of national finance Capital aided by the dismantling of the Keynesian control on its cross-border flights coalesced to form International Finance Capital.

The international finance formed by the coalescence or fusion of national finance does not have a national character. It is a corpus fund, the sole aim of which is to multiply itself. It is in a speculative mode and relocates itself to that region where its prospectus is better than anywhere else. It views as its playground the entire globe. Every block of finance Capital whether it has come from the capitalist or erstwhile communist or the newly independent former colonies stands stripped of its national identities and affiliations, once it is a part of the International Finance Capital.

During the days when finance Capital remained national, rivalry between imperial powers was the norm. The multitude of internecine conflicts culminating in the two world wars were triggered by each financial block's desire to encroach on the other and multiply itself. With such national financial blocks coalescing to form International Finance Capital devoid of any national character, the business case for war between nations does not arise. The remarkable bonhomie that exist among the European powers that were at each other's throat until the twentieth century is rooted in the very nature of the present day capitalism. Muting of inter-imperialist rivalry in the current conjuncture in short is owing to the very nature of contemporary capitalism, characterized by the emergence of International Finance Capital devoid of the trappings of nationality. The narrative that the peaceful existence of European nations is due to the balance of power among the advanced capitalist countries under the aegis of the UN brokering peace is just wishful thinking.

The formation of international finance entails fundamental changes in the economy. The speculative character of international finance that refuses to be tied down to any particular geography also means capital-in-finance is its most preferred means of engagement than capital-in-production. The domestic capitalist class, in the new regime that facilitates the coalescence of national blocks of Capital into International Finance Capital, makes common cause with it in its speculatory transits across the globe. That they no longer be subservient to the writ of any national government is beneficial to them. This makes the present conjuncture of neoliberalism markedly different from the bygone era of colonialism. During the colonial days, the colonial power to further its financial interests systematically pursued the de-industrialisation of the colonies as a matter of policy. Such a policy unseated the domestic industrial-capitalist class, resulting in them making common cause with the freedom movements.

Chicago School Leads Counter-attack on Keynesianism

'Chicago always had a strong tradition of a belief in the power of markets. Chicago's contribution was to show the power of markets and people's choices, not only in public policy but also in economic science. The department also had very strong leadership. There was a lot of self-confidence that we had the right answers and the rest of the profession was wrong. We saw economic analysis as a powerful way to understand behaviour, providing a lot of insight not only into the economy itself, but also how society organised. I think that at most places economics was taught as a game; it was not clear that teachers elsewhere thought economics was a powerful tool. Chicago did'.

– Gary Becker,
an alumnus of the University of Chicago and
the winner of Nobel Prize for Economics in 1992.

'Planning is coming. Of this, there can be no doubt. The only question is whether it will be democratic planning of a free society or totalitarian in character ... whether fascist or communist'.

– Prof Charles E. Marriam,
University of Chicago

The Chicago school right from its inception stood for free market principles. The paternalistic government was to its abhorrence. It was much more concerned about the extension of government power than about the dangers of monopoly capitalism. The school professed that market knowledge outwits government knowledge, a belief that market fundamentalists still hold dear, despite all evidence to the contrary.

Milton Freidman (1912–2006), a founding member of the Mont Pelerin Society joined the University as a faculty in 1946. He held that *'private unregulated monopoly'*, was the lesser of the evils *'when compared to government regulation and ownership'*. In Hayek, the founder of Mount Pelerin who joined the University in 1950, Friedman found his intellectual Guru. The Chicago School which stood for free market principles was on a proselytizing mission soon.

In the 1950s in order to curb left-wing tendencies across the globe and Latin America in particular, the US State Department organized a training programme for global economic development in association with the University of Chicago. Funded by the Ford Foundation and Rockefeller Foundation, the University of Chicago's Department of Economics set up scholarship programme with Chile's Private Catholic University. The intention was to create a chunk of economists bred in free market fundamentalists to be its harbingers across the world. They came to be referred to as the *'Chicago boys'*. In the decades to come, they occupied positions of power in many countries and were to champion free-market orthodoxy. Ironically, neoliberalism was first experimented in Latin America, Chile to be precise, long before it came centre stage in the US and Britain.

Nobel Prize for Economics: Branding Neo-Liberal Economics

Sixty-seven years after the first Nobel Prize was granted, the Nobel Prize for Economics was instituted in the year 1968 by a grant by the Swedish Bank to the Nobel Foundation. Mont Pelerin Society too pitched in to create the fund. Hayek was awarded the Nobel Prize for Economics in 1974. Milton Freidman followed suit in 1976. In the subsequent decades, members of the Mont Pelerin Society George Stigler, Maurice Allais, James M. Buchanan, Ronald Coase, Gary Becker and Vernon Smith won the Nobel Memorial Prize in Economic Sciences. Since 1974, eight professors from

Chicago and another 11 associated at some time with Chicago won Nobel Prizes in economics.

The institution of a Nobel Prize in Economics and the awarding of the same to the free-market economists lent an aura of scholarship to the free-market paradigm. Free market fundamentalism was on its ascend. A systematic attempt to discredit Keynesianism by holding it accountable for the stagflation was on. Since his retirement, Milton Friedman had been on a mission. His 1980 TV series *'Free to Choose'* based on his book by that title was a comprehensive attack on any government that intervened in the market. MIT Economist and Nobel Laureate Paul Krugman would later write that Friedman's *'long campaign against the ideas of Keynesian economics'* transformed him into *'the world's best-known economist'*.

The Rise and Rise of 'Supply Side Economics'

As opposed to *'demand side'* economics, *'supply-side economics'* championed by the neoliberals rests upon the premise that tax cuts on the rich will *'free up'* the amount of Capital available for investments. Such a spurt in investments, it argues, will generate high amounts of tax revenue which will more than compensate for the initial loss of tax revenue owing to the initial tax cuts. The *'Laffer Curve'* is a crucial theoretical component of supply-side economics. It even *'graphically illustrates'* that increases in taxation rates will not translate to an increase in taxation revenue. As tax rates approach 100 percent, as per the curve, revenue will drop as citizens will have no incentive to work harder. The growing evidence refutes the claim. A reduction of taxes on the highest bracket never ever in history has translated to higher tax revenue till date, but supply-side economics still have its followers in the hallowed institutions of the capitalist world.

Neoliberals lurking in the wilderness were eyeing for the most opportune moment to pierce its claws into the politico-economic landscape. In Chile, under the military dictatorship of Pinochet they found an opportunity to practice their gospel of free market fundamentalism. Friedman knew the value of crisis. The late 1970s gave him the most perfect crisis. Friedman sincerely believed his ideas could transform the world -- and, arguably, they did. Though not for the better.[19, 20]

---

[19] *'Inflation is entirely made in Washington and nowhere else'* Friedman.

[20] 'Washington Consensus', an umbrella term for a set of financial institutions and policies designed by the shylocks of Wall Street to further their interests across the world.

Chapter 17: Neoliberalism on Either Side of the Atlantic

> *For decades we have piled deficit upon deficit mortgaging our future and our children's future for the temporary convenience of the present...you and I, as individuals, can, by borrowing, live beyond our means, but for only a limited period of time. Why then, should we think that collectively, as a nation, we're not bound by that same limitation? We must act today in order to preserve tomorrow. And let there be no misunderstanding: We are going to begin to act, beginning today.*
>
> *'In this present crisis, Government is not the solution to our problem. Government is the problem'.*
>
> **– President Ronald Reagan**
> **Inaugural Address, 20th January 1981 .**

From just $70 billion President Reagan took the fiscal deficit to $175 billion. Through the decade the national debt would soar from $1 trillion to $4 trillion.

In the late 1970s, Democrat President Jimmy Carter (1977–1981) and Labour Prime Minister James Callaghan (1976–1979) turned to monetary policies to stave off stagflation. Arresting inflation that was stifling growth and there-by prospects of employment for the baby boomers who were being added to the labour pool topped their priority. But, the monetarism that was resorted to was well within the framework of a Welfare State. Neither of them had in their wildest of imaginations thought about dismantling the Welfare State that they had inherited. Their successors President Reagan and Prime Minister Thatcher who encashed the crisis of stagflation to make electoral gains and come to power took the purported fight against inflation to such levels and irreparably dismantled the Welfare States of the capitalist world that their centre-left successors, Bill

Clinton and Tony Blair, could not even attempt to restore the social order, their parties advocated for. From a broader perspective, however, the cumulative effect of the two conservative politicians amounted to a full-blown assault on a parental state committed to a state-led redistribution of private wealth.

The long-standing and deeply entrenched economic orthodoxy that gained prominence during the New Deal, Keynesian fiscal and monetary policies with full employment as the key objective, was abandoned in favour of a policy designed to quell inflation, no matter what the consequences might be for employment and welfare.

Reagan's Attack on Labour

Until Ronald Reagan, the social contract borne in the depths of the Great Depression was the mantra by which all Presidents had functioned, Republican or Democrat. President Reagan, the most transformative President since Roosevelt though not for the better, within weeks of his inauguration systematically undercut and eventually dismembered the entire fabric of a Welfare State. President Reagan is singularly responsible for the elimination of the greatest middle class.

The deregulation of the airline industry which resulted in the proliferation of the service providers in the previous years had over-burdened the Air Traffic Controllers. Professional Air Traffic Controllers Organisation, PATCO called for a reduced 32-hour work week citing safety concerns, a $10,000 pay increase for all Air Traffic Controllers and a better benefits package for retirement. The negotiations stalled and PATCO went on strike on 3rd August 1981. Ronald Reagan's response was swift and severe. He served the striking employees with an ultimatum.

---

[21] By the end of the Reagan era, the income of the lowest 90 percent rose by 17 percent while those of the top 10 percent rose by 106 percent. The benefits of increased productivity have not gone to the deserving middle class since the early 1980s.

'They are in violation of the law and, if they do not report for work within 48 hours, they have forfeited their jobs and will be terminated'.

The fight against the middle class was on. Several of the strikers were jailed. The Union was fined and eventually rendered bankrupt and decertified. Many of the strikers, though belonging to trade unions, were leading middle-class lives even without a college degree. PATCO was in effect a white-collar trade union. As a result of being blacklisted for federal employment the members lost their middle-class status and slowly inched towards abominable poverty. In the 1980 Presidential election, the Union had endorsed Ronald Reagan in return for written assurances that their grievances would be looked into. The President's firing of the 11,000 PATCO employees was a message to both labour and to the big Business. The decline of real wages which began in the 1980s could partly be attributed to Reagan's tough stand against labour.

President's Tight Embrace of the Supply Side Economics

Reagan's initial tax cuts in the early 1980s, led to a decline in government revenues. It did not free up additional resources and scale up investments, as was reasoned by the votaries of supply-side economics. Tax revenue fell far short of what was required to cover existing spending commitments in social policy and dramatic increases in military expenditure. Reducing taxes and increasing military expenditure at an astronomical scale, while trying to balance the budget turned out to be inconsistent objectives. As a result, contrary to what the President had resolved on the day of inauguration, his administration was forced to resort to enormous levels of deficit spending to cover these revenue shortfalls.

Winning Political Legitimacy In Lieu of The Lost Legitimacy In The Economic Front In The Neo-liberal Era: President Reagan Shows The Way.

> 'My fellow Americans, I'm pleased to tell you today that I've signed legislation that will outlaw Russia forever. We begin bombing in five minutes....'
>
> – remarked Reagan jokingly, while he was riffling on his own speech and joking with the National Public Radio audio engineers during soundcheck

> "Using Nicaragua as a base, the Soviets and Cubans can become the dominant power in the crucial corridor between North and South America. Established there, they will be in a position to threaten the Panama Canal, interdict our vital Caribbean sea lanes and ultimately move against Mexico."
>
> – President Reagan cautioned the nation

Ronald Reagan who assumed the office of the Presidency on behalf of the finance capital, with great rhetorical skills practised and perfected the art of inventing *'enemies at the gate'*. Reagan's Presidency was marked by the upping of the Cold War ante and an obsession with Central America. Though the previous Carter years had seen the relations with the Soviet Union turn sour due to the *'Soviet invasion'* of Afghanistan, Ronald Reagan unilaterally withdrew from the détente and increased the military budget. He dismissed off the then prevailing logic of **M**utual **A**ssured **D**estruction as not a sufficient deterrence for nuclear adventurism. The launch of **S**trategic **D**efence **I**nitiative was part of a well-scripted plan of inventing new enemies.

The US interests in the Middle East are well known. But Reagan's Presidency was to witness a shift, if not an obsession, with Central America, much beyond the demands of the Monroe Doctrine (1823), to the point of insanity. In repeated addresses to the nation and the joint sessions of the Congress, he specifically convened to reflect on the *'threat that Central America posed'*, he deplored the *'developments of strategic importance to the US'* in that region. He was convinced about an imminent attack on the US by the combined forces of Sandinistas, Cubans, East Germans and even the Italian brigades. *'Nicaragua's armed forces are the largest Central America has ever seen'*, he cautioned the nation. All that Nicaragua had was a rag-tag army. All throughout the 1980s, the Soviet Union had consistently declined Managua's request for arms just not to antagonise the US. Soviets wanted to get out of the arms chase with the US as it was bleeding the Union.

Even a narrow air strip in Grenada constituted an existential threat for the Commander-in-Chief of the world's most powerful armed forces. In March 1983, President Reagan began issuing warnings to the American citizens of a possible attack against America from Grenada. For Ronald Reagan, the *'excessively long'* airplane runway being built and the *'numerous fuel storage tanks'* constituted a potential threat and signalled military adventurism. Representative Ron Dellums after travelling to Grenada on a fact-finding mission on being invited by the country's Prime Minister Maurice Bishop stated before the Congress in 1983, *'Based on my personal observations, discussion, and analysis of the new international airport under construction in Grenada, it is my conclusion that this project is specifically now and has always been for the purpose of economic development and is not for military use... It is my thought that it is absurd, patronizing, and totally unwarranted for the United States government to charge that this airport poses a military threat to the United States' national security'.*

The President's near obsession with any welfare measure in Latin America that contrasted with his penchant for dictators in Latin America who towed the American line is well-documented. On the genocidal dictator of Guatemala Reagan stated *'President Ríos Montt is a man of great personal integrity and commitment... I know he wants to improve the quality of life for* all Guatemalans and promote social justice'. When Reagan was asked about human rights violations in Guatemala he said, 'I am inclined to believe they've been getting a bum rap'.

War On Drugs – High Incarceration Rates – Private Prisons

The Soviet Union and Central America rationalised the burgeoning defence budget of the US. But, the most potent weapon in Reagan's arsenal in his fight for political legitimacy was to be in the domestic front. His declaration of war on drugs at a time when less than 2 percent of the Americans identified drugs as a major threat afflicting the country was two-pronged. Like his Star War programme and his obsession with Central America, he successfully created a national panic on drug use that he sought to get the nation rid of, thus enhancing his legitimacy. Harsher and longer terms of sentences with minimum parole were intended to overwhelm the state prisons and eventually make a case for privatisation of prisons. The prison population in the US exploded during President Ronald Reagan's Administration. From just 3,29,000 the prison population almost doubled to 6,27,000. This rise in incarceration hit communities of colour the hardest and are disproportionately incarcerated even to this day. 5 percent of the world population now accounts for 25 percent of the world's prison population

'Thatcher, Thatcher, Milk Snatcher'

> '...who is society? There is no such thing! There are individual men and women and there are families and no Government can do anything except through people and people look to themselves first'.

After WW II the Labour government of Clement Attlee in pursuance of its resolve to establish a Welfare State had introduced the Free Milk Act. The

Act entitled all under-18 years of age ⅓ of a pint of milk every school day. In 1971, Thatcher as Education Secretary, oversaw the restriction of this scheme to only those children under seven. In 1980, under the Thatcher Government, it was further reduced again to the children under five.

Thatcher right from the beginning made it clear which side of the great debate she was on. She abhorred Keynesian measures of high government spending to ensure full employment and welfare of the population. The lady Prime Minister embraced supply side economics to extricate Britain from the quagmire of stagflation. She threw her weight behind deregulation, privatisation, and tax cuts for the *'captains of the industry'*. Perfectly solvent government companies were thrown into the private hands for a pittance. This involved many of the crown jewels of the British government like Rolls Royce, British Petroleum, British Telecom, British Aerospace, British Airways, Jaguar British Gas, British Steel, and several Water and Power utilities. A fire sale of government-owned enterprises at dearth cheap prices was a windfall for the private Capital. The rationale provided was such privatisation would enhance the quality of service. However, in reality all it delivered was a body blow to the middle class. The Prime Minister was in a haste as she knew that once privatised it was irreversible. Job cuts following privatisation busted trade unions and undermined its power to bargain on behalf of labour. All forms of social solidarity which had the potential of being a bulwark against organized Capital was dissolved. All throughout the privatisation spree she kept insisting *'There is no alternative'.* The miner's strike in 1984, which was provoked by the closure of many coal mines as imported coal was cheaper, saw her stand eye ball to eye ball with Union leaders. As with the members of PATCO in the US, labour blinked first and conceded defeat. Coal miners represented the last bastion of the socialist mindset in the UK. From then on labour was on full retreat. Labour was tamed and Britain was transformed into a country with very low wages. Even conservative politicians dissented at times. *'You turn if you want to – this Lady is not for turning'* she boldly declared when conservative members within her own Tory Party stated that they could no longer tolerate her tough anti-inflation policies which were impacting employment, wages and the welfare of the people.

One by one she put the government-owned enterprises, the commanding heights of British economy that had made it a Welfare State, on sale. In Britain the battle over who should be in control of the commanding heights was over. *'Popular Capitalism is nothing less than a crusade to enfranchise the many in the economic life of the nation'* she contended. She repeatedly cited that the entire world was moving towards privatisation. *'From France to the Philippines from Jamaica to Japan from Malaysia to Mexico from Sri Lanka to Singapore privatisation is on the move'*, she proudly declared.

After Reagan... After Thatcher

The first-wave of neoliberalism in the 1980s dismembered the welfare states in well-functioning democracies. Still both in the US and Britain, the leaders could get re-elected in consecutive terms with landslide victories. The secret behind their electoral success lies in the fact that the two blended neo-conservatism with neoliberalism to ensure that they could blur, if not mask, they were acting on behalf of Capital. The hyper-nationalism both of them espoused bordering on showmanship came to their rescue. Reagan's war on drugs, upping the Cold War ante and the new-found enemies in Central America and Thatcher's victory in the Falkland war, a war in which Reagan and the much-dreaded Chilean dictator Pinochet came to Thatcher's rescue, cemented their electoral performance.

It goes to the credit of the two leaders that the forces of the democratic left that succeeded them incorporated the crux of the neoliberal agenda into their own political rhetoric and governance. More than Reagan it was the Democrat President Bill Clinton who oversaw the annulment of many of the New Deal initiatives of Roosevelt ranging from welfare provisions to ensuring safeguards to prevent another depression. President Clinton announced in the Congress in his 1996 State of the Union Address that *'The era of big Government is over'*. In 1996, Clinton signed the Welfare Reform Act, which replaced the Federal programme of Aid to Dependent Children, founded in 1935 as part of Roosevelt's Social Security Act. The President consistently claimed that his business-friendly policies in no way interfered with his progressive social programmes. But, his friends in the left who went on to be his critics as soon as he effected his triangulation politics minced no words in their critique of his attempts to replace *'Welfare as we know it'*. Bill Clinton tore apart many of the safeguards that were erected in the face of the Great Depression. The Financial Services Modernization Act of 1999 virtually removed the Keynesian regulation enacted into law by the Glass-Steagall Act during the Great Depression by Roosevelt. The legal divisions between Commercial and Investment banking as well as those between insurance companies and brokerage houses were undone by the 1999 Act. Such reckless deregulation was the precursor to the global financial crisis of 2008–2009. As the Great Recession unfolded provisions of the Glass-Steagall protections had to be reinstated.

Bill Clinton's ideological somersault must have made the task of his British counterpart, Tony Blair, all the more easier. Prime Minister Blair and his Minister for Exchequer, Gordon Brown signalled the abandonment of the Labour party's socialist moorings. In Gordon Brown's own words *'The problem for the left in the past was that they equated public interest with public ownership and public regulation and therefore they assumed that markets were not in the public interests. What we had to explain both to ourselves and to the country and now I believe it is possible to explain to the rest of the world well is that markets are in the public interests'* Blair argued that the *'New Labour'* he and Brown represented championed *'social advancement through individual achievement'* by facilitating the release of

---

[22] Margaret Thatcher famously visited the Chilean dictator Pinochet following his arrest in London in 1998 on a Spanish warrant issued under international law seeking to try him on charges alleging human rights violations during his 1973-1990 regime. The former Prime Minister thanked him for his support in the Falkland War and noted," *I'm also very much aware that it is you who brought democracy to Chile"*

the entrepreneurial energies of the individual. The Prime Minister aimed at fundamentally changing the *'paternalistic'* relationship between the state and its citizens to one based on a *'social partnership'* among individuals.

Conclusion

> *'The limits of tolerance are passed when protestors in the name of some spurious cause seek to inflict fear, terror, violence and criminal damage on our people and property'.*
>
> **– Prime Minister Tony Blair**

> *'I want my child to grow up in America. I don't want her to be a part of the generations of Americans to do worse than their parents did... I don't want her to be a part of the country that is coming apart instead of coming together....'*
>
> **–President Bill Clinton**

The world, as we know it today, is an outcome of the neoliberal turn that the US and Britain took in the 1980s. By the time Clinton and Blair took centre stage of politics of their countries, the neoliberal order had become so entrenched that all they could do was to bring a semblance of welfare to placate their electoral base. Having been in the political wilderness for a long time, the Democrats in the US and the Labour in England deemed it necessary to effect such a somersault of sorts. Triangulation of politics that was necessitated by electoral compulsion was effected by both parties. *'For every blue-collar worker we lose in Pennsylvania, we will pick up two moderate Republicans in the suburbs of Philadelphia and you can repeat it in Ohio, Illinois and Wisconsin'*, A popular strategy evolved in the 1990s stands institutionalized in American politics even to this day.

Neoliberalism is fundamentally a social order. It is all-pervading as it encompasses every aspect of human life. Neoliberalism sweeps across the fundamental structure and texture of the State to the most granular level. The State's nature of engagement with its people fundamentally changes as neoliberalism creeps in. The multitude of agreements with the various financial institutions and trading blocs compound the problem. Once sucked into the black hole of neoliberalism, there is no escape. Nursing the state back to its pre-neoliberal state is unthinkable. Even the new government that is inaugurated, determined to undo the dismemberment of the Welfare State, continues to be in a state of awe. In its heydays during the 1990s, neoliberalism hovered around the world like a mighty colossus. It had its way through the communist bloc with ease... like a knife slicing through a piece of butter.

Neoliberals often cite Adam Smith to be their forerunner. Those who regard him to be a *'Reaganite'* or a *'Thatcherite'* do not get the context right. There is no denying the fact that classical liberals like Smith, did preach the virtues of the *'free market'* and *'laissez-faire'* economics. But the freedom they espoused, the non-interference of the state they stood for was in opposition to the mercantilism of the Royalty and the nobility who exercised near absolute and unquestioned control over their nation's economy to satiate their whims and fancies of indulgence and bloody conquests. Citing the classical liberals' abhorrence for the *'meddling of the state'* in such a varied context as what we have today is deceptive, outlandish and propagandistic.

Chapter 18: German Unification: The Colonization of the East by the West

> 'To the Germans in the GDR, I can say what Prime Minister de Maziere has already emphasized: No one will be worse off than before. And many will be better off'.
>
> – Helmut Kohl,
> West German Chancellor

As it turned out the only purpose of the German unification was to place the nukes closer to the Soviet border.

The West German Chancellor Helmut Kohl's promise of transforming East Germany aka German Democratic Republic (GDR) into a *'blooming landscape'* on the eve of German unification was as good as the promise to the Soviet Union by the West on NATO's eastward expansion. As events turned out, the two promises were made to allay the fears and win the trust of the constituencies they were addressed at and cut a deal.

West Germany had a free-market capitalist system. An economic integration would be possible after re-unification, only if the State-Owned Enterprises of the East were also privatised. It was said that these enterprises would be transferred to the very citizens whose toil had created it. However, as it turned out, the trusteeship of these Enterprises were handed over to handpicked West Germans who represented big business. All assets were privatised at breakneck speed. After being acquired by the West German investors the Enterprises were promptly closed down throwing millions out of work. East German industry was labour intensive. Jobs were for a lifetime. East German life revolved around the workspace. Each organization had its own childcare and health services. Companies often

---

[23] In the book *'WHY WOMEN HAVE BETTER SEX UNDER SOCIALISM'* the author Kristen R Ghooseargues, based on verifiable data and case studies that, women had a better life under the so-called totalitarian Communist systems.

provided recreation facilities. It was not just that people were affiliated to their workplace. Most of them derived their very identity from work.

Post re-unification, birth rate fell among the East Germans. The marriage rates too fell drastically. East Germans had a higher birth rate than their western counterparts prior to reunification. Mortality rates peaked. From being euphoric about the fact that their leadership was no longer on a short leash from the Kremlin, the East Germans soon were in a state of despondency. Even East German human rights activists confided all they wanted was reforms within the framework of the GDR and never an abolition of it. *'Another East Germany was possible'.*

West Germany had been the recipient of Marshall aid to the tune of 1.4 billion dollars. As the bloodiest battles were fought in the East between the Red Army and the Nazis, West Germany was comparatively better off. With full integration with the western capitalist bloc, it enjoyed an affluence that the East Germans had come to envy. The East Germans had thought that through post-unification they could keep all the benefits of social security of GDR and enjoy the consumption habits of the West. In the re-unification process dictated by the West, they lost what they had but never appreciated. Their aspirations for the opulence of the West never materialised. Opponents of Helmut Kohl had urged for a gradual approach as the track record of shock therapy was poor. They reasoned that without the institutional frameworks and regulatory bodies shock therapy would wreak havoc. And it did. The people in the East had taken it on themselves to *'tear down the wall'.* But, as it turned out it was a colonisation of the East by the West. It was a triumph of neoliberal conservatism under the banner of German reunification.

---

[24] 9th November 1989 the day the Berlin wall fell marks the colonisation of the East by the West.

Chapter 19: The Greatest Geopolitical Disaster of the 20ᵗʰ Century

17ᵗʰ March 1991 Referendum

> *'Do you consider it necessary the preservation of the Union of Soviet Socialist Republics as a renewed federation of equal sovereign Republics in which the rights and freedom of an individual of any ethnicity will be fully guaranteed'?*
>
> 113, 512, 812 Soviet citizens, close to 80 percent, voted YES.

---

[25] Throughout 1992 the Russian Parliament refused to ratify the undemocratic and unconstitutional dissolution of the Soviet Union.

[26] In 1993, the Russian Parliament impeached the President of Russia Boris Yeltsin 636-2 for having illegally dissolved the Soviet Union and unleashing neoliberal market economy.

[27] In 1995 the newly constituted Russian Parliament passed a resolution abrogating the illegal and undemocratic dissolution of the Soviet Union.

The Greatest Welfare State Abolishes Itself

> 'The President of Russia (Boris Yeltsin) and his entourage, in fact, sacrificed the Union to his passionate desire to accede to the throne in the Kremlin'.
>
> **— Mikhail Gorbachev**

> 'Soviet Union did not die of natural causes... It committed suicide'.
>
> **— Fidel Castro**

> 'The dissolution of the Soviet Union was the greatest geo-political disaster of the twentieth century'.
>
> **— Vladimir Putin**

> 'By the grace of God, we won the Cold War'.
>
> **— President George Bush Sr**

In the 1980s, six decades after the Russian Revolution, from being a semi-pastoral society untouched by the industrial revolution, the Soviet Union was one pole of a bipolar world. By any such measures as life expectancy, caloric intake, and literacy, the Soviet Union had reached the ranks of the developed countries, though starting from a primitive era without any resort to slave labour or the plunder of any colony, instead being at the beck and call of the former colonies of the Third World, over-coming external armed aggression, civil war and economic boycott. Across the ages, great nations have declined often but never crumbled so rapidly within a few days. The sudden demise of a nation that was economically and militarily powerful, which had in its infant stages withstood external aggression and an internal upheaval nothing short of full-fledged civil war, in the absence of any debilitating factors comparable to those, is unprecedented in modem history.

The Soviet Union ever since its inception was a bulwark against capitalism and its inevitable offshoot, colonialism. It was a beacon of hope for the entire Third World. While recessions and depressions are fundamentally inherent in the capitalist system, the Soviet economy never knew of any recession, let alone depression. The very fact that the Soviet economy made giant strides at a time when the capitalist world plunged into the greatest depression until then speaks for itself.

The Rise of Gorbachev

The Soviet Union in the 1980s witnessed a series of successions to the top job. After Brezhnev's death in 1982, an ailing Yuri Andropov who replaced him died in office in just 2 years. His successor Konstantin Cherenkov died in just 6 months. Cherenkov was the third Soviet Leader since Ronald Reagan had come to office. It was a bit embarrassing for the Soviet leadership when Ronald Reagan, who had upped the Cold War ante unilaterally, sarcastically remarked when asked about the progress of talks with his Soviet counterpart that he could not help if the Soviet General Secretaries did not outlast him. This paved the way for the rise of the virtually unknown young Mikhail Gorbachev. The charismatic Gorbachev was fondly referred to as '*Gorby*' in the western countries.

Reforms of Gorbachev

During the 1980s the Soviet economy experienced stagnation. Rampant corruption, slow adoption of technology and a sense of entitlement and complacency contributed towards this stagnation. The labour market, as in any socialist economy with constitutionally provided right to work, was a seller's market and never a buyer's market. Inefficiency marred every sector of the economy which is hardly indicative of a tyrannical system as the Soviet system is often accused of.

Adding insult to injury, the oil glut in the 1980s compounded the problem. Oil was Soviet Union's chief source of hard currency. Saudi Arabia, on Ronald Reagan's insistence, started to produce oil at full capacity with the sole purpose of creating an oil glut that effectively reduced the oil price which had peaked at $35 per barrel in 1980 (equivalent to $124 in 2022 dollars adjusted for inflation) to below $10 per barrel in 1986 (equivalent to $27 in 2022 dollars). The intention was to strangulate the Soviet Union, as oil alone fetched its hard currency.

The new General Secretary embarked on an ambitious reform programme. His reforms were intended to effect a paradigm change in both the economy as well as the body politik of the Union. The Union needed it. The new General Secretary's initiatives *perestroika* (re-construction), *glasnost* (open-ness) *uskarenia* (acceleration) were well-intentioned. The intention was to build on what was good in the Soviet system while expunging the unsavoury aspects that had crept into the Soviet system. The reforms were to revamp both the political and the economic system. But, as fate would have it, the well-intentioned reforms, which we shall see later in this chapter, took a life of their own and played into the hands of social groups with an ideological stake in private property and free market capitalism.

In the Soviet Union, ever since the reforms were launched, there were three forces at work. Three factions were battling it out. First there was the Gorbachev faction which wanted to bring a paradigm shift in the Soviet administrative apparatus and in the very way the Republics federated to form the Union. Opposed to this faction was the one led by the hardliners in Kremlin who wanted just a cosmetic change to the Soviet system, as any further devolution of powers to the Republics threatened to reduce their power, prestige and material endowments. A third faction led by Yeltsin, the elected President of Russia, favoured doing away with the socialist system in its entirety and embracing the free market economy. As it was difficult to embrace the market economy while being within the Soviet system as every Republic was on a very short leash from the Kremlin with regard to economic matters, the Boris Yeltsin faction harboured plans to part ways with it, even if that meant dismemberment of the Union. As the hardliners, alarmed at the devolution of greater powers to the federating Republics, took on the Gorbachev faction in the August 1991 coup resulting in a pandemonium that discredited both, the third faction under Boris Yeltsin hovering around the side-lines moved in and encashed the opportunity. From then onwards it was all Yeltsin. It was a *'revolution from above'.*

Referendum on Whether to Retain the Soviet Union Under a New Union Treaty

Lenin had insisted right from the beginning on the recognition of the principle that nations should have the right of self-determination including the right to secede. A federation of equal Republics was thus envisaged as a means of maintaining the integrity of the multinational state that was the USSR. It was only in a federation of Republics of equal standing that the nationalities could bloom to the fullest extent possible. The Gorbachev faction was favouring further devolution of powers to the federating Republics transforming the USSR into a confederation of Republics.

On 17th March 1991, a nationwide referendum as to whether the Republics preferred to stay within the Soviet Union was conducted in the Republics. It asked whether or not the Soviet citizens approved a new Union Treaty between the Republics, that was drafted to replace the 1922 treaty that created the USSR.

Boris Yeltsin, President of the Russian Federation had been harping on the dissolution of the Soviet Union for a long time. For him, from being the President of the Russian Federation to acceding to the throne in the Kremlin, the most plausible way was to dismember the Union in its entirety. On 9th March as the date of the referendum approached, he declared *'We* do not need a Central Government like this—huge and bureaucratic . . . We must get rid of it'.

The verdict of the Soviet citizens a week later on 17th March was unambiguous and was in favour of preserving the Union. 80 percent of the Soviet citizens voted in favour of retaining the Union. 73 percent of the Soviet citizens in the Russian Republic, in spite of Boris Yeltsin's appeal to the contrary, voted in favour of retaining the Union.

In the Republic of Kazakhstan, the wording of the referendum had a cosmetic change by substituting *'equal sovereign states'* for *'equal sovereign Republics'*. Six Republics, the three Baltic Republics of Latvia, Lithuania and Estonia together with the Republics of Armenia, Georgia and Moldova with deep-seated nationalist sentiments boycotted the referendum. By the time of the nation-wide referendum in March, voters in these three Baltic Republics had overwhelmingly declared themselves in favour of independence from the Soviet Union. Their Parliaments had issued decrees to that effect. These Republics were added to the USSR during World War II by Stalin, to serve as a buffer in the event of frontal attack on Russia by Germany. The Republics of Georgia, Moldova and Armenia Republics conducted referendum independently in which an over whelming majority opted for Independence.

Nine Republics with an overwhelming majority close to eighty percent opted to remain in the Soviet Union. Gorbachev, the General Secretary of the CPSU, therefore, received a strong mandate to proceed with a new Union Treaty. The New Union Treaty was to take the first and biggest Welfare State from being a Federation to a Confederation. In the month of August 1991, as the Supreme Soviets of the federating Republics buoyed by the YES vote in the referendum were deliberating on the nuances of the new Union Treaty, the hardliners who stood to lose staged a coup. Yeltsin's defiance as epitomised by the *'man atop the tank'* imagery when Gorbachev was held incommunicado at Crimea by KGB aborted the coup.

Unlike Gorbachev, Boris Yeltsin had won the Presidency of the Russian Federation by direct vote and his call to all Muscovites to line up in the street against the military tanks was heeded. Coup plotters, the hardliners stood discredited. Though abortive, the coup undermined the Gorbachev's position very much. In the ensuing pandemonium, the Yeltsin faction gained the upper hand. From then on, the fate of the Union and that of Gorbachev was sealed.

The Anatomy of the 'The Greatest Geopolitical Catastrophe of the 20th Century'

> *'Aren't we all very dependent on each other...we are greatly corporatized...we cannot destroy that under the pretext of the need for sovereignty... that is not what sovereignty demands...'*
> — **Mikhail Gorbachev**

8th December 1991 Belovezha declaration: *'The Union of Soviet Socialist Republics as an entity under international law and a geopolitical reality has ceased to exist'.*

Heads of three Republics, namely Russia, Belarus and Ukraine signed an accord effectively ending the Soviet Union. The very people in these Republics by a huge majority had willed to retain the Union in the referendum of 17th March 1991.

The Belovezha Accord was secretive, treacherous, illegal, unconstitutional and was in direct violation of the people's mandate. Treacherous because the three signed an agreement to establish a Commonwealth of Independent States (CIS) just to hoodwink the people into believing that the CIS that was being proposed was both in content and form very much akin to the Union that was being discussed in the Supreme Soviets of the Republics. Such was the overwhelming majority of the referendum favouring the Union that the three could not risk signing an accord that appeared in direct violation of the people's will.

In effect, the Belovezha Accord bluntly put an end to the existence of the USSR. Undeniably, each Republic had the constitutional right to secede from the Union. But, the fate of the multinational state could not be determined by the leaders of the three Republics alone. The question of secession should have been decided only by constitutional means with the participation of all the sovereign states and taking into account the will of all their citizens. The will of 113, 512,812 of the Soviet citizens being invalidated by just the 3 Heads of State was unconstitutional. The undue haste with which the declaration was made with the provision of a CIS, the purpose of which was to deceive, reflects on the sinister intentions of the perpetrators. It was never discussed by the citizens nor by the Supreme Soviets of the Republics in whose name it was signed. The declaration was made at a time when the draft treaty for a Union of Sovereign States, drafted by the State Council of the USSR was being thoroughly discussed by the Parliaments of the federating Republics. Instead of preserving, renewing, and reforming the Union, it was dismembered by a stroke of criminal ingenuity by 'Boris Yeltsin and his entourage'.

> 'It is disgraceful. To tell the President of the United States and not bother to tell the President of your own country. it is shameful. absolutely contemptible. It is dirty'.
> **– Mikhail Gorbachev on TV on his being kept in the dark**

President Bush was privy to the Belovezha Accord. Gorbachev made no attempt to conceal his anger. Gorbachev had basked in the limelight of international politics. Every western leader had warmed up to him. He was young, charismatic and open to (their!) ideas. The West rewarded the affable Gorbachev with Nobel Peace Prize. The West had invested heavily in him. But following the August coup, which saw his standing in domestic politics dwindling and being eclipsed by Boris Yeltsin, they double-crossed him and eventually dumped him for their new man. It was Boris Yeltsin who pulled the real coup. Boris Kagarlitsky, a prominent Soviet dissident said *'In fact there was no coup at all…and the leaders of the so-called coup never even seriously tried to take power'.* As a Kremlin insider noted, *'I believe that if [Soviet leader, Yuri] Andropov had been fifteen years younger when he took power in 1982, we would still have a Soviet Union with us'..*

Implications for the Third World

'We have arrived at the end of history'.

– Francis Fukuyama

In the Great anti-communist celebration that followed the dissolution of the Soviet Union the triumphant right-wingers were on a proselytising mission. The western media broadcasted stories of a popular assault taking on the old guards and hardliners and eventually winning. They were quick to highlight the dissolution as the inevitable outcome of a systemic failure of socialism they had been highlighting and, hence fighting since the days of its inception rather than a human error. The dissolution of the biggest Welfare State was heralded as the invalidation of the socialist welfare cause and the vindication of the neoliberal policies, that had been doing the rounds since the turn of the 1980s. It was for them a standing testimony that any form of social solidarity against Capital was not sustainable. It was the kind of crisis that Milton Friedmanites had been craving for. The right-wingers hammered into the consciousness of millions that the Soviet experiment was an accident or aberration of history born in the labyrinth of violence and sustained by coercion, and fundamentally incompatible with democracy and human freedom. The dissolution of the Union due to an unfortunate turnaround of events was projected to be what the Soviet system was heading to since 1922. In a state of shock, the uncritical mind is receptive to the *'ideas that are lying around'.*

Protagonists of unfettered free-market economics seized upon the Soviet fiasco as proof that any form of state intervention in the economy was a recipe for disaster. The Soviet system was inching towards a disaster entirely due to *'Government meddling'* is a believable narrative as the system crashed in the absence of any external armed aggression. Western Capital had their man in Kremlin something unthinkable quite a few days ago. The Third World lost an all-weather friend.

Neoliberalism pulverised economy after economy ever since socialism failed to be viewed as an alternative to predatory capitalism. Socialism was invalidated beyond redemption. Even among the lowest strata of the society of the capitalist World or in the Third World countries, except, of course, Cuba, a discredited socialism found no takers

Yeltsin's defiance of the coup catapulted him to world attention. He raced to the White House, making a memorable speech from atop the turret of a tank onto which he had climbed. He was dubbed *'Man atop the Tank'.* It was Yeltsin's finest hour. He pulled a second coup and dismembered the Union. He was to shell the White House soon.

17th March 1991 Referendum in the Soviet Union	
Republic	**For the Union**	**Against the Union**
Russia	73 %	27 %
Azerbaijan	94.12 %	5.88 %
Byelorussia	83.72 %	16.28 %
Kazakhstan	95.0 %	5.0 %
Kyrgyzstan	95.98 %	4.02 %
Tajikistan	96.85 %	3.15 %
Turkmenistan	98.26 %	1.74 %
Ukraine	71.48 %	28.52%
Uzbekistan	94.73 %	5.27 %

'I am convinced that decisions of such scale should have been made on the basis of a popular expression of will'.

– **Mikhael Gorbachev**

Russia on Sale

1992 Russia

> 'What did capitalism accomplish in 1 year that 74 years of communism could not'?
>
> *Make communism look good'.*

> *Throughout the free market reforms the use of force was elevated to a principle of Government policy.*
>
> **– Mikhail Gorbachev**

> 'The contrast between Russia's transition, as engineered by the international economic institutions, and that of China, designed by itself, could not be greater: While in 1990 China's gross domestic product (GDP) was 60 percent that of Russia, by the end of the decade the numbers had been reversed. While Russia saw an unprecedented increase in poverty, China saw an unprecedented decrease'.
>
> **– Joseph Stiglitz**

> 'No region in the world has suffered such reversals in the 1990s as have the countries of the former Soviet Union and Eastern Europe'.
>
> **– UN report in 1998**

The Robber Baron Capitalism in the Aftermath of the Soviet Catastrophe

On 17th March 1991, the people of the Soviet Union had willed by a landslide in a referendum that the Union was to be preserved, though with more devolution of power to the federating Republics. Still, the

Soviet Union was dissolved on 26th December 1991. In 1992 the Russian Duma repeatedly declined to ratify the dissolution. The newly constituted Russian Parliament in 1995 even passed a resolution abrogating the dissolution of the Union, a symbolic gesture to signify the USSR still does exist.

Very much akin to the dissolution, the free-market economy was introduced in Russia against the will of the people. By mid-1992, barely after six months of shock therapy, the Parliament and the President were on a warpath. By September 1993 Yeltsin dissolved the Parliament; a move that was unconstitutional. The Russian Parliament impeached the President for gross violation of the constitution and laid siege to the Parliament. Moscow witnessed the bloodiest of all street fights since the October Revolution. On the orders of the President the Parliament was shelled.

Like in Chile, free market arrived in Russia against the interests of its people. The Welfare State was dismembered within weeks of the dissolution of the Soviet Union. In Russia, however, the government continued to retain a pretence of being a democracy. All throughout the 1990s the West saw to it that Boris Yeltsin remained in power.

The Context of Russia as it Embraced the Market Economy

In the 1980s, the Soviet Union witnessed a stagnation. The slash in the global oil prices and the war in Afghanistan took their toll on the Russian economy. The subsidies to its allies and its efforts to catch up with the US in defence of the alternative socio-politico-economic model it championed, the Welfare State, did strain its exchequer. A stress on heavy industry and weaponry necessitated by the capitalist encirclement meant the Soviet system had to neglect the production of consumer goods, which did impact the material comfort of its citizens. But, it was a Welfare State that liberated the largest number of people, unprecedented in the history of mankind. It had succeeded in creating an egalitarian society.

Prices of basic necessities, like food, energy and natural resources were government-administered. It ensured their affordability to every stratum of the society. The per capita calorie intake in the Soviet Union was higher than that of the capitalist West. There was no unemployment in the Soviet Union. The State enterprise never fired any employee. Places of work had day care facilities to take care of the children of its employees. It took care of its employees even after retirement. Let us not forget that when the capitalist world was reeling under the greatest depression in the 1930s, the Soviet Union was making giant strides in every walk of life.

The dissolution of the mammoth Welfare State of the Soviet Union signalled the end of the Cold War. The defence cuts were expected to give a breathing space for the Russian economy. It could, it was hoped, concentrate on consumer goods and provide a better standard of living for its people. *'Seldom has the gap between expectations and reality been greater than in the case of the transition from communism to the market'* writes Joseph Stiglitz, in *'Globalisation and its discontents'* on the Russian experience of embracing neoliberalism.

All Shock and No Therapy!!!

The Soviet Union disappeared on 26th December 1991. The next week, on the 2nd of January 1992, the first working day after the formal dissolution of the USSR, Russian President Boris Yeltsin vested with sweeping powers to rule by decree by the Russian Parliament dismantled the planned economy, inaugurating a market economy in its place. Across Russia, the State control over eighty percent of wholesale prices and ninety percent of retail prices were removed just like that. It was the first time that an economy in which the government planned every activity at the minutest level for decades was left to be managed by market forces in a few hours.

The concerns over the ramifications of introducing a market economy in Russia, given its non-capitalist history, was never heeded. With absolutely no institutional framework, neither legal nor political or regulatory, to oversee the market mechanism, the transition was done in undue haste. *'You can't cross a chasm in two leaps'*, the shock therapists argued. Those opposed to the shock therapy, the gradualists as they came to be known, reasoned about crossing the river by feeling the stones. Shock therapists prevailed.

With the abolition of price regulation, Russia witnessed an inflation of 2600 percent in 1992, the first year of *'reform'*. It wiped out the savings of the middle class. Wages for workers and pensions for the elderly were not indexed to the new cost of living. Government subsidies to industry were slashed as per the gospel of market economics. Industrial production crippled. The Russian economy was on a downward spiral. GDP more than halved. The state of Russia in the 1990s was worse than the hardliners had forewarned the citizens against. Food shortage was common. It was all shock and no therapy.

When a much-trumpeted policy initiative fails to achieve any of its declared objectives and instead, ruins the entire system, debate is inevitable. The protagonists would highlight that their recommendations were not implemented in their entirety and that it would have been different had that been so. The case of Russia was no different. The debate still continues. Till date shock therapy has never worked in any economy.

Privatisation in Russia

The privatisation of the Russian State–Owned Enterprises (SOEs) was to be implemented through privatisation vouchers. The rationale was to ensure the ownership of the country's wealth be distributed among the citizens equally. Vouchers worth 10,000 Rubles were distributed among the citizens. With vouchers, they could buy shares of the SOEs.

Seven decades of communist rule had moulded the Russians. They were completely ignorant about the concept of shares and stocks. The people were unaware of the wealth of the vouchers. Hard-pressed for money and due to financial illiteracy, they exchanged it for a few dollars or for food and clothing. A handful of unscrupulous *'entrepreneurs'* who had amassed wealth in the initial years of economic reform bought off all the vouchers from the people. With these vouchers they bought many of the State-Owned Enterprises. Thus, national wealth was usurped by a select few by purchasing all the vouchers for privatisation.

Why the Undue Haste?

Boris Yeltsin and his team of apparatchiks went ahead with privatisation with a haste, un-paralleled in the history of free market economy. Even in Chile, the Chicago boys who were under the spell of Milton Friedman were much more cautious. Even in Russia, a sizeable chunk of the reformers learning lessons from the Latin-American debacle had recommended a gradual approach. The gradualists, were side-stepped. But, why?

Though Boris Yeltsin had declared communism to be dead, he feared the return of the communists by the ballot. The communists never lost power in Russia. In the pandemonium precipitated by the failed August Coup of 1991, they lost traction over the events unfolding. The Russians both in 1993 and 1995 had returned a Duma which was decisively left-leaning. Pro-Kremlin parties were decimated in both elections.

Fearing a return of the communists, given the economic ruin the first weeks of liberalisation had caused, Yeltsin and his coterie wanted to take the baton of neoliberalism to such a farthest extent possible that the communists once restored to power would not even think of reversing it. Thatcher and Reagan had so thoroughly and systematically pulverised the fabric of their respective welfare economies built on post-war consensus that their successors Tony Blair and Bill Clinton chose not to reverse it, but to desert their own constituencies in deference to the dictates of neoliberal mantra. Thatcher in her days of retirement would relish that her best achievement was *'We could change Tony Blair and his party'*.

In retrospect, it is evident that under the pretext of conferring the ownership of the SOEs to the individual citizens through privatisation vouchers, a sinister intention of placing the ownership of the SOEs into a few private hands was achieved. Heavens would not have fallen had the SOEs continued to be state-run. After all, the SOEs in Russia that had come into existence by legislative acts of the Soviet Parliament belonged to the people even after the dissolution of the USSR. People exercised control over SOEs through the Parliament to which the enterprises were accountable. The scheme was rushed through on a holiday, a couple of days prior to the recalcitrant Russian Parliament was to vote against the privatisation of the SOEs. As Deputy Prime Minister Anatoly Chubais, who as an Yeltsin apparatchik oversaw the voucher scheme proudly stated in an interview years later, *'We sneaked them through the Supreme Soviet during the holiday. They were issued on 28th August*[28] *and on 3rd September there was to be a vote banning privatisation. The first vouchers were handed out on 1st September. We beat the Supreme Soviet by two days. No member of Parliament with any sense would dare oppose something that was already in the people's hands. We presented them with a fait accompli'*. The over zealousness of distributing the vouchers to the people, bypassing the Parliament that had become critical of the reforms, was just to transfer the state assets to a select few entrepreneurs close to Kremlin. By the time the ploy became evident, it was too late. Privatisation of State assets was accomplished without Parliamentary approval. The people and their Parliament had been duped. It was destined to recur once more.

The 1996 Presidential election was the next most opportune moment for the *'entrepreneurs'* to usurp more of the wealth of Russia into their own hands. By then the economy had taken a nose dive. The communists had swept the polls in the 1995 elections to the Russian Duma. The leader

---

[28] 28th August 1993 was a Saturday.

of the communist party Gennady Zyuganov was elected the Speaker of the Russian Duma. He was leading in the opinion polls and was clearly the favourite. Western media even predicted the return of a communist President by the ballot. Yeltsin's popularity had plummeted to as low as 3 percent. With multiple heart attacks and bypass surgeries, Yeltsin spent most of his time in hospital.

Davos Pact

At the World Economic Forum Summit at Davos in February 1996 Gennady Zyuganov was being courted by the captains of big businesses the world over. In the words of Anatoly Chubais, *'The problem was the behaviour of my good friends and comrades... the captains of the western business community... people I knew well ...carefully considered people who were falling over themselves trying to butter up Zyuganov currying his favour so blatantly that it was revolting to watch'*.

With a communist takeover imminent, he was in a way *'The President-elect'*. Once he was even asked whether his return would signal the reconstitution of the Soviet Union. At Davos, he went on air that he was critical of privatisation in Russia. Privatisation, he contended, which was to bring in efficiency had not delivered in Russia. *'Privatisation is supposed to make a company work better and achieve corresponding profits. So the word privatisation is out of place. Pure and simple, it is theft and destroys the production base'*. The GDP that was in a downward spiral vindicated his concerns. In the Russian context, he lamented privatisation was just a transfer of state assets to private hands by Presidential decree bypassing a legitimate Parliament. He let it known that on his return, misappropriation of national wealth at such a scale would be checked and undone. His bashing of the private monopolies that sprung up from nowhere did not go down well with the Oligarchs attending the Summit.

Alarmed at the standing of Gennady Zyuganov and the prospect of being put in jail or put up against the wall, the Oligarchs of the Russian delegation decided to bury their differences and animosities and to join hands, in what would be known as the *'Davos Pact'*, and throw their financial weight behind Yeltsin to ensure his re-election in the upcoming Presidential election in June.

Loans for Shares

The pact at Davos gave birth to a new round of privatisation. Thus, was born the *'loans-for-shares'* scheme. As per the scheme, the government reeling under financial constraint pledged the shares of some of the remaining State-Owned Enterprises as collateral in return for the loan from private banks that had sprung up in the 1990s. These private banks accepted the shares of highly profitable State Enterprises and loaned the government. The government in tacit understanding with the private bankers promptly defaulted on loan repayments and the bankers as was scripted in the Davos Pact ended up owning the State enterprises. The bankers in turn contributed towards the election campaign of Boris Yeltsin. It was privatisation without Parliamentary approval a second time, a convenient way to bypass a communist-dominated Russian Duma. The Russian Parliament was duped a second time.

The most obscene aspect of the loan-for-share scheme was yet to come. Banks loan depositors' money. The depositors are either institutions or individuals. In Russia, inflation had eaten up all the savings of the common man. Hence, in Russia, in the context of inflation, the depositors of a bank were the institutions, namely, the State-Owned Enterprises. In a way, the state was being loaned back its own money for which the collateral, namely, the stocks of SOEs pledged were usurped by the banks. The amount loaned was just a fraction of the worth of these highly profitable cash cows in natural resource extraction and trading. That was how the Russian *'entrepreneurs'* who had become millionaires graduated into billionaires overnight.

IMF Facilitated the Plunder of Russia

The IMF on its part against all conventional wisdom insisted that Russia should maintain a high exchange rate. Towards this end, all through the 1990s the institution even loaned billions of dollars to Russia. Why did the IMF loan such large amounts to Russia to help maintain parity between the Ruble and the Dollar? The only possible explanation was to help the Oligarchs. Every Russian Ruble could now purchase a higher number of dollars than at any time in the past. Concerned about the fate of their ill-gotten wealth in the event of a return of the communists, the Oligarchs stashed their ill-gotten wealth in Swiss banks, thus, earning them a nickname *'kleptocrats'*. IMF was facilitating the plunder of Russia at the behest of its masters.

An over-valued currency made imports cheap and exports expensive. Luxury cars could be imported to Russia as only a few Rubles were needed to be spent on it. There were traffic blocks caused by luxury cars in the previously deserted streets of Moscow. The Russian retail shops were filled with imported goods that had become affordable overnight. The influx of imported foreign goods into the country, due to an overvalued currency, hit the domestic producers hard. They were edged out of the domestic retail shops by foreign goods that had become cheap. Not just that, their exports' competitiveness in the global market spiralled under the over-valued Ruble. Russia was soon home to starving millions and a handful of millionaires very much in line with Marx's observation that capitalism creates wealth at one pole and poverty and deprivation at the other.

West's Meddling in the 1996 Russian Presidential Election

The free market economy, the well springs of democracy as they had been lectured to be, seemed not to be to the liking of the Russians. Russians in less than five years had enough of it and were gearing up towards a *'totalitarian communist state'* through democratic means. Yeltsin was prodded by the West to state that communism was dead in Russia.

But Russians had been electing left-leaning Parliaments all through the *'reforms'* unleashed by Boris Yeltsin. A triumphant return of the communists by the ballot would have discredited the West's rhetoric of a free-market economy and laid bare the hollowness of it. The prospect of a democratically elected communist Russian President was not in the West's interests. After all, they had tirelessly worked to dismantle the Soviet Union ever since its inception.

A US PR team managed Yeltsin's campaign. The media that had been under the Oligarch's control relentlessly aired Pro-Yeltsin campaign. None of the opposition candidates could get across the electorate through any media. Russians were warned of a civil war in the event of a communist President. World leaders air-dashed to Moscow and held *'talks'* with Yeltsin. Six weeks prior to the election, Moscow was host to G 7 Summit. The Nuclear Summit was intended to shower upon Russia the status of a world power and to its President the pretensions of a global leader. Halting NATO's eastward expansion on Yeltsin's insistence was the icing on the cake. President Clinton made statements praising Yeltsin and lectured the Russians on the political freedom that the free-market economy would deliver, as it had in his country! He reminded the Russian people that transition though torturous was temporal and worth a price to pay. It appears that in 1996 President Clinton was obsessed with getting Yeltsin elected one more time than his own re-election later that year. The two leaders were in constant touch. Under Clinton's insistence, Michel Camdessus, Managing Director of IMF, granted a loan of $ 10 billion to Russia. It was promptly siphoned off for electioneering.

Undemocratic Nature of the Russian Wave of Neoliberalism

The Parliament of the Russian SFSR elected in 1990 during the Soviet days functioned as the newly independent Russian Republic's legislature following the dissolution of the USSR. Moreover, having been elected during the Soviet years, 86 percent of the Russian Parliament were members of the communist party of the erstwhile Soviet Union. On 1st November 1991, more than a month before the Belovezha declaration of 13th December, which dismembered the Soviet Union in the subsequent weeks, the Russian Parliament had granted President Yeltsin the power to rule by decree in the area of economic reform for a period of two years. The Parliament had vested such powers in Yeltsin at a time when retaining the Union within the socialist framework with further devolution of powers to the Republics was being discussed across the Soviet Union. With the dissolution of the USSR Yeltsin exercised his plenipotentiary powers to embark on a path virtually unthinkable during the Soviet days. He wasted no time. The very first working day after the dissolution, i.e. 2nd January 1992 saw the President dismantling price control, the first of the neoliberal reforms. By late 1992, as the economy crashed following the reforms being under the dictates of the IMF. The Russian Parliament and President Yeltsin were on a war path. Though it had invested Yeltsin the power to rule by decree, the disastrous route the reforms took cautioned the Parliament from extending his plenipotentiary powers any further beyond 1992. The President had breached his limits. He wanted the same to be reinstated before the next round of shock therapy. The Russian Parliament refused to grant the President the power to rule by decree. Neither the people nor the Russian Parliament did endorse the reforms that were being carried out by Yeltsin by decree.

Constitutional Crisis of 1993

In March 1993, the Parliament made a crucial decision. It repealed special powers that were granted to Yeltsin to proceed with free-market capitalism. Yeltsin declared a state of emergency which was ruled illegal by the Constitutional Court.

By September 1993, the stand-off between the President and the Parliament reached a flash point. President Yeltsin went the Pinochet way. On 21st September Yeltsin dissolved the Parliament. Electricity and water connection were cut off to coerce the Parliament into submission. It was an unconstitutional move. The Parliament, braving all odds, passed a resolution 636-2 impeaching the President under candlelight and laid siege to the Parliament. The capital witnessed the bloodiest of all street fights and arson since the October Revolution. The West threw its weight behind Yeltsin. The day the Parliament was dissolved, the US Vice President Al Gore declared, *'We feel that Boris Yeltsin is the best hope for democracy in Russia'*. Warren Christopher, the US Secretary of State who air-dashed to Russia in a show of camaraderie stated: *'The US does not easily support the suspension of the Parliament. But these are extra-ordinary times'*. On 4th October 1993, an emboldened President Yeltsin ordered the army to shell the Russian White House to bully the Parliamentarians into submission. Ironically, it was the same building that Yeltsin defended during the abortive coup by communist hardliners.

1993 Russian Parliamentary Elections

Following the 1993 constitutional crisis, elections were declared to be held to elect a Parliament for a transitory two-year term. In the pre-election debate, the Russian communist party leader Mr. Zyuganov stressed that privatisation, the way it was proceeding then, would be put on hold. And promised a referendum on the restoration of the Soviet Union. President Yeltsin appealed to voters not to *'allow the forces of the past to seize power again'*.

The election results were a decisive blow to the Pro-Kremlin parties. Their standing in the Duma was such that they could not command the Parliamentary agenda nor force the will of the President on the Duma. The election result was a shot in the arm for the nationalists, communists and their affiliates critical of the economic reforms that threw the economy into disarray letting Yeltsin and his apparatchiks usurp to themselves the wealth of the nation. The results reflected the humiliation and disillusionment of the population on the pathetic and diminutive status of their country.

1995 Russian Legislative Elections

In the 1995 Russian Legislative elections to constitute a new Duma after the end of the two-year transitory period, pro-Kremlin party, Our Home – Russia with access to resources that the Russian communists could not even think of, fared poorly. Such was the disgruntlement among the Russian populace on the turn towards a market economy that in the 1995 Parliamentary election the communists emerged victorious. The communists and their left-leaning affiliates controlled a little less than half of the seats in the Duma. Together with other parties, it was a dominant force to reckon with. The belligerence of the Russian Parliament is reflected in the passing of a resolution abrogating the dissolution of the Soviet Union. Though inconsequential, it symbolized the people's will to return to the Soviet days. It was to serve as a grim reminder that unlike the secessions of the Baltic States of Lithuania, Latvia and Estonia based on a referendum, the dissolution of the Soviet Union was undemocratic and in violation of the will of its people. All throughout the 1990s the communists and nationalists fanatically against the dissolution of the Union and the introduction of the market economy had a decisive majority in the Russian Parliament. Russian President Boris Yeltsin ruled by decree. Neither the people nor the Russian Parliament did endorse the reforms. Consistently the Parliament was duped in furtherance of the reforms.

Conclusion

It must be said that in spite of pretensions to the contrary, in Russia the fabric of democracy was dismembered in pursuit of reforms. The legislature was rendered virtually impotent. The Presidential elections were rigged. The West had always been obsessed with Russia since the Tsarist days. American and European aristocracy had vast investments in this resource-rich land mass. The Bolshevik revolution was a blow to the investors. Decades of war, embargo, diplomatic isolation and a world war could not deter Russia. Neoliberalism by a mole in the Kremlin achieved precisely that.

Chapter 20: Yugoslavia: NATO Obliterates the Last Holdout of Collectivism in Europe

> 'Kosovo is the heart of Serbia. Stop the violence'.
>
> – **Novak Djokovic**

> 'Many say that this (Russian invasion of Ukraine) was the first conflict on European soil after World War II, but the truth is that the territorial integrity of a country in Europe, Serbia as a matter of fact, that did not attack any other sovereign country was violated is constantly unspoken'.
>
> – Aleksander Vucic, President of Serbia addressing the UN General Assembly on 22nd September 2022

Why NATO Spit Fire from The Yugoslav Skies for Seventy-eight Days From 24th March to 10th June 1999?

Slobodan Milosevic was no messiah. He had his failings. In Serbia, it was mayhem time. But why did NATO pick him up and make him the poster child of ethnic cleansing while the West in general and the US, in particular, had consistently warmed up towards murderous dictators elsewhere like the Batista of Cuba, Somoza of Nicaragua, Salazar of Portugal, the Shah of Iran, Marcos of the Philippines, Suharto of Indonesia, Noriega of Panama until he fell out of favour, Pinochet of Chile and a host of those of Latin America and Africa?

The Federal Republic of Yugoslavia was a stumbling block for the eastward expansion of western Capital. As communist and socialist governments fell like a pack of cards in eastern Europe with many of the federating Republics torn apart by ethno-nationalism, Yugoslavia being no exception, witnessing a breakaway of Slovenia and Croatia, the socialist government in what was remaining as the Federal Republic of Yugoslavia, stood its ground. Federal Republic of Yugoslavia (FRY) remained the only nation in that region that would not voluntarily discard the socialist principles.

NATO's attacks on what remained as Yugoslavia revealed the western plot. Following the seventy-eight -day aerial terror the Confederation of Trade Unions of Serbia came up with a list of 164 factories destroyed by the bombings. Not even a single foreign-owned firm was damaged. Those owned by the State and the cooperatives were razed to the ground in their entirety.

Michael Parenti in his book *'To Kill a Nation: The Attack on Yugoslavia'* notes that during a visit to Belgrade after the bombing he noticed the state-owned *Hotel Yugoslavia*, iconic by its size, was severely damaged while the Hyatt Hotel, a pride of the western Capital was left unscathed. Buildings of Panasonic, Coca-Cola, Diners Club International, and McDonald's were never in the NATO list.

Yugo! The Pride of Yugoslavia

The Yugo car was very economical and offered a semblance of competition to many European brands. It was the most preferred car in Yugoslavia. The Zastava factory churning out the Yugo cars was promptly bombed into a dysfunctional state thus throwing thousands of workers out of a means of livelihood. Any feeble competition it offered to the world brands was nipped off and the Yugoslav auto market was prised open to foreign brands. Kragujevac, the renowned industrial city in Central Serbia with its mammoth infrastructure that churned out trucks, tractors and jeeps which were in high demand in the West, and had irked the European companies was razed. ICN Pharmaceuticals in Yugoslavia is a telling example of how selective and vengeful NATO bombing was. The worker-owned ICN pharmaceutical company in Yugoslavia which catered to the medical needs of the Yugoslav population was bombed. ICN began as a joint venture of the Yugoslav State and private Capital, the controversial Serbian born US-based Milan Panic contributing a lion's share of the private part of the equity. Panic attempted to buy out the government. Milosevic, in response to his overtures, turned it to the workers. It was demolished in the very first weeks of the aerial bombing. Incidentally Panic had run against Milosevic unsuccessfully for the Presidency earlier. Every enterprise in every sector in Yugoslavia that could quote a lower price in the European market thereby triggering a competition that ate into the profitability of the MNCs was razed to the ground in those seventy-eight days of bombing.

It comes as no surprise that the Yugoslav opposition television channel, Studio B, was untouched by NATO bombs while three of Yugoslavia's government TV channels and dozens of government-owned local radio and television stations were bombed.

Yugoslavia was the first country to have been expelled from the UN and Slobodan Milosevic was the first sitting head of state to be charged with war crimes. Refusing counsel, he faced his accusers alone. He contended that the International Criminal Tribunal for the Former Yugoslavia (ICTY) was a tool of the UN Security Council, which set up the tribunal, and not the broader UN General Assembly. He stated the ICTY was an illegal body set up by his western enemies to produce false justification for the war crimes of NATO committed in Yugoslavia. On 11th March 2006, Slobodan Milošević was found dead in his prison cell in the tribunal's detention centre after being in confinement for five years. His death occurred shortly after the tribunal denied his request to seek specialised cardiac medical treatment in Russia.

Chapter 21: Critique of Neoliberalism

'Laissez-faire is finished'.
– French President, Nicolas Sarkozy

'The old world of the Washington Consensus is over'.
– British Prime Minister, Gordon Brown

'The global financial crisis is a crisis which is simultaneously individual, national and global. It is a crisis of both the developed and developing world. It is a crisis which is at once institutional, intellectual and ideological. It has called into question the prevailing neoliberal economic orthodoxy of the past 30 years – the orthodoxy that has underpinned the national and global regulatory frameworks that have so spectacularly failed to prevent the economic mayhem which has been visited upon us'.
– Australian Prime Minister, Kevin Rudd

'But then it is easy, too easy, to sermonise about the dangers of paternalism and the need to take responsibility for our own lives, from the comfort of our couch in our safe and sanitary home. Aren't we, those who live in the rich world, the constant beneficiaries of a paternalism now so thoroughly embedded into the system that we hardly notice it'?–
– Abhijit V. Banerjee
Indian-American Economist and Nobel Laureate

New Avatar of IMF: The Inflation Monitoring Fund

'Working to foster global monetary cooperation, secure financial stability, facilitate international trade, promote high employment and sustainable economic growth, and reduce poverty around the world'.

— **IMF's Stated Mission**

'Keynes would be rolling over in his grave were he to see what has happened to his child'.

— **Joseph Stiglitz**

IMF and the International Bank for Reconstruction and Development are public institutions that came into being as a result of the United Nations Monetary and Financial Conference in July 1944 in Bretton Woods, New Hampshire. The two institutions were founded on the learnings of the Great Depression that markets far from being perfect often generate high levels of unemployment and if left to themselves generate persistent unemployment. The twin objectives behind the founding of these institutions were the reconstruction of a razed-down Europe and to prevent the occurrence of another economic depression as domestic economic stability was a pre-requisite for world peace and tranquillity, a learning from the depression years.

Purge of the Keynesians and the Ideological Somersault of Bretton Woods Institutions

'We are victims of language. The very word inflation leads us to think it is high prices. Inflation is not just high prices. It is a reduction in the value of our money'.

— **President Ronald Reagan**

The functioning of the Fund till the early 1980s was very much in keeping with the Keynesian prescription to tide over economic downturn. Since the ascendance of President Ronald Reagan (1981–1989) and Prime Minister Thatcher (1979–1990) these two Bretton Woods institutions have been viewed more as tools to spread the free-market ideology that the two Heads of Governments championed. Beginning with the 1980s, Keynesian Economists have been purged and replaced with market fundamentalists. IMF, a public institution founded on the premise that the market often failed has since then been pioneering market fundamentalism.

Since the 1980s IMF while assisting a government in tiding over a crisis, prescribes contractionary measures of austerity and a rollback of welfare measures. The IMF manned by market fundamentalists believes that markets work perfectly well and that it is the governments that need a dress down. It is an irony as IMF is a brainchild of John Maynard Keynes who believed that markets were far from being imperfect and government intervention was necessary. The irony does not end there. The Bretton Woods institutions of the IMF and World Bank are put to use for the very dismemberment of the Keynesian measures across the world.

IMF's Obsession with Inflation

Inflation is a problem only when it gets to a point that it slows growth. As growth slows down it affects employment. Economists tame inflation only if it has a debilitating effect on employment. As living standards improve due to the welfare measures there will be an increased demand for many of the goods and services. This rise in demand will naturally translate to slightly higher prices. Such low rates of inflation are unavoidable and should never be a cause of worry. But IMF's almost fatalistic obsession with even very low rates of inflation even when it is very much below the threshold of affecting growth and employment is to serve the interests of the Capital. As discussed in detail in the Chapter, 'Post-War consensus to Washington Consensus', the value of money is sacrosanct in a capitalist system. If the value of money erodes, then money can no longer be used to store wealth. It also ceases to be a medium of exchange. IMF's insistence on financial austerity and a roll back of welfare schemes and even employee guarantee schemes to tame inflation is reflective of its resolve to unabashedly further the interests of Capital often at the cost of the welfare of the people of the nation it is supposed to be serving. After all, for the financier who has lent his money out for a long term, inflation and non-payment of his loan are the only two real dangers he is prone to. Inflation may mean that the dollars he gets repaid will not be worth the dollars he lent years back. IMF as the guarantor of International Finance Capital steps in to ensure that inflation is under control. Its role in safeguarding the interests of the finance Capital explains its anathema for any reprieve or even a standstill in loan repayment even when the recipient nation is facing a financial crisis.

Against overwhelming evidence to the contrary, the IMF hardly entertains an objective evaluation of its actions since the 1980s and is committed to pursue a course that has turned minor crises into international disasters. The remarkable consistency with which this Bretton Woods institution has pursued policies and actions, with scant regard to historical context that had birthed it into existence, that ruined nations and its populations to abject poverty and destitution is appalling. Its obsession with curbing inflation often at the expense of the welfare of the people suggests that even without a formal revision of its mandate and objectives, there is a change in the constituency it has come to serve over the years. It is pursuing budgetary constraints and hiking taxes at times of financial distress, contrary to the Keynesian prescription. Far from fulfilling the objectives of the post-war consensus, it has become a tool to further Washington Consensus. World Bank has unabashedly played second fiddle to its sibling. It grants loans only if IMF conditionalities are met. Together the two institutions are furthering the interests of the Capital.

From Crisis to Disaster...Revisiting East Asian Crisis of 1997

'Instead of dousing the fire, the IMF in effect screamed fire in the theatre'.

– **Jeffrey Sachs**

'IMF demands that if we borrow from them they take control over our economy and that we can't afford, because we are in the process of affirmative action to level off the growth of different communities in this country. So, if you leave it to the IMF, they would not care about the political effect of their management. Secondly, they will take over the control of the economy of this country and they focus entirely on the loans and not on growth. Then this country will regret'.

– **The Malaysian Prime Minister Dr Mahathir Mohammad on why he rejected IMF's overtures to help during the 1997–1998 East Asian Crisis.**

The countries that availed IMF loans Thailand, Indonesia and South Korea were forced to undergo Structural Adjustment Programmes (SAP) that involved steep hikes in interest rates, budget cuts that effectively choked off economic growth. It was the *'beggar thy neighbour'* policy which the very constitution of IMF sought to avoid. In an economically integrated region like East Asia, it is the best recipe for disaster as one country's imports are another country's exports. Such financial austerity contrary to Keynesian prescription bankrupted companies causing massive unemployment. Soon a contagion set in. The austerity pursued by these countries affected Russia which was recuperating from the shock that was administered to it in its embrace of neoliberalism, as these countries slashed imports of oil from Russia. Malaysian Prime Minister Dr Mahathir Mohammad was the only leader in the region who could stand up to IMF pressures. He rejected IMF's offer to help and steered his country out of the crisis in a way that is worthy of emulation. He pegged the Malaysian Ringette at 3.8 to the dollar and imposed Capital control measures to shield the country from speculative pressures. The countries that submitted to the dictates of the IMF were pulverised and took years to reach the kind of economic vibrance they had experienced prior to the crisis.

IMF Loans... Whom Do They Serve?

The billions of dollars that IMF loans to the developing countries to maintain high exchange rates has dubious intentions. When a country's native currency is overvalued two things happen. Firstly, for each unit of the native currency, more dollars could be purchased and stashed in foreign banks. The imports become cheaper as a lesser amount of native currency need to be spent to buy imported items. This serves the purpose of the elite in the recipient developing nations. While facilitating stashing of dollars in foreign banks an over-valued native currency facilitates the import of luxury goods for a pittance. But, it also means exports become costly. The domestic economy nose dives. The billions loaned under the pretext to stabilise the native currency are used to retire loans availed from foreign creditors. Most often the loans must have been availed by private institutions. The debt to the IMF will have to be paid back by the developing country through a rollback of the welfare schemes. IMF rationalises fiscal austerity under the pretext of investor confidence. The foreign creditors i.e., the financial institutions are thus, saved in the event of a recession. In effect, the debt of the private institutions stands nationalised. The paradox in the neoliberal era is that IMF insists on privatisation of national assets but nationalises private debts. There is a greater paradox involved. Why should the IMF which has started to view markets as perfect intervene in the forex market? Usually lending institutions do buy insurance to protect themselves against unexpected and unfavourable exchange rate fluctuations. But, with IMF standing on guard to protect the financial institutions, hardly any institution buys insurance. Put bluntly, the IMF is serving global finance interests rather than serving global economic interests.

IMF's handling of bankruptcy is appalling. In a loan agreement, there is always a creditor and a debtor. Always a provision of bankruptcy is written into every loan agreement. In case of a bad loan, the debtor files for bankruptcy. The creditor too bears the brunt. This is how market economies across the world worked until the onset of neoliberalism seconded by the IMF. Bankruptcy is an anathema for the IMF. IMF insists that western creditors should always be bailed out of bankruptcy. This makes the western creditors to be less prudent. Loaning huge amounts to the third-world governments and private firms has become not only risk-free but highly lucrative. Even a temporary suspension of loan repayments to let the debtor country recoup and stabilize is not to the liking of the IMF. IMF cites that such standstills affect the investor confidence. IMF loaning huge amounts to countries is essentially to maintain high exchange rates with the sole intention to help the loans to the financial institutions to be paid back, come what may. IMF unabashedly is furthering the interests of the financial institutions and the domestic elite to the detriment of the population it professes to serve.

Debt Enslaves Nations

> 'Finally I turn to the other slavery ...Our 26 billion dollar foreign debt. I had said that we shall honour it. Yet half our export earnings 2 billion dollars out of 4 billion dollars which is all they can earn in the restrictive markets of the world must go to pay just the interest on a debt whose benefit the Filipino people never received'.
> — **President of Philippines Corozona Aquino, in the US Congress in 1986**

During the 1980s, one Filipino child died every two hours because of the increase in debt service payments. Vast tracts of rainforests were cut down to grow cash crops to pay off the debt. In the Third World countries, the amount is paid by the poorest to the rich as interest payments on loans most of them never asked for or they knew it existed. The burden of debt falls on those who are the least responsible for it. A huge part of the budget goes to servicing the debt. Billions of dollars leave the country for deals that benefit only the rich. Anti-slavery society termed debt as a contemporary form of slavery. The Fund insists on cutting government spending. The Structural Adjustment Programmes of the IMF drive down social spending, employment opportunities and real wages. The 1980s have been a lost decade for the developing world in general.

The debt is often used to bully the Third World nations into submission. A secret US Treasury report in the 1980s said, *'We are capable and willing to pursue important policy objectives in the banks by exercising the financial and political leverage at our disposal'*. Debt was used to make Egypt, Iran and China toe the American line in the run-up to the first Gulf War. Egypt was promised that its 14 billion dollars would be written off. Iran received the first loan of 250 million dollars from the World Bank since the Islamic Revolution, the day before the ground attack began. A senior US diplomat told Yemen's Ambassador to the UN who voted against the UN Security resolution *'It was the most expensive No vote you had ever cast'*.

The Flawed Capital Market Liberalisation

The pretext IMF provides for insisting that developing countries to liberalise their capital market is that it opens up new avenues of investment to the developing nations. Capital market liberalisation pursued by the developing countries at the dictates of the IMF is in no way a measure to pull up a failing economy. On the contrary, it is very much in line with the IMF's new avatar as an agency to spearhead neoliberalism. The only purpose such capital market opening had served is to open up new avenues for the

Shylocks of Wall Street. A liberalisation of the capital market often results in sudden entry and exit of speculative Capital that results in high exchange rate volatility. The exchange rate volatility that the IMF seeks to address is just a symptom of a much deeper disease of entry and exit of speculative Capital facilitated by the liberalisation of the capital market. But, instead of addressing the core issue of capital market liberalisation, which would entail safeguards against sudden flight of Capital across borders and risk-mitigating measures, the IMF tries to cure the symptom of exchange rate volatility. Towards this end the IMF loans billions of dollars to countries to maintain abominably high exchange rates.

Double Standards at Times of COVID Pandemic

> 'The European Union should not put economic recovery in danger with the suffocating force of austerity.... Don't rush into tightening monetary policy because you may throw cold water on prospects for growth.... In the Eurozone inflation is transitory. It is driven by the energy price, supply disruptions and also by the fact that we are seeing more demand picking up after the years of close-downs'.
>
> **– Kristalina Georgieva,
> Managing Director - IMF**

> 'The situation is deteriorating in a complex environment and urgent actions are required to mitigate a plausible fast and serious degradation of the nutritional situation during the 2022 lean season'.
>
> **– UNICEF Report on
> the nutrition situation in the West and
> Central Africa region**

While the IMF supported fiscal stimulus to the tune of 10 percent of their respective GDPs by rich nations, it imposed fiscal austerity on the Third World. The Third World nations were cautioned and restricted from similar fiscal stimulus. In India, the government could announce only 1 percent while in the rest of the Third World things were worse. The cap on the fiscal deficit that a Third-World government can run to trigger its economy, insisted by the International Finance Capital for its own advantage, came in the way of national efforts in tackling the pandemic.

Oxfam reported that of the 91 loans IMF negotiated with 81 countries after the onset of COVID in March 2020, in 76 cases IMF insisted stringent austerity measures that impacted efforts in tackling the pandemic. IMF recommendations at the dictates of International Finance Capital included cuts in public healthcare expenditure at a time when it was most needed. In the curious case of Ecuador, the IMF agreed to grant a $6.5 billion loan, but it required Ecuador to cut healthcare expenditures, reduce fuel subsidies and stop cash transfers with immediate effect to the people who are unable to find work. 9 countries of the Third World, which include Angola and Nigeria, have been required to increase or introduce value-added taxes which impact the poor the most in their attempt to procure food, clothing and medical care. IMF encourages governments in advanced countries to pursue policies of fiscal expansion but recommends the Third World countries to administer extreme measures of unprecedented austerity. By such obscene double standards IMF desires the inflation rising out of expansionary policies of the First World is more than compensated by the contractionary methods of the Third World. It is clear on which side of the Suez the institution feels accountable to.

This blatant discrimination of IMF between countries is here to stay. There is no escaping it. In its rhetoric, it articulates its willingness to stand by the Third World. The purpose of any such rhetoric is to stave off the simmering opposition of the Third World governments to its functioning. The IMF is held by metropolitan financial institutions on a tight leash. The double standards in sanctioning loans and in imposing conditions are very much in keeping with its commitment to those whose funds it manages.

The blatant and unabashed double standards hold true with regard to capital controls by the Third World to protect its economy from the vagaries inflicted on it by the speculative flight of International Finance Capital across its borders. Though the institution of late has started to favour re-institution of capital controls by the Third World in the light of adverse effects on the Third World economies, no concrete action has been taken on this front. It is hell-bent on keeping the economies of the Third World open to free Capital flows at the instance of Wall Street.

The International Monetary Fund's bail-out of Greece raised many eyebrows in Asia, as they genuinely worried that Athens got an easier ride than them during the Asian financial crisis in 1997–1998. The IMF was widely criticised for the severity of conditions in its $41.3bn bail-out programme for the three Asian tigers Thailand, Indonesia and South Korea. The conditionalities required bank closures, substantial public spending cuts and higher interest rates. The leniency shown in the case of Greece as opposed to East Asia reflected the substantial voting power of European countries on the IMF board. One official joked that the *'European Monetary Fund is located on 19th Street'*, the fund's address in Washington.

An Open Letter to Milton Friedman

Milton Friedman!

The Neoliberalism that you championed is the single most vicious attack on the Welfare State till date. Do you know that it has thrown more families into destitution and despair than the two World Wars? The erstwhile communist bloc countries, pursuing neoliberal policies since the 1990s, witnessed a virtual decline in the population for the first time since World War II. Life in the former Soviet Republics following the carefully orchestrated disintegration, was worse than the archaic communist hardliners had forewarned their citizens about.

Against all evidence to the contrary, the neoliberal economists who consider you as their intellectual Guru in much the same way you considered Frederick Hayek as yours, still proselytise that actions pursued by individuals in pursuit of self-interest will by the working of the *'invisible hand'* result in public good? Where has it ever happened? To believe that private vices lead to public good is to be insane.

The Great Depression, you theorise, to be the outcome of perverse monetary policies of the government. According to you, the government created depression and is the single major source of instability and, hence, should be curtailed. Your stand for minimal government undermines democracy. The democratic representative government that derives its authority from the people and is socially contracted to further their well-being playing second fiddle to the private players virtually annuls democracy. For you, the most legitimate place for social change is the market and not politics. How can you gloss over the fact that taking things from the democratic sphere to the oligarchic sphere will make a mockery of Governance? Around the world, since the onset of neoliberalism, the common man is no longer welcome to the inner councils of decision-making. The democratic process is being rendered more procedural and farcical than authentic. It is the best recipe for disaster.

In the 1960s and 1970s, the democratically elected governments of Latin America had been heavily investing in their people. Universal education, health care and housing were being implemented. These governments were upstaged and replaced with military juntas owing allegiance to Washington. It was under these military Juntas' patronage the economists of your breed ran amok in that part of the world. Why is it that neoliberalism, which you argue is the wellspring for human freedom, was first experimented in Latin America under the patronage of military Juntas that had toppled well-functioning democratic governments? Why neoliberalism, which as you always claim unleashes human freedom, require the services of the dictators? 'Shocks', crises and absolute curtailment of civic freedom were the pillars on which the free-market economy was erected. Your prescription of Shock Therapy, as it turned out, was all *shock and no therapy*.

Ever since your retirement, you were on a proselytising mission. Travelled far and wide for the video series on *'Free to choose'*. In one of the videos, you walk through one of the most impoverished streets of India, a country barely into the third decade of her independence from being a colony of four different European nations for centuries and holds Central Planning responsible for its backwardness. You cite the opulence of Japan to be an outcome of the free-market policies which incidentally Japan had to adhere to, given the post-war context. How shallow is your *'analysis'*?

Milton Friedman, no two nations and hence, no two people are similar. Each is a captive of its own unique history and a host of contingency factors. Aren't you aware that Japan had been a superpower a century before? By the turn of the second half of the nineteenth century Japan had embarked on a path of modernising with a missionary zeal. In what is referred to as the *'Meiji restoration',* Japan had reinvented herself. The goal of restoration that touched every sphere of Japanese life was to combine western technology with traditional Eastern values. It had turned itself into a military power. The 1905 war with Russia in which the mighty

Russians were trounced or the Manchurian invasion or the occupation of Korea prove the point that Japan had turned itself into a formidable power by the turn of the twentieth century. Japan was the first Asian country to come out of the Great Depression. The Pearl Harbour attack on the US by a belligerent Imperialistic Japan speaks for itself. The hollowness of the conclusions that you derive from comparing two countries which simply don't share the same history, and hence, are at various stages in their evolution is symptomatic of the lack of depth that the literature on neoliberalism is fundamentally afflicted with.

On the traditional weavers of India, in a sarcastic note, you mention them to be paying homage to the Mahatma as they sit and spin making clothes *'with patterns that never vary with methods that never change'*. You miss the employment potential of the cotton industry in a country like India which was and is still experiencing a spurt in its growth of population.

In another video, you walk through the offices of Washington DC where lobbyists are busy influencing the Senators and other elected officials. You lament that too much of power rests on too few elected individuals and your prescription is to entrust the entire economy to the very people whom the lobbyists represent. How is it this a solution for lobbying?

Have you ever pondered over the high living standards of Scandinavian Nations? Those countries have a highly interventionist governments.

Norway is a Telling Example

The North Sea is flanked by Great Britain and Norway. When oil was struck in the North Sea in 1969 the Norwegian public sector company STATOIL took up a commanding position in oil exploration. The profits were directed to the Norwegian Sovereign Fund. But in Britain, indiscriminate privatisation of all the profit-making government oil companies under Margaret Thatcher who embraced the neoliberal mantra meant the profits were pocketed by a few. Norway transformed itself from being a predominantly agricultural and fishing country to an energy giant and is in the top five in per capita income with the lowest inequality among its citizens. Education and health are universal. Every Norwegian is properly housed. Britain, a colonial power, is not even placed in the first ten in per capita income. And inequality in Britain... The less said... The better...

You cite the agriculture in the US to make a point. By employing a tiny fraction of its working population, the US was able to feed its millions as well as those in the Soviet Union, its satellites and countries like India and China. Hence, the argument concludes that it was the principles of the free market that finds validated and the very concept of centralised planning that stands invalidated. You conclude *'The fecundity of freedom is demonstrated most dramatically and clearly in agriculture'*. But you gloss over the fact that the entire American agriculture was built on the most inhuman and pitiable human conditions of slavery. Also glossed over is the fact that geography was too kind to the Americans. Prairies, the land between the Appalachians and the Rockies constitute the greatest stretch of agricultural land in the entire world. With comparatively fewer people to feed within the borders of the New World, unlike the great cradles of civilisation to its East, and a highly mechanised agriculture, thanks to the industrial revolution that America was able to encash and leverage unlike Russia, India and China, it will be in an advantageous position.

In *'Free to Choose'* you state *'The key insight of Adam Smith's Wealth of Nations is misleadingly simple: if an exchange between two parties is voluntary, it will not take place unless both believe they will benefit from it'*. But do we see voluntary exchange between economic agents? The element of coercion is writ large in the economic sphere. A set of economic agents coerce another set and bully them into submission. The Third World, ever since the days neoliberalism dawned on them, has been yoked under the West for a second time. Many a time, most of them are just price takers.

Three functions of the government outlined by Adam Smith in *'Wealth of Nations'* include

- the duty of protecting the society from the violence and invasion of other independent societies.
- the duty of protecting, as far as possible, every member of the society from the injustice or oppression of every other member of it, or the duty of establishing an exact administration of justice.
- the duty of erecting and maintaining certain public works and certain public institutions, which it can never be for the interest of any individual, or small number of individuals, to erect and maintain; because the profit could never repay the expense to any individual or small number of individuals, though it may frequently do much more than repay it to a great society.

The second and third duties outlined by Adam Smith clearly call for a highly interventionist state. By the *'Exact administration of justice'* he meant a government that interferes in every aspect of the civic life of a citizen and not just confine itself to the ivory towers of the judiciary.

Balance Sheet of Neoliberalism

The Promise of the Neoliberal State...

The fall of the Berlin Wall, the upheavals in Eastern Europe and the sudden and unexpected disintegration of the Soviet Union invalidated any collective cause and led to the unprecedented dominance of the neoliberal model in the 1990s across the world. Those were the days of triumphant capitalism marking the beginning of the unchallenged rule of American-style free-market capitalism.

Dismantling the active state that intervenes in the economy and restructuring the same along the lines advocated by neoliberals, we were told, would unshackle every economic agent from the prohibitive restraints of the government thus bringing in optimal economic performance. The interventions of the government on behalf of labour were henceforth referred to as meddling. The visible hand of the government was to be replaced with the *'invisible hand'* of the free market. A lowering of the taxes on business and the wealthy, it was reasoned, would incentivize them to invest more. A deregulation of the financial sector would provide the much-needed funds for investments. Such high rates of increasing investment would then increase the growth rates of output which would *'trickle down'* to the labour class. Reiterating the adage *'A rising tide lifts all boats'* neoliberal measures, we were tutored, would wipe out poverty and all the wanton squalor that capitalism was afflicted with.

With neoliberalism piercing its claws deep into the politico-economic framework of every country, national governments find themselves in a pitiable position with their hands tied. Unlike in the post-war decades during which Keynesianism was the widely accepted economic mantra which held that Capital shall remain national, national governments are no longer in a commanding position to rein in the Capital. With controls over cross-border flows of Capital, a Keynesian measure to ensure that the writ of the national government extends over the nation's Capital done away with, Capital leaves a national territory in which its possibilities of self-aggrandizement stands checkmated by the interventionist government. Any attempt to run a fiscal deficit to give a fillip to the employment generation schemes is institutionally curtailed. There is a cap on the fiscal deficit that a country can run insisted by Capital as the country embraces neoliberalism. For instance, in India, the government was coerced into enacting a *'Fiscal Responsibility Act'* that capped the fiscal deficit, to just 3 percent of its GDP (The wording of the act is reflective of the neoliberal state: being responsible to Capital and not to the people). With its hands tied the nation now becomes exclusively committed to promoting the interests of International Finance Capital, with which the domestic corporate-financial Capital is in league.

Neoliberalism in Former Communist States

The Free Market was hailed as the precursor and the wellspring of democracy. But the irony is that Presidents of Russia, Poland and Czechoslovakia demanded their Parliaments be suspended so that they could rule by decree to ram through the free market reforms. To bring in the free market, they felt the elected Parliaments were a hindrance as these representative bodies were stuffed with ideologues of a bygone era. Properties that were nationalised during the communist days were returned to the *'rightful'* owners. Many State-Owned Enterprises were privatised for a pittance. Promising power to the people through the market, they embarked on capitalist restoration. The difficult period that was promised to be transient turned out to be protracted and ended up taking these countries to a state that was worse than their pre-communist state.

In 1992 Russia's birth rate fell below the death rate for the first time since 1945. Russia witnessed gangster capitalism. The entire country was up for sale. Many of the industries of East European countries were acquired by western capital and simply closed down to arrest competition. To cite an example, the Smederevo steel factory in the Serbian province of former socialist Yugoslavia was built with 600 million dollars. On being commissioned, the plant used to churn out steel worth hundreds of millions of dollars yearly. In the tailored pandemonium that followed the break-up of Yugoslavia, the steel plant was sold to US Steel in 2003 for a paltry sum of 23 million dollars. The land on which the colossal plant stood alone would have fetched more dollars. German unification witnessed the largest expropriation of public wealth in European history. Almost all socialised property including factories, farms, apartments and high-tech companies were taken over by giant West German firms and were promptly closed down. In Croatia, the best hotels on the scenic Adriatic coast were bought by German and Austrian companies for a tiny fraction of their real costs. In Czechoslovakia, former aristocrats and their descendants restored the lands their families had held before 1918 under the Austro-Hungarian empire.

Free healthcare, housing, education and assured employment that turned the job market into a seller's market vanished at the wink of an eye. Nutrition levels plummeted. The decadent socialist system that was a monstrosity and had to be done away with had provided basic amenities for millions. Capitalist efficiency and free market dismembered it. Such is the ruthlessness of Capital that the German unification, which marked the coming together of people of the same descent after a span of just four decades, was soon resented by those in the East. East was simply colonised by the West.

East Europeans embarked on the free market odyssey in the hope that they could taste all the indulgent consumerism of the capitalist world which they thought everyone in the West was entitled to, while retaining all the social gains their welfare states had provided which they took for granted. They could not make it. They lost what they had.

The State Under Neoliberalism

With the onset of the neoliberal Era, it is often said that the governments of nation-states have retreated into oblivion and that markets have taken over. Though there is definitely market centrism, to conclude that the state has retreated is to mistake the symptom for a worse malaise underlying it. The highly clichéd *'retreat of the state'* needs closer scrutiny. Did the State really retreat? The fact of the matter remains that the government of the day has not retreated. On the contrary, it continues to be as interventionist, if not greater than it had been at any time in the history of organised government. It is just that the purpose of its engagement and on whose behalf it intervenes that has changed. On the domestic front, it has usurped to itself more power. Every neoliberal state has highly militarised its police to further the cause of free-market reforms. The neoliberal State, on behalf of the capital, enforces strong individual property rights, ensures the integrity of the currency in which the business operations take place, provides an optimal *'investment climate'* for investment and tears down every protective barrier that has been instituted like tariffs, quantitative restrictions, punitive taxes for the purpose of ushering in free-market.

Inflation is tightly under control thanks to government intervention. The cap that is placed on the government of the day on the extent to which it can borrow from its Central Bank to finance the welfare of its own people cannot be brushed aside as a retreat of the state. From intervening in the economy to protect labour from the capital and society from monopoly power, the State in the neoliberal era intervenes to ensure the demands of International Finance Capital placed on it are met. The neoliberal government of any state is in league with the IMF and has turned itself to be the bill collector for the G-7 nations. Debt service payments as a share of the total budget far outstrip the expenditure on health. With shrinking fiscal space, the government of the day finds its hands tied in investing in human development.

Fundamentally Unstable

Financial assets demand negligible carrying costs and for this sole reason come to be courted by speculators. Unlike other assets, the speculators are not interested in the yield of the financial assets but hold it for reaping a reward by selling it off at a higher price. In anticipation of a price rise, more speculators come to buy these assets. This speculative behaviour results in the rapid rise of the value of the assets. In such bouts of euphoric price rise, many such assets come to be over-valued. In a bullish financial market speculators in pursuit of an immediate return seldom are guided by the risk involved or an objective evaluation of the intrinsic value of the assets. At some stage scepticism as to whether the market value of such assets bears any resemblance to its true intrinsic value sets in. Such a scepticism sends alarm bells in the market. In the event of speculators busying themselves to offload such assets from their portfolio, the market turns bearish and the prices slide down. The boom is replaced by a bust. Such unsustainable booms based on a euphoric price rise and its eventual bust have come to be the mainstay of the neoliberal era.

The lessons learned from the Great Depression were put into legislation by the Glass-Steagall Act which erected a Chinese wall between investment banking and ordinary banking. Such a quarantine between the two wings of the operation was necessitated by the learning that ordinary banking needs to be quarantined from speculative high-risk behaviour. In November 1999, during heydays of neoliberal politik, President Bill Clinton publicly declared *'the Glass–Steagall law is no longer appropriate'* and repealed it. Economists of all hues hold the view that the repealing of the Glass-Stegall Act was a contributing factor to the 2008 financial meltdown.

Jobless Growth Nose-diving Wage Rates

In an economy close to full employment a demand for labour will not be easily met by a sudden gush from the ranks of unemployed. In such circumstances, the labour obviously will command a higher wage than it would have in the context of high unemployment with swelling labour reserves. Capital even if it is to its dislike has to concede to this higher demand of wages by the labour even if this high wage rate eats into the profit that is being appropriated by the Capital invested. It is in perfect harmony with the demand-supply logic. In the pre-war years and even up to the 1960s and 1970s long before neoliberalism rose its head, the world economy was severely segmented. With severe controls on Capital flow across countries, Capital even if it wanted to enter the less developed countries in search of profits, found itself to be confined to the developed industrialised countries. When Capital stands confined within the national borders, the workers in these developed countries are favourably disposed. A hike in labour productivity is translated to a commensurately higher wage. As labour productivity rose through technological breakthroughs and upskilling, the wage too increased proportionately. An average blue-collar worker could raise his family in moderate comfort on his income alone. With strong labour unions, he had a sense of security from being fired.

As data would show, the trend continued until the neoliberal era set in. With the dawn of the neoliberal era, Capital in the developed countries, thanks to the easing of controls on its cross-border flight which Keynes had severely resented, started its predatory flight across countries in search of speculative profits. Vast chunks of international capital finance gravitated to the newly independent Third World, where, due to historical reasons, the labour had been in plenty and cheap. The labour in the industrialised capitalist countries soon found itself to be pitted against the cheap labour of the Third World. The compromise between labour and Capital that had been effected during the depression years and resolved to be observed with the institutionalisation of Keynesianism as an article of faith across the capitalist nations went out of the window. Labour was on the defensive. The golden age of capitalism in which labour found itself poised to enjoy the fruits of the rise in its productivity came to an end abruptly. The unsuspecting labour was caught off guard. The real wages started to freeze in the 1980s. Capital had, at last, gained the lost ground in the industrialised West.

Real wages started to decline over time though productivity was rising every year. Even families with two wage earners found it difficult to make both ends meet. Pressure at work grew while job security plummeted. Most of the good industrial jobs fled the country. The social safety net was cut back. Public services, including public education, were squeezed year after year. Art and music shrank or disappeared in the schools, with physical education not far behind. The gap between the rich and the rest of society grew rapidly

The Third World to which the Finance capital gravitated was administered severe austerity measures at its diktats. The existence of a vibrant economy with very low levels of employment militates against the interests of international capital. An increased government activity that ensures higher employment is abhorred by the Capital. Capital always prefers a buyer's market, never a seller's market in labour. Hence, the government intervention that created huge employment opportunities that had curtailed unemployment was rolled back. The rank and file of the Third World labour were to be at Capital's exclusive disposal. With the IMF insisting on the exact amount a national government could borrow from its Central Bank to finance its activities, it was in effect directing its broad economic imperatives. The Third World was recolonised.

The Declining Job Elasticity

In India, a developing economy from the Third World, every 1 percent growth of GDP resulted in 2 lakh new jobs in the formal sector during 1980–1990. From 1990 to 2000, the decade India embraced globalisation, it came down to 1 Lakh jobs. From 2000 to 2010 as international finance became entrenched in the Indian economy formal sector jobs created for every 1 percent rise in GDP came down to 52,000. Since 2010 Central Bank of the country has not released data on how well the employment generation fared in relation to the rise in GDP. It is estimated by proxy data that only 32,000 jobs have been created.

It is clear that the correlation between GDP growth and formal sector jobs has declined. This divorce of GDP growth and jobs is reflective of the nature of economic development with stress on capital-driven efficiency that the country is witnessing. It does not augur well for a country that adds an Australia to its population every year.

In the US or in China or Sri Lanka, a unit increase in the GDP does not produce as many jobs as it used to, a decade back. Employment intensity of economic growth has fast declined and GDP ceases to be a measure of societal well-being. An expanded dashboard that includes parameters centric to each country may serve a better gauge.

The tall claims of the neoliberal think tank were based purely on theoretical beliefs rather than any empirical data. With mounting evidence accumulated over more than forty years of neoliberal shade of capitalism, an objective analysis of how it had fared is possible. Ninety percent of the Americans born in 1940 bettered their parents in education and income. It has come down to 40 percent since 1980. Credit goes to Alan Greenspan, former Federal Reserve Chairman, who was candid enough to admit in front of the US Congressional Committee on Oversight and Government Reform that neoliberal ideology was a total disaster. Across the spectrum that extends to even far-right conservatives, there is growing consensus that free markets are not self-regulating and perfectly efficient, a viewpoint John Maynard Keynes always held and which the Great Depression laid bare beyond a shred of doubt.

Gaining Political Legitimacy During Neoliberal Times

> *'Although it may be good to possess power that is based on guns, it is better and more gratifying to win the hearts of the people.'*
> – **Joseph Goebbels, Minister for Propaganda, Third Reich**

> *'How do we use the attacks'*
> – **Secretary of State Condoleezza Rice, in a meeting with top US officials following 9/11.**

A state, dictatorial or democratic, can never carry on without legitimacy. A brutal dictatorship that can resort to any means in cowing down public dissent too needs political legitimacy to continue for long. Invoking the tenets of national glory or righting the wrongs of the past serves to be the source of political legitimacy in many instances, as was the case in Nazi Germany. In the pre-war period with strict controls over cross-border flow of capital finance, Capital was strictly national. Nations found themselves pitted against each other. In such a scenario the government that found its legitimacy being questioned could silence its critics and win it by invoking the national question. In Germany, Hitler could tap into the wounded German pride to gain legitimacy.

The Spectacle That Was The Armistice of 22nd June 1940: Resurrection of The German Pride

Adolf Hitler after the fall of France in WW II selected the Compiegne Forest as the place for the negotiations. It was in Compiegne Forest that the 1918 Armistice was signed which ended World War I with Germany's abject and humiliating surrender. For Hitler and the rest of Germany, it was the supreme moment of revenge of Germany over France. Hitler insisted that the signing of the armistice should take place in the same rail carriage, the *'Compiègne Wagon',* in which the Germans had signed the 1918 Armistice. War correspondent William Shirer, who was present on that day, reported, *'I am but fifty yards from him. [...] I have seen that face many times at the great moments of his life. But, today! It is afire with scorn, anger, hate, revenge, triumph. Then, on 21st June 1940, in the same railway carriage in which the 1918 Armistice had been signed (removed from a museum building and placed exactly where it was in 1918), Hitler sat in the same chair in which Marshal Ferdinand Foch had sat when he faced the representatives of the defeated German Empire. After listening to the reading of the preamble, Hitler – in a calculated gesture of disdain for the French delegates – exited the carriage, as Foch had done in 1918'.* The carriage itself was taken to Berlin as a trophy of war.

From then on the Germans stood by their Fuhrer who took them to all the suffering which they endured with unquestioned loyalty.

In the neoliberal era with all welfare schemes being rolled back, the State has its authenticity under check. To gain political legitimacy the fear of the enemy at the gates is often invoked… at times it could be the enemy within or a combination of both. President Reagan unleashed a war on drugs, unilaterally upped the Cold War ante, called for a Star-War program, identified a threat in Latin America, and launched 'Operation Urgent Fury' against Grenada and punished Ghaddafi in distant Libya. Margaret Thatcher capitalised on the Falkland Wars and turned herself into the Iron Lady as she sold off iron and steel and other industries to the captains of industry.

ISLAMIC TERROR! The Mother of All Lies

There is a manufactured paranoia that afflicts the population of any nation that often helps capital to rope in the unsuspecting citizenry to its agenda of usurping to itself even a greater share of wealth, while purportedly fighting the enemies at the gate. Much is said and reams of literature written on the Islamic terror that the US government, the military outfit of the western Capital, is supposed to be guarding us against. A closer analysis debunks the very notion of Islamic terror. It is the International Finance Capital that aided and abetted the fringe elements of Islamic conservatism and catapulted them to seats of power.

Afghanistan had a progressive government led by the People's Democratic Party of Afghanistan (PDPA). Established on 1st January 1965 it was Marxist–Leninist. The progressive government undertook the most radical reforms which included land reforms, a total literacy movement, women's emancipation, agricultural reforms and other initiatives that would take the country from medieval times to the modern era. The Soviet Union had a cordial relationship with Afghanistan since the 1920s even during the days of Royalty. Lenin took the lead in establishing diplomatic ties with King Amanullah who steered his country to complete independence from any British influence. Soviet Union ably supported the progressive government's modernisation drives. Soviet involvement in Afghanistan in its drive to modernity was very substantial. The reforms initiated however were far ahead of its times. The entrenched privileged classes were alarmed at the course of the reforms. The situation started to get volatile. The internal feuds within Afghanistan had the potential to dismember the country. This alarmed Kremlin as it shared a 2000 kilometres border with Afghanistan. The deteriorating situation in the country necessitated the entry of Soviet Army. Its presence provided the missing ingredient for the conservatives. for a holy war against the infidels. The conservative aristocracy irked by the far-reaching reforms could now cast a shadow on the administration branding them Un-Islamic. They reorganised themselves into Mujahidin and it was none other than the most lovable US President, Jimmy Carter, who initiated the arming of the Mujahidin against the Soviet Red Army. The US and the rest of the capitalist world termed the Russian presence as aggression and even boycotted the 1980 Moscow Olympics. The Soviet Union never had any interest in making it a client state, a fact well documented in the Brest-Litovsk treaty[29] signed by Bolsheviks with the Axis powers in 1918 that brought the Russian involvement in the war to an end.

> *'Afghan people do not have a history of being religious zealots. To create the CIA desired jihad required the recruitment of Arab, Egyptian, and Pakistani extremists. So the fundamentalism that emerged in Afghanistan is a CIA construct'.*
> **– Ahmed Rashid, Journalist.**

To recruit close to 50,000 jihadists from across 40-plus Islamic countries is no mean task. Saudi-born millionaire Osama Bin Laden was the kingpin of organising these recruitment drives. Code named *Operation Cyclone*, the CIA financed the Mujahideen in Afghanistan from 1979. The CIA in 1977 supported right-wing military coup in Pakistan that toppled the socialist government of Zulfikar Ali Bhutto and had him hanged, making Pakistan the perfect staging ground for the CIA training of Mujahidin.

Earlier Iraq had witnessed the assassination of Abd al-Karim Kasim, a progressive communist leader who nationalised the Anglo-American dominated oil industry. He was killed in a coup by Ba'ath party loyalists with CIA assistance in 1963. The Ba'ath government awarded lucrative contracts to US oil companies in return for the CIA support in toppling the communist regime. Later it was seen as a bulwark against the Ayatollah on his triumphant return to Iran following the Islamic revolution that had toppled the Shah Pahlavi who was enthroned by the CIA replacing a democratically elected Mohammad Mossadegh with socialist leanings. Indonesia which is home to a radical Islamic movement had the third biggest communist party in the world. CIA had it annihilated by its protégé Suharto who toppled the legendary Sukarno and assumed the

---

[29] Article VII of the Brest-Litovsk treaty between the Bolshevik Government and the Axis powers signed on 3rd March 1918. *'In view of the fact that Persia and Afghanistan are free and independent States, the contracting parties obligate themselves to respect the political and economic independence and the territorial integrity of these states'.*

Presidency following the coup in 1965. Sudan had the biggest communist Party in the whole of Africa which too was decimated by the CIA. In many Islamic countries, progressive movements very much ahead of their times were spearheaded by the socialists or communists. Colonel Qadhafi and Saddam Hussein, who championed Pan-Arab nationalism had ensured the best social care programme in their countries the Arab world had ever known. The toppling of their governments and their lynching once again underscore the point that western capital views nationalism as a trojan horse for socialism.

Today Afghanistan, Iraq, Sudan, Indonesia and Libya are home to factions of radical Islam, entirely of the making of International Finance. It is this radical Islam, that the US fomented in the first place to upstage truly democratic and socialist progressive governments, that is projected as the enemy of mankind which the US claims to fight to win legitimacy. Fighting terrorism is advantageous to the finance capital. In the name of fighting international terrorism, US troops can march into any territory and serve the interests of the Capital. Any criticism of the marauding international capital or its defender, the US troops, could be spin-doctored into a stand on behalf of the terrorists and hence discredited. Following the 9/11 a US trade official's statement to the effect that whoever opposed the US at WTO was with the terrorists should be seen in the light of the US parading itself to be the saviour of humanity. Post-9/11 patriotic infection conferred immunity for the US excesses in Afghanistan against any objective scrutiny. The war in Afghanistan was doomed from the start.

> 'The goal is an endless war...not a successful war.'
> **– Julian Assange, founder of Wiki leaks.**

From President Bush to Obama to Trump every US President promised to pull back, but on being inaugurated sent more troops to Afghanistan. It is good that President Biden at last decided to call it a day in Afghanistan. The very war that is doomed was by itself an enterprise. The three companies that profited the most from the war were Lockheed Martin, Boeing and Raytheon. President Trump appointed Lockheed Martin's Senior Executive John C. Rood as Under Secretary of Defence for War Policy and Raytheon Senior Executive Mark Esper as the Secretary of Defence who replaced Boeing Sr Executive Patrick Shanahan.

Heads of States presiding over vast resources who refuse to toe the line dictated by Wall Street, are demonized with immediate effect. The real triumph of International Finance Capital is that as it posits fighting for modernity, freedom and the rule of law, even the stratum of the intelligentsia which can see through its perilous and predatory intention end up being silent and, at times, wilful partners in these aggrandising deeds of the Capital for fear of being discredited of its zeal of modernity. The invasion of Iraq serves as a prime example.

Conclusion

The premise around which free-market ideology is centred is that government regulations and public spending are costly and wasteful burdens detrimental to general well-being. It holds that the *'Nanny State'* doling out freebies is an incubator for inefficiency churning out parasites by their millions. The private enterprise, an epitome of efficiency with its pristine resource allocation measures can outdo the government that is held at ransom by its bloated bureaucratic system. So goes the free-market catechism.

PART 6

THE REAL CRIME OF CUBA

'The Real crime of Cuba is its demonstration effect'.
— **Noam Chomsky**

'Cuba demonstrates how much nations can do with the resources they have if they focus on the right priorities – health, education, and literacy'.
— **Kofi Annan, UN Secretary General**

'It was the first time that a country had come from another continent not to take something away, but to help Africans to achieve their freedom',
— **scribbled the longest-serving political prisoner in his cell in Robben Island, South Africa**

'No other Third World country had ever projected its power beyond its immediate neighbourhood'.
— **Prof. Piero Gleijeses, Johns Hopkins University**

> 'Cuban doctors are the first to arrive and the last to leave. Cuba can teach the world about its health system based on primary care, with significant achievements, such as lower mortality, increased life expectancy and universal coverage.'
>
> – **Ban Ki-Moon,
> UN Secretary General**

Chapter 22: Cuba

'Perhaps the most frank and objective response would be Nothing. Nothing for or against us. Just leave us alone',

– Che

'Children of Chernobyl'

'.... this meeting was on a Thursday...On Saturday our country's top leadership responded...all the three best specialists in common childhood diseases were ready and would be immediately travelling to Ukraine... and within few days. I think Monday or Tuesday they were already on the way'.

– As recollected by the Cuban ambassador Sergio López Briel in the documentary, 'Cuba and Chernobyl'.

The Cuban ambassador was reflecting on the meeting with the first secretary of the Ukrainian Komsomol during which the latter sought Cuban assistance in treating the children who were suffering from acute radiation-related diseases following the Chernobyl disaster of 1986.

Two Cuban planes with nearly 140 children arrived in Cuba on 29th March 1990. It marked the beginning of the Chernobyl Children's Medical Treatment Programme in Cuba. The group was received at the Havana Airport by Fidel Castro himself. Castro offered to help 10,000 children from Ukraine, Belarus and Russia. In the documentary, López recalls Castro telling him, *'I do not want you going to the press, or the press going to the consulate. We are carrying out a basic duty to the Soviet people, to a sister nation. We are not doing it to get publicity'*. The *'Children of Chernobyl'* camp was set up at a polyclinic in Tarará, ten miles outside Havana in the most pressing circumstances.

Within a couple of months, the socialist bloc collapsed. the Soviet Union disintegrated. The world as we knew it, came to an end. The world we know today began to take shape. Cuba, refusing to budge before free market capitalism stood isolated. The loss of trading partners sent the economy into a freefall. Over the next 23 years, close to 30,000 people of which nearly 22,000 of them children, received free treatment in Cuba far exceeding Castro's promise. A Cuban medical team worked in a Ukrainian sanatorium. With the collapse of the socialist bloc and disintegration of the Soviet system, Universal health care became a thing of the past in the erstwhile Soviet Republics. Not so in the *'satellite'* State of Cuba. Children of Chernobyl from Ukraine, Belarus and Russia were looked after free of cost by the Cubans. Cuba consistently refused to disclose the expenses incurred. Some unofficial estimates put Cuba's expenditure at more than $300m.

The Cuban Odyssey

Cuba, a tiny island 90 miles off the coast of Florida, is a country of contradictions. A poor country with human development indicators comparable to that of the Scandinavia; a tiny speck in the Caribbean island that has mobilized its troops in almost every continent to support the liberation movements, the most sanctioned country that has mobilised the world's largest international humanitarian assistance; formally rendered a pariah in the world, but with millions of defenders around the world. Though Cuba meets most of the Sustainable Development Goals set by the United Nations in 2015, it hardly finds any mention in the official literature of the UN.

Sanctions... Sanctions... Sanctions... But Cuba Lives On

The US policy towards Cuba is a default to hostility. Over the years the premise for the sanctions against Cuba kept changing. To begin it was in

---

[30] Cuba calculates the cost of the US blockade to be 144 Billion dollars over 6 decades, i.e., 12 million per day.

response to the expropriations and nationalisations of the US commercial entities in Cuba. The Bay of Pigs invasion forced the Cubans to the Soviet camp. After landing Cuba in the lap of the Soviet Union, the new pretext for renewed hostilities was its adoption of a socialist pattern of society and close ties with the Soviet Union. Its military internationalism was cited as the new reason. Then came human rights and of late came its support for Venezuela. There could be a détente with the Soviet Union though a brief one from 1969 until the Soviet *'invasion'* of Afghanistan. But with Cuba, there is no respite. Even after the crumbling of the Eastern bloc in its entirety, Cuba prevailed. The more under-developed and harassed the economy is, the more the demonstrative power of its survival.

It was John F. Kennedy who imposed sanctions with the aim of crippling the revolutionary government in 1961. The Bay of Pigs invasion during his tenure in fact cemented the revolution. White House Aid Dick Goodwin said of Che '...*went on to say that he wanted to thank us [the United States] very much for the invasion – that it had been a great political victory for them – enabled them to consolidate – and transformed them from an aggrieved little country to an equal'*. The overwhelming support for the revolution convinced Washington, Cuba was no Guatemala or Iran and Fidel was no Jacobo Arbenz or Mohmmad Mossadegh. It dawned on the US establishment that the *'only foreseeable means of alienating internal support is through disenchantment and disaffection based on economic dissatisfaction and hardship'*. Thus, began the most inhuman regime of sanctions.

The embargo intended to suffocate the island nation is enforced through the

- Trading with the Enemy Act of 1917
- Foreign Assistance Act of 1961
- Cuban Assets Control Regulations of 1963
- Cuban Democracy Act of 1992

- Helms–Burton Act of 1996
- Trade Sanctions Reform and Export Enhancement Act of 2000

In the words of Senator Torricelli who spearheaded the 1992 Cuban Democracy Act, the sanctions were meant to *'wreak havoc on that island'*. Such is the perverse nature of the sanctions that even US subsidiaries in other countries are banned from trading with Cuba. Ships docked within Cuban ports are blocked to travel to US ports for the next 6 months.

Cuba following the disintegration of the Soviet Union, embarked on an ambitious programme to boost its tourism industry. Provision of the act barred travel to Cuba by the US citizens. Though the EU resented the sanctions that curtailed the operations of US subsidiaries located in its territory, as it amounted to dictating terms to them on how to conduct the business, the sanctions are still operative.

Cuban American National Foundation (CANF) modelled on the Israeli lobby is powerful in the US. Founded immediately after the Ronald Reagan's ascension to Presidency, in states like Florida its capacity to swing votes is primarily responsible for the slew of sanctions against Cuba. The US embargo costs the tiny island $12 million daily. The UN General Assembly pass a resolution every year, since 1992, demanding the end of the US economic embargo on Cuba. By 2019 the UN General Assembly had overwhelmingly voted against the brutal and criminal US blockade 28 times. Only two nations voted against the resolution. The usual two. However, the embargo proved to be ineffective in enforcing a regime change or bending it to Washington's will. The real crime of Cuba is that the social experiment on this island convinced that universal education, health care and housing were possible with the meagre income from the tropical crops of sugarcane and tobacco.

On 21st January 1962, Cuba was suspended by the Organisation of American States (OAS), by a vote of 14 in favour, one (Cuba) against with six abstentions. The expulsion was not authorized in the OAS Charter. The expulsion was soon followed by multilateral sanctions. Castro referred to the OAS as a *'Ministry of Colonies'* of the US. Though the suspension was lifted on 3rd June 2009, which was welcomed by the Cubans, Cuba chose not to return.

---

[31] *'Are you a Communist or a Marxist'?* queried the journalist Erik Durschmeid.

'There is no communism or Marxism in our ideas. Our political philosophy is representative democracy with social justice in a well-planned economy', said the young revolutionary who was waging a war from Sierra Maestra mountains.

Chapter 23: Cuba Internationale
Cuba's Principled Intransigence

> ... 'Our Revolution is not a revolution of millionaires. Instead, it is one carried out by the poor, and is one which dreams of ensuring the well-being not only of our own poor, but rather of all the poor in this world. And that is why we talk of internationalism'.
>
> – Fidel Castro

> 'We will never forget how you [Cubans] cared for our orphans and our wounded,'
>
> – Ahmed Ben Bella,
> Prime minister of the fledging Algerian Republic,
> stated on his arrival in Havana on 16th October, 1962.

Following his triumphant entry to Havana on 8th January 1959, Castro reached out to the US. America was his first port of call. President Eisenhower declined to meet him. It was his deputy, Richard Nixon who received him on 19th April 1959. The CIA orchestrated Bay of Pigs Invasion in April 1961, at a time when Cuba had not yet declared the revolution to be Marxist-Leninist nor betrayed any intention to be one, convinced the Cuban revolutionaries that they were up against a formidable enemy. The invasion, though abortive, was a sign of things to come. To win an unequal war against the US and save the revolution for its people, Cuban leaders resolved that Cuba should engage the US on multiple fronts across every continent. Internationalism was to be the cardinal principle on which the foreign policy of the young island nation was based on. At times it engaged US-backed troops in multiple countries simultaneously. The early 1960s saw Che touring the continent of Africa meeting the revolutionary leaders. He was excited by the opportunity they presented to Cuba to take on the imperialist forces on multiple fronts. Cuba intervened in no less than 17 revolutionary movements in Africa.

In the post-Soviet period, medical internationalism has come to be the mainstay of Cuban foreign policy. It has come to be the means of combating Yankee capitalism. It also served to showcase the financial viability of a planned Welfare State.

Military Internationalism

> 'Hammarskjöld was on the point of getting something done when they killed him. Notice that I said "when they killed him"'.
>
> – Harry S Truman

In December 1964, Che Guevara in the UN General Assembly referred to the *'tragic case of the Congo'* and denounced the western powers' *'unacceptable intervention',* referring to *'Belgian paratroopers, carried by US planes, who took off from British bases'.* Che was referring to the assassination of Patrice Lumumba, the first Prime Minister of the Democratic Republic of Congo (2nd July 1925–17th January 1961).

Cuban internationalism had begun as early as 1959 April within months of its revolution. Cuban troops intervened in Panama and the Dominican Republic. It was involved in the Algerian War of Independence. In 1966 Cuba hosted a gathering of leaders of Afro-Asian and Latin American countries and anti-imperialist movements from 3rd January to 16th January 1966. The conference emphasised the political alignment of the three continents of Africa, Asia and Latin America. It was well attended, the most notable attendees included Salvador Allende of Chile and Amilcar Cabral of Guinea Bissau. For Fidel, it was an opportunity to gauge the revolutionary leaders he intended to support. Che by that time had embarked on his mission in Bolivia and could not attend and had his speech sent to the conference. As fate would have it, that was his last mission.

Though the tri-continental conference was very much in keeping with the spirit of the Bandung Conference of newly independent Afro-Asian nations in 1955 in Indonesia, that called for camaraderie of the Third World with a firm conviction on non-violent resistance eventually giving birth to the Non-Alignment Movement, it un-equivocally championed the cause of a violent armed attack against imperialism. It condemned imperialism, colonialism and neo-colonialism. The global state of affairs in the prevailing Cold War scenario had a bearing on the conference. The systematic overthrow of democratically elected governments in Iran and Guatemala in the previous decade, the brutal murder of Patrice Lumumba, the highly partisan stand of the UN peacekeeping troops in Congo, the assassination of the upright UN Secretary-General, Dag Hammarskjold, and the raging war in Vietnam had convinced the organizers of the necessity of violent and armed struggle against the imperialist forces. Indonesia which had hosted the Bandung conference had witnessed a violent takeover by a US-supported dictator in 1965, thus, effectively putting an end to its tryst with democracy under the legendary Sukarno. The conference set the stage of Cuban internationalism. In Latin America, the impact of the conference was mixed. But, it was in Africa that it made a real impact.

Reversals Did Not Deter Cuba

It is said that the Egyptian leader Colonel Nasser in his discussions with Che on his decision to lead a contingent of Cuban soldiers in Congo had cautioned him *'not to become another Tarzan. It can't be done'*, he had said. Guevara did not heed the warning. Che contended that Congo surrounded by eight countries, the Central African Republic, Sudan, Uganda, Rwanda, Burundi, Tanzania, Zambia and Angola could be the epitome of anti-imperialism in Africa. It was not to be. Nasser was right. Che's Congo mission was a disaster.

The Context of Angola

> 'Angola is rich in mineral resources. Cabinda has oil. But, we shall take back only the mortal remains of our soldiers and doctors.'
> — **Fidel Castro**

> 'Gentlemen... This is the map of Africa and here is Angola, and in Angola we have three factions. There is the MPLA; they're the bad guys; the FNLA, they're the good guys. And, there is UNITA and Jonas Savimbi. we do not know too well.'
> — **CIA director Bill Colby (as quoted by John Stockwell, Head, CIA Task Force, Angola).**

On 25th April 1974 a group of leftist military officers staged a bloodless coup in Portugal that toppled the extreme right-wing government of Portugal in what came to be known as the Carnation Revolution. The new revolutionary government declared its intention to grant independence to the three Portuguese colonies in Africa, Guinea-Bissau, Mozambique and Angola. Unlike the two countries Guinea-Bissau and Mozambique, Angola was too rich to be left to the Angolans.

Angola was Portugal's gem. Cabinda, an exclave province of Angola, was rich in oil reserves. Angola was second only to Nigeria in the production of oil in the continent of Africa. It was dubbed *'The Kuwait of Africa'*. The vast deposits of oil and minerals of this soon-to-be independent colony attracted the capitalist forces. No sooner did the progressive left government of Portugal decide to grant independence to Angola than did the US and the apartheid regime of South Africa join hands to take over the country. Angola was to be mired in a bloody civil war for the next three decades.

---

[32] A total of 300,000 Cuban troops, doctors and teachers served in Angola.

Angola was home to three nationalist factions of liberation movements jostling for power. MPLA (People's Movement for the Liberation of Angola which declared itself to be Marxist-Leninist) was headed by Agostinho Neto. The MPLA was by far the most inclusive and Pan-Angolan outfit with a presence across Angola. It had cultivated deep roots among the intelligentsia, scholars, poets and professionals. It received training from Cuba and arms from Moscow. FLNA (National Front for the Liberation of Angola) operated from the North with bases in what was known as Zaire (Congo) and UNITA (National Union for the Total Independence of Angola) headed by the charismatic leader Jonas Savimbi operated from the South. The US was averse to an MPLA takeover. It started to support UNITA and FLNA. As the country was inching towards its independence, a civil war between these warring factions wreaked havoc. The fate of Angola was soon cast in blood.

Cuban Involvement

Cuban involvement in Angola began as early as 1965, at the request of the MPLA leader, Agostinho Neto. Neto had met Che in Zaire where he was spearheading the revolutionary movement against the despotic regime of Mobutu Sesesko. Cuba committed its support for the MPLA cause. Cuban trainers were dispatched to train the MPLA cadres on guerrilla warfare. But, the scale and intensity of the Cuban involvement in Angola touched new heights as the country was inching towards independence.

On the eve of Angolan Independence in 1975, when it became apparent that the popular support of MPLA was not yielding sufficient military dividends in the battlefront when pitted against the combined might of FNLA, UNITA and the regular troops of Zaire and South Africa augmented by US fire power, Cubans threw in their lot in favour of MPLA. Cuba airlifted its soldiers to the Angolan war front. Thanks to the Cuban contingent of 40,000 soldiers, MPLA managed to capture the capital Luanda and proclaim the first independent government of Angola with its leader

Agostinho Neto as the first President on 11th November 1975. Cuban troops were instrumental in repelling the FLNA back into Zaire. Its military wing was blunted. The South African troops and UNITA were checkmated and driven out of Angola. A Marxist-Leninist government in its vicinity was not to the liking of the apartheid regime of South Africa. South African administration viewed the presence of UNITA as a natural buffer between the Marxist MPLA and itself.

'In Angola, Black troops...Cubans and Angolans... have defeated White troops in military exchanges,' a South African analyst observed, 'and that psychological edge, that advantage the White man has enjoyed and exploited over 300 years of colonialism and empire, is slipping away'. 'Black Africa is riding the crest of a wave generated by the Cuban success in Angola,' noted the 'World', South Africa's major black newspaper. Black Africa was *tasting the heady wine of the possibility of realizing the dream of total liberation.'*

The East bloc recognised the MPLA government of Neto. The new President requested the Cuban troops to continue as UNITA was still active and supported by the US and South Africa. The US found it hard to digest the establishment of a Marxist-Leninist government in Angola with the support of the Soviet Union and Cuba. The US did not recognise the Republic of Angola until 19th May 1993.

US-Sponsored Civil War Was to Continue

UNITA re-grouped under its founder Jonas Savimbi and continued waging a guerrilla war against the Angolan government. From 1981, with Ronald Reagan in Washington, the Angolan civil war was kept alive by the steady supply of military hardware. Jonas Savimbi was projected as the saviour of Christianity. His video footage with Christian clergy and the nuns was shot and widely telecasted in the US media. He cultivated a deep-standing relationship with the influential conservative right-wing think tank '*The Heritage Foundation'*. This helped him fund his guerrilla activities. Such was the backing he enjoyed that the Foundation had

Clark's Amendment of 1976, that barred aid to non-state players engaged in military or paramilitary operations in Angola, repealed in 1985. This is often considered a feather in Savimbi's cap. It also bolstered the CIA's efforts in equipping Savimbi's forces. In 1988 he stated, *'Whenever we come to Heritage Foundation, it is like coming back home'*. Interestingly during the entire period of operation of the Clarke's amendment (1976–1985), Israel was used as a proxy to supply arms to UNITA cadres. During the late 1980s, a failed invasion of Angola by South Africa and UNITA forces eventually paved the way for the freedom of Namibia, the end of apartheid and the release of Nelson Mandela.

Namibia Marches to Freedom in 1990

Angolan independence in 1975 with the ascension of MPLA to the seat of power and Cuban military intervention on behalf of the young republic had a great bearing on the future of Namibia. Namibia, formerly known as South West Africa, was a colony of Germany. Following Germany's defeat in WW I, it became a protectorate under South Africa. South African administration viewed Namibia as its colony for all practical purposes. While the UN engaged in prayers and protests against the inhuman practice of apartheid in South Africa, it promptly extended the legislation of apartheid into Namibia as well. Namibia continued to be an anachronism. In Namibia the South West African People's Organisation (SWAPO) was waging a War of Independence against South Africa. MPLA provided the military wing of SWAPO, the People's Liberation Army of Namibia (PLAN) sanctuaries in Southern Angola for its guerrilla warfare against the South African troops.

1987-1988: The Battle of Cuito Cuanavale: The *'Black Stalingrad'*

Buoyed by the US support, UNITA cadres and troops of South Africa invaded Angola from their bases in Namibia in August 1987. The South

---

[33] *'This man needs Stinger missiles… Give him'*: President Reagan conceded to UNITA leader Savimbi's demand for Stinger missiles without batting an eye in a meeting in the Oval office.

African intention was to take the city of Cuito Cuanavale which had all the trappings of a capital and transform it into a full-fledged one in the event of UNITA wresting control of the Southern parts of Angola. Cuban and Angolan troops ably guided by Soviet military advisors fought against the regular troops of South Africa. It was the biggest conventional battle in the African continent since WW II. The battle of Cuito Cuanavale was indecisive, though all the combatants claimed victory. There was never going to be a decisive military victory in southern Angola which was witness to a civil war since 1975. By all means, it was a tactical military stalemate that led to a strategic political realignment. Peace was brokered by March 1988 due to the UN intervention. A ceasefire agreement on the total withdrawal of the South African forces from Angola was reached. The withdrawal of Cuban troops was timed with specific tangible milestones with regard to Namibian independence. It was agreed for a UN-supervised election in Namibia, leading to its independence in March 1990. The SWAPO leader, Sam Nujoma, was elected to the Presidency of Namibia. It also led to the lifting of the ban on ANC and the end of apartheid and the release of Mandela from prison.

Medical Internationalism

'Money and materials are important but those two things alone cannot stop Ebola virus transmission... . . . Human resources are clearly our most important need. We need most especially compassionate doctors and nurses, who will know how to comfort patients despite the barriers of wearing PPE (personal protective equipment) and working under very demanding conditions'.
                                    – Margaret Chan, Director WHO

When the rich countries threw finances, supplies and military personnel to distress call for international assistance following the Ebola outbreak,

Cuba was the first country to respond to the WHO appeal, sending the largest medical contingent – to Guinea, Sierra Leone and Liberia

Cuban medical internationalism is multi-pronged.

i) Emergency response medical brigades that are sent overseas;
ii) Maintaining public health infrastructure in foreign countries to cater to the needs of the local residents;
iii) Foreign patients brought to Cuba for free medical treatment and
iv) Providing medical training for foreign nationals, both in Cuba and overseas.

The exodus of professionals from the island especially that of doctors following the 1959 revolution virtually incapacitated the island's already impoverished health services. It was only as late as 1976 that the pre-revolutionary ratio of doctors to citizens was restored in Cuba. But, nothing could prevent the revolutionary zeal of the new government. In May 1960, Valdivia province in Chile was struck by the most powerful earthquake ever recorded. Cuba was the first country to respond with medical assistance. In the 1960s, Cuba extended its medical assistance to Algeria, Congo and North Vietnam. When Angola won her independence from Portugal it witnessed the sudden exodus of the Portuguese health professionals. The country was left with just four doctors. Cuba contributed handsomely towards bridging the gap left by the Portuguese departure.

US Students study in Cuban Medical School

> 'I know of no other medical school that offers students so much, at no charge. I know of no other medical school with an admission policy that gives first priority to candidates who come from poor communities and know, first-hand, what it means to live without access to essential medical care. For once, if you are poor, female, or from an indigenous population, you have a distinct advantage. This is an institutional ethic that makes this medical school unique.'
> **– Margaret Chan**

In 1999, the Cubans established the Latin American School of Medicine (ELAM), probably the world's largest medical school, to train foreign students.

In June 2000, a US Congressional Black Caucus (CBC) delegation met Castro. Representative Bennie Thompson of Mississippi mentioned to Castro that his district had a shortage of doctors. Castro responded by offering full scholarships for US nationals from Mississippi at ELAM. Later that month, in a meeting with the CBC in Washington D.C, the Cuban Minister of Public Health expanded the Castro offer to all districts represented by the CBC. In a September 2000 speech in New York City, Fidel Castro further expanded the offer allowing several hundred places at ELAM for medical students from low-income communities from any part of the US. The US State Department classified ELAM offer to US students as a *'cultural exchange'* program to avoid the restrictions of the US embargo against Cuba. The first intake of US students into ELAM occurred in the spring of 2001. Ever since thousands of US nationals pursue their medical studies and graduate in Medicine from Cuba.

Cuba, Katrina Hurricane, Henry Reeve International Contingent of Doctors

In 2005 after the Katrina hurricane and the extremely negligent US response to the disaster, Cuba offered 1586 doctors, 36 tonnes of medicine and diagnostic help to the US. The omni-potent POTUS George Bush rejected it. As a revenge (!) Fidel Castro rechristened the Cuban medical brigade to *'Henry Reeve International Contingent of Doctors Specialised in Disasters and Serious Epidemics'* in memory of the great American soul who died fighting the Spanish colonisers.

The Revenge of Cuba

Mario Teran Salazar... who shot dead Che Guevera on 9th October 1967 was treated by Cuban doctors 40 years later almost to the date... Under a Cuban medical programme 'Operation Miracle' for Latin America.

PART 7

THE SHAM OF MULTIPARTY DEMOCRACY

> *The remarkable trajectory of the pristine bullet according to the Warren Commission that probed the assassination of President Kennedy defies logic.*

> *'We live in a world where the powerful deceive us. We know they lie, they know we know they lie, they don't care. We say we care, but we do nothing'.*

---

[34] **4th June 1963** Executive Order 11110 called for a transfer of power from the Federal Reserve to the United States Department of the Treasury by replacing Federal Reserve Notes with silver certificates.
11th October 1963: National Security Action Memorandum (NSAM) 263 issued which called for a withdrawal of troops from Vietnam.
22nd November 1963 John Fitzgerald Kennedy killed by a lone assassin.

Chapter 24: The Blitzkrieg of Unstoppable Self-Propelling Capitalism Pulverises Institutions of Democracy

"The capitalist is just "Capital personified".

– Karl Marx

I don't know what would have happened to Walmart if we had laid low and never stirred up the competition. My guess is that we would have remained a strictly regional operator. Then eventually, I think, we would have been forced to sell out to some national chain looking for a quick way to expand into the heartland market. Maybe there would have been 100 or 150 Walmarts on the street for a while. But, today they would all have K-Mart or Target signs in front of them, and I would have become a full-time bird hunter.

– Sam Walton

'In a Darwinian struggle for existence, a capitalist is just an instrument in the hands of "immanent tendencies" of capitalism. His actions are not by his volition, but coerced by the competition. He is not a sovereign of his circumstances'.

– Prabhat Patnaik, Indian economist

"Marconi is a good fellow. Let him continue. He is using seventeen of my patents",

– Nicola Tesla

In a capitalist landscape, each enterprise is pitted against every other. A Darwinian struggle for existence is inherent in such a socio-economic milieu. It is inescapable. Such a struggle to exist causes the economic agents to act in a certain manner in their battle for survival. His own volition has no role in his choice of action. His actions are never the outcome of the exercise of his free will. His actions are just responses to the logic of the situation he finds himself in. The capitalist is compelled to act in ways dictated by the logic of the capital. He lacks initiative. Every participant in the capitalist system experiences this coercion. No economic agent is the sovereign of his circumstance in such a system. He is predisposed to react. The decision to outsource, to lay off or to employ labour-saving machinery to maintain high reserves of labour, to tame domestic labour, consigning it into a mere *'price taker'*, or to colonise new territories in search of raw materials and markets to leverage scale economies is thrust upon the capitalist. Whether it is predatory pricing to drive out competitors, mergers and acquisitions to exert monopoly power, or lobbying the government to create favourable conditions for unfettered expansion in both domestic and international arena, these actions are thrust upon the capitalist by the system. Not to respond to the logic of the situation is a sure recipe for his ruin. In effect, every entity in the capitalist force-field is subject to an impersonal coercion to act in a manner as deemed fit by the logical necessity of the circumstance. The very *'he'* who is rightfully held responsible for the dismemberment of local petty business owners and their livelihood is very much a victim of his circumstances. All his actions could be interpreted as frantic efforts to stay in the race. The built-in Darwinian struggle for existence among the participants of the capitalist system renders every participant, even the capitalist, the much-pilloried villain in the entire capitalist order, a mere plaything or an instrument through which the immanent tendencies of the capitalist system get played out.

> *'Business complications do strange things to our patriotism and to our ethics.'*
>
> **– Elanor Roosevelt, the US First Lady in NY Times on 20th September 1945**

Trading with the Enemy Act (TWEA) of 1917 enacted on 6th October 1917, gives the President of the United States the power to oversee or restrict any and all trade between the United States and its enemies in times of war. Amended in 1933 and 1977, it provides the legal means for the US to sanction a *'belligerent'* country. As of 2023, Cuba is the only country that is being sanctioned.

During World War II President Roosevelt described his country to be the *arsenal of democracy*. But, in effect, the US Inc had turned itself into an *'arsenal of fascism'*. Many reputed US companies like Coco Cola, IBM, Ford, Standard Oil, Kodak and General Motors, to say a few, had subsidiaries in Nazi Germany. These subsidiaries won lucrative contracts from the Nazi government and aided the Nazi war machine by producing what was required of them by the Nazi officials. They employed slave labour which was available in plenty under the Third Reich. Many plants were located near prison camps to ensure a steady supply of slave labour and to cut on logistics. The killing profits that these subsidiaries made by aiding the German war efforts were funnelled back to the US, profiting its American shareholders. Except for a few organisations like Kodak which paid namesake compensation for the surviving victims of slave labour, none paid any reparations, nor issued any apology.

During World War II, there prevailed a gentlemen's agreement between the warring nations not to raze down plants from which capitalists on both sides were making blood profits. Amid the devastation after years of merciless bombing razing Germany to rubble, invading American ground troops were shocked to discover huge war plants churning out arms, ammunition and war machinery, virtually unscathed. Plants in which American and British capital were invested which were the lifelines for the Nazi military apparatus were never a target. Many a time, these plants functioned as rescue shelters for the German elite. Gen. Arnold, Chief of the U.S. Army Air Forces when pressed to respond to the reasons for *'missing'* those plants in bombing missions passed off the whole matter laughingly, saying *'I could say something about that, but I won't'.* GM plant was accidently bombed on 6th August 1944. Post-war, GM was compensated by the American tax payer to the tune of 32 million dollars. Luckily no Air Force pilot was court-martialled for an act of insubordination!

IBM had an undeniable role in the Holocaust. IBM trained SS employees on how to use the IBM machines and punch cards to identify, locate and track the Jews. IBM employees trained the officials in using punch cards to co-ordinate the trains to bring the Jews to death camps. Killing Jews on an industrial scale was a lucrative business for IBM. IBM till date has not apologised. The US company BAYERS collaborated with the German company IG Farben to produce Zyklon B gas that was used in the gas chambers.

'Operation Paperclip' was a clandestine US intelligence program in which close to 2000 German scientists, engineers and technicians, majority of them holding high ranks in the much dreaded SS, were taken from the former Nazi Germany to the U.S. Many of them had committed atrocious acts but were granted immunity. Post-war there was a clamour for denazification of Germany. In West Germany, the denazification meandered into nothingness. The economic value of many of the Nazis came in the way of denazification. The surrendered Nazi officials' records were bleached out and were absorbed into the US government. They had enviable careers in the US. Though the Nazi political leadership was sent to the gallows or for long terms in prison, the Nazi officials who were potential assets for the impending war with the Soviet Union were never brought to justice. As the allied troops marched on to Germany, the high-ranking German Nazi officials fled West. They preferred to surrender to the US-British forces invading from the West rather than to the Red Army closing in on from the East, as they could negotiate better terms. The scientist Von Braun who was spearheading rocketry in Germany, a senior SS official, went on to become a high-ranking NASA official and was instrumental in the success of the Appollo programme which landed man on moon and secured a semblance of equality with the Soviets in the space race. While being a SS official in the Third Reich he employed Jewish slave labour and often sent many, who could not complete the quotas, to the gas chambers. The V2 rockets his team developed, that devastated London, is said to have killed more people in their development than in their deployment in the war.

Surgeon Shirō Ishii, Director of the much dreaded Unit 731 biological warfare unit of the Imperial Japanese Army, and his team were granted immunity by Douglas MacArthur, Supreme Commander of the Allied Powers in spite of the fact that they had conducted the most atrocious experiments on live human beings, including many of the US Prisoners of War. They were never charged with war crimes and were never tried by the Tokyo Tribunal much to the chagrin of the Soviet authorities. The US microbiologists who investigated, held that information was *'absolutely invaluable'*; and that it *'could never have been obtained in the United States because of the scruples attached to experiments on humans'* and *'the information was obtained fairly cheaply'*. But their counterparts working in Manchuria under Japanese occupation, taken into custody by the liberating Red Army, were not so lucky. No wonder Japan preferred a surrender to the Americans than to the Soviets.

The 9/11 Pinto Madness

The late 1960s witnessed the US car markets being flooded with highly fuel-efficient German and Japanese cars. The legendary President of Ford, Lee Iacocca made it clear that he wanted a 1971 model that weighed under 2,000 pounds and that would be priced at less than $2000. Thus, was born the *Ford Pinto*. The product development of Ford Pinto, right from conception through delivery, was completed in a record time of 25 months when the automotive industry average time in the US was 43 months. Any decision or afterthought that threatened the schedule was frowned upon. Ford formally introduced Pinto on 9/11 1970. The mad rush to the market did take its toll on the safety of the car. When hit from the rear with sufficient speed the fuel tank burst and the car would be in flames. Ford knew that it had an issue with the fuel tank that could seriously put the passengers' lives in danger. $11 was all that was required to fix it. Ford chose otherwise. Ford, after a cost-benefit analysis, reasoned it was profitable to meet the claims in case of death and burns suffered by the passenger and damages incurred by the car rather than fix it for the entire vehicles that were going into production.

Ossification and Opaqueness of Democracy

'I feel like I've been struck by a bolt of lightning... If you ever pray, pray for me now'.

– President Harry S Truman

During the course of World War II US had two Presidents, Franklin D Roosevelt and Harry S. Truman. England had three different Prime Ministers; Neville Chamberlain, Winston Churchill and Clement Attlee. Joseph Stalin had a better grasp of the nuances of the conduct of the war and negotiations and had the better of his peers in the conferences of Teheran (1943), Yalta (Feb 1945) and Potsdam (July 1945). He had a hypnotic hold over the negotiations. Even Churchill and Roosevelt consistently conceded territory to Stalin. The British diplomat Alexander Cadogan writes on the negotiations at Yalta Summit in which Stalin, Churchill and Roosevelt deliberated: *'I must say I think Uncle Joe is the most impressive of the three men. He is very calm and reserved. When he speaks he never uses superfluous words and gets straight to the point'*. The British Secretary of State A Eden was no less impressed. *'By more subtle methods he got what he wanted without having seemed too obdurate',* he noted.

And at Potsdam, things were far worse for the *'free world'*. Roosevelt had died and was replaced by Truman. As the conference progressed, Churchill having been defeated in elections, was replaced by Clement Attlee, about whom Churchill himself had commented, *'A modest man with much to be modest about'.* Attlee was no replacement for Churchill. Neither Truman nor Attlee could fully fill the vacuum left by their predecessors. Little-known Missouri Senator Harry S. Truman was no replacement for the longest-serving US President FDR. He had been the Vice President only for 3 months and in those 3 months Roosevelt had met him in private only twice. Despite his failing health, Roosevelt had kept Truman pitifully ill informed. Truman never knew of the Manhattan Project. He had made a late entry into politics and had been Senator for only 10 years. Roosevelt had chosen him to be his running mate purely for electoral reasons as is often the case with Vice Presidents in the US. The former shirt and tie sales personnel from Missouri found himself to be the Commander-in-Chief of the world's largest military. He was not even privy to discussions of the Big 3 at Yalta. To replace FDR in the White House is one thing. To rub shoulders with world statesmen like Stalin and Churchill was another. Truman on his part never made any attempt to pretend that he was the man for the job. In his brief exchange with the Press, there was no President talking when he said *'You boys have been good to me. I don't know whether you have ever had a load of hay fall on you. But, when they told me yesterday what happened, I felt like the moon, stars and all the planets had fallen on me. If you ever pray, pray for me now'.* His advisors worried, *'Can a tie salesman from Missouri hold against the tyrant Stalin against whom the seasoned politicians Churchill and Roosevelt had no luck with'.* On Stalin, President Harry S Truman noted in his diary, *'He is honest, but cunning as hell'.*

Stalin, a seasoned statesman, had a formidable mind, a sharp memory and the capacity to get to the heart of any problem. He radiated a seductive charm. A marvellous listener, in meetings he would say little waiting for his moment. *'Never once in any of his statements did he make any strategic error, nor did he fail to appreciate all the implications of a situation with a quick and unnerving eye. He stood out when compared with Winston Churchill and*

Roosevelt', remarked Alan Brooke, Britain's highest-ranking military officer on Stalin.

> 'The roughest thing in my life. He beat the hell out of me. He savaged me'.
>
> **– President John F Kennedy**

In the Vienna Conference of June 1961 at the height of the Cold War when the newly inaugurated President Kennedy was to meet an uneducated, moribund Soviet Leader Nikita Khrushchev, things could not have been worse. In the context of the Vienna Summit, 4th –6th June 1961, the US was on a sticky wicket. The Soviet Union had an edge over the US in space. Yuri Gagarin had made it to space on 12th April 1961. President Kennedy could not conceal the failure or shrug off the blame for the botched Bay of Pigs invasion (17th–20th April 1961) that had driven the Cubans to the Soviet camp. The assassination of Patrice Lumumba and the mysterious air crash that killed UN Secretary General Dag Hammarskjold weighed heavily on the young and untested President. The two had met in 1959 during Khrushchev's visit to the US. Khrushchev had then remarked on Kennedy, who was then a Senator from Massachusetts, *'Too young to be a Senator'*. The US Secretary of State felt that the Summit would be a risky gamble. He preferred a back-channel operation with diplomats rather than letting the inexperienced President take on the mammoth leader. He never wanted the President to tangle so soon with the hardened Soviet Leader and feared Khrushchev would browbeat the young Kennedy barely 6 months in office into a deal. Very protective of the Commander-in-Chief of the world's biggest war machinery indeed!

As the meeting progressed Kennedy was sucked into a battle of ideologies with Khrushchev which Kennedy could not have won given the socialist onslaught in Europe and the Third World. Soviet support for national liberation could not be contested. Kennedy's points were deflected to his disadvantage. Khrushchev's haranguing of the US patronage for the despotic Shah of Iran, the crisis in Belgian Congo and Algeria knocked the President off balance. The General Secretary's allegation that many of Hitler's Generals were top commanders of NATO could not be contested. Many dreaded Nazi officials taken prisoner by the Soviets were sent to the gallows or were languishing long years in jails but those who surrendered to the US were leading flamboyant lives with a meteoric career in the US. The President's aides confided that their President was taking one hit after the other.

Kennedy was no novice to international relations and diplomacy. His thesis in Harward was titled, *'Appeasement in Munich'*. It was on British Prime Minister, Neville Chamberlain's negotiations with Hitler in Munich in September 1938. It was later refurbished into a book by the title *'Why England Slept'*. But with Khrushchev, the young President found no luck.

The Transient Political Leadership is Held Hostage by The Entrenched Vested Interests.

> *'I had entered the Pentagon with a limited grasp of military affairs and even less grasp of covert operations. This lack of understanding, coupled with my preoccupation with other matters and my deference to the CIA on what I considered an agency operation, led me to accept the plan uncritically... The truth is I did not understand the plan very well and did not know the facts. I had let myself become a passive bystander'.*
> **– Mc Namara on the 'Bay of Pigs Invasion'**

The existence of a near-permanent bureaucracy, military, police, state personnel, judiciary, business houses, media houses and religious institutions have rendered the political establishment to be a mere ornamental embellishment over the polity of a country. Even the most powerful office of the land is rendered transient. The government of the day is incapable of fulfilling the collective will of the people of which it is a reflection of. It has greater implications than one can possibly even imagine.

Kennedy's Secretary of Defence Mc Namara's memoir is a compendium of confessions on how the Kennedy administration and later that of Lyndon B Jhonson were taken hostage by the entrenched interests in Pentagon, DoD, and the CIA. In fact, Kennedy's predecessor Eisenhower in his farewell speech had warned about the *'permanent armaments industry of vast proportions'*. In spite of the outgoing President urging the citizenry to *'guard against the acquisition of unwarranted influence whether sought or unsought by the military-industrial complex'*, the political leadership, representative of the people's will, finding itself to be in a sense of awe and be deferent to the permanent powers, is more a norm than an exception. Very often it is the case that the bureaucracy could brow beat the political leadership into submission.

The tussle between the President Kennedy and the CIA director Allen Dulles was a battle for American democracy. Assassination of the democratically elected Prime Miniter of Congo Patrice Lumumba (17th January 1961) was rushed ahead of John F Kennedy's inauguration (20th January 1961) as the CIA director Allan Dulles rightly feared that the new President with sympathies for Pan African nationalism would be a stumbling block. Suffice it to say that the CIA director Allen Dulles whom Kennedy had fired following the Bay of Pigs fiasco and is widely believed to have masterminded the President's assassination was a member of the Warren Commission that probed into it.

---

[35] Kennedy is said to have stated *'I will splinter the CIA into a thousand pieces and scatter it into the wind'.*(National Security Action Memoranda 55, 56, 57 meant to hold the Joint Chief of Staff wholly responsible for all covert actions during peacetime, thus signalling the end of the reign of the CIA came to nothing because of 'bureaucratic resistance')

The long career of John Edgar Hoover, the longest-serving FBI director speaks for itself. President Calvin Coolidge appointed Hoover as Director of the Bureau of Investigation, FBI's predecessor, in 1924. He went on to serve as the first Director of the Federal Bureau of Investigation (FBI), which he was instrumental in founding, from its inception in 1935 until his death in 1972, 37 years later. From 1924, when Hoover had not even turned 30, until his death in 1972 aged 78, he outlasted seven US Presidents. It must be said that successive Presidents in spite of entertaining thoughts of removing him as the director chose not to, for fear of the political cost. Truman had even said that Hoover had transformed the FBI into his private secret police. Presidents Harry Truman and John F. Kennedy considered dismissing Hoover as FBI Director, but weary of the political backlash, let him continue. President Lyndon B. Johnson, successor to Kennedy even went to the extent of waiving the then-mandatory U.S. government Service Retirement Age of 70, allowing Hoover to remain the FBI Director *'for an indefinite period of time'*. President Richard Nixon was recorded in 1971 as stating he would not fire Hoover as he was afraid of Hoover's reprisals against him.

Iran-Contra Affair: US President Capitalised on the Ossification of Democracy

> *'Let me put this in capital letters…I did not know about the diversion of funds'*
> **– President Ronald Reagan,**

> *'It just defies logic that people at the level of field grade officers would be making foreign policy for the United States'''*
> **– Jim Wright, Speaker of the US House of Representatives (1987–1989).**

By the time Ronald Reagan was at the Oval Office the dismemberment of the Presidency had been so institutionalized that he could even claim immunity under it in the Iran-Contra affair for transgressing the Boland Amendment which the Congress had passed into law.

Reagan's obsession with any welfare measure aimed at poverty eradication, employment generation and health care in Latin America is well-documented. Keeping in line with this obsession, Reagan announced that his administration perceived Nicaragua to be *'an unusual and extraordinary threat to the national security and foreign policy of the United States'*. He henceforth declared a *'national emergency'* and a trade embargo against Nicaragua to *'deal with that threat'*. For the President, Contra rebels that were fighting the Sandinista government in Nicaragua were *'our brothers'* and held them to be the *'moral equivalent of our forefathers'*. BOLAND amendment in 1982 had effectively curtailed any US funding to the Contras. The amendment effectively prevented the DoD and the CIA from financially supporting the Contras. Ronald Reagan was to find an opportunity in Ayatollah's Iran against whom the US trade embargo was in effect. In what was to be later known as the Iran-Contra affair, under the pretext of securing the release of Americans held hostage in Lebanon, Iran in return for brokering their release was to receive 30 million worth of US weapons. As it turned out, 8 million of the cache was siphoned off to fund the Contras.

In the investigations that followed once the deal surfaced, National Security Advisors, Lieutenant Colonel Oliver North, 4 CIA officers and 5 government contractors were found guilty. Reagan was never implicated. The President's *'lack of oversight'* did find mention, however. For the

President the entire *'Iran-Contra mess'* was all about the wrong people failing the right processes. In effect, the Commander-in-Chief of the world's largest fighting machinery was taking refuge in the very ossification of democracy rather than rectifying it.

Citizenry Duped by the Political Leadership
Pearl Harbour Attack: The Perfect Pretext President Roosevelt Wanted

> *'The question was how we should manoeuvre them into firing the first shot... It was desirable to make sure the Japanese be the ones to do this so that there should remain no doubt as to who were the aggressors'.*
>
> **– Henry Stimson**
> **US Secretary of War (1940–1945)**

Democracy is the most acceptable form of government. But instances abound in which the citizenry is often taken for granted, if not duped by the political leadership.

After the US involvement in WW I Americans were reluctant to get entangled into yet another *'European civil war'*. The US Congress throughout the 1930s in response to growing threats of war in Europe passed a slew of acts affirming neutrality and non-interventionism bordering on isolationism. Such was the abhorrence of the Americans to enter the overseas war in Europe that even after the fall of France in June 1940, 85 percent of Americas were opposed to sending troops. Less than 16 percent agreed to send aid to the allies.

1940 was an election year. Roosevelt was running for an unprecedented third term. He never wanted to appear to be a warmonger in an election year. Roosevelt promised the Americans *'Your boys are not going to be sent into any foreign war'*. It was a promise to the American people their

President never intended to keep. But once re-elected to power, he did everything in his capacity and left no stone unturned to ensure that Pearl Harbour did happen, thus presenting the perfect pretext to enter the war. Japanese assets in the US were frozen. Ninety percent of Japanese requirements for oil were met by the US. It was promptly cut. Japanese felt castrated, to say the least. The US pumped up its aid to China which has been fighting Japanese invasions since 1941. The US also positioned B17 bombers in the Philippines at a striking distance from Japan. Adding fuel to the fury US Pacific fleet sailed out from California to Pearl Harbour in Hawaii. The Japanese attack on Pearl Harbour was only a question of when and not whether. 'A date that will live in infamy' was left to the Japanese to decide.

Did Reagan Manipulate The Hostage Release To His Electoral Advantage?

> 'There was a flurry of activity in their Iranian Parliament that they were going to vote on whether or not to release the hostages just before the votes were cast in this country that Parliament decided under Khomeini's pressure that they would not release the hostages and this devastating negative news about hostages swept the country that election day. I have always been convinced that this was a major factor'.
>
> **– President Jimmy Carter
> in an interview to PBS News.**

The Carter Presidency was marred by the Iranian hostage crisis. During the 1980 US Presidential election which saw Ronald Reagan take on the incumbent Jimmy Carter, William J. Casey, Director of President Reagan's campaign is widely believed to have reached out to the Iranians and promised them a better deal under Reagan to dissuade the Iranians from reaching a settlement with the US Administration. The release of hostages could have swung the tide in favour of Carter. It did not happen. Reagan won a landslide. Within minutes after having delivered his inaugural speech on 20th January 1980 Iran released the hostages after 444 days of agonizing captivity in Iranian prison. By all probability, it appears that they could have been released at least 100 days prior to the date.

On being elected Reagan promptly rewarded his campaign director William J. Casey with the directorship of the Central Intelligence Agency.

Democracy More Procedural and Farcical than Authentic

The procedural democracy with all its much-trumpeted ceremonial rites of Parliamentary debates, elections, no-confidence motions, impeachments and the emblematic change of the mantle of governance *'from one generation to the other'* offers a convincing spectre. It is still a distant cry from the authentic democracy we have been tutored on that will bloom under a capitalist system. Freedom, democracy, the much-trumpeted blooming of the individual and other shibboleths of capitalist democracies seem to elude capitalist countries. Unlike in many of the Latin American countries, where the Welfare State had been dismantled by military dictators on orders from Washington, Reagan and Thatcher could dismantle it in their countries in the most democratic manner. Both of them could get re-elected with a landslide margin. The worst was yet to come. Their successors Bill Clinton and Tony Blair though hailing from the far end of the political spectrum of their predecessors catering to a different electorate, continued with their *'reforms'* and presided over the complete dismemberment of what was left with the Welfare State that was built over the decades. Why does not a change in government correspond to a paradigm change in the policies of the nation? The political party that comes to power by a landslide victory seldom pursues a policy that had been vocalised during the electioneering. Why?

'The Failure of the Parliaments'

Very often it is the case that Parliament sets the broad contours of a law or measure and it is up to the executive to hammer out the nuances of it. In this process, the executive usurps to itself a greater share of the pie of governance much to the undermining of the very Parliament to which it is answerable. The supremacy of the Parliament quickly erodes and is reduced to a forum to criticize the executive and censure its actions from time to time. As Harold J Laski said, *'Our Government has become an executive dictatorship tempered by fear of Parliamentary revolt'*.

Spontaneity of Capitalism is Incompatible with Democracy

The Darwinian struggle inherent in the capitalist ecosystem has an overwhelming influence on its participants, be it on the capitalist, the labour or the democratically elected government. Every entity making frantic efforts to retain its position behaves in a manner that is the most logical in the given circumstances. Like the fervently patriotic American car buyer who left Ford, Chrysler and GM and shifted towards the fuel-efficient German and Japanese cars on account of rising gas prices in the 1960s and 1970s, an act unthinkable during affluent times, every economic agent faced with an existential threat in Darwinian struggle for survival typical of capitalist ecosystem, promptly proceeds to embrace a sequence of actions never under the exercise of his free will or volition, but under coercion. This impersonal coercion exercised by the economic circumstances renders every economic agent a mere object with no recourse to exercise his free will. This objectifying nature of capitalism which is an outcome of the Darwinian struggle for existence makes the capitalist system spontaneous. In the economic realm of social life every agent is just a plaything of the capitalist system.

Obviously, a question arises. Even if we concede the objectification of the individual in the economic realm of things, why can't a recourse to the political process in a democracy rein in the economic forces, riding roughshod over the human life, and restore the fully bloomed individual capable of critical thinking in the exercise of free will? In a democratic polity with universal adult suffrage, why can't the citizen be a sovereign of his circumstance rather than its mere plaything? Why can't the vast majority that stands dismembered by the economic forces, with the exercise of adult suffrage in the political sphere, earn their rightful place in the economic realm? It defies logic when even in a democracy, concerns of the impoverished majority seldom resonate in the inner councils of government.

In a capitalist framework, it is economics that calls the shots. It won't be an exaggeration if one says that economics drives politics. The political parties, comprising of individuals who are mere objects in the economic realm, internalise the helplessness. And with minimal government intervention in the economic realm being the norm, laissez-faire as they call it, the political apparatus is structurally incompetent to stand up against the economic forces and secure for the citizens what is their due. The political apparatus of a capitalist country lacks the teeth to enforce its will.

The Very Brief Post-War Golden Era of Capitalism

The first time in the history of capitalism the government took upon themselves to ensure the welfare of their own people was during the Great Depression. The Great Depression convinced everyone that the government of the day had a greater role to play in the economic well-being of its citizens. But still, though the urge was felt, it was taken up in right earnest only in the US. But even the US, the government found its hand constitutionally tied. The Supreme Court of the US was in the forefront in combating the New Deal initiatives of Roosevelt, striking down many laws passed by the Congress citing that they violated the provisions of the Constitution. The President's attempt to tame the predominantly Republican Supreme Court by appointing more judges who would be sympathetic to the New Deal found no success. In the US as early as 1937 when the economy showed signs of recovery, the government was in a mode of retreat from welfare initiatives with unemployment levels still high. It was the WW II that really got the economy ticking and unshackled the labour from being a price taker.

The strong showing of the worker's republic of the Soviet Union during the war had a great influence on the US economic policies. In the US it was realisation time, a growing realisation that the political rights guaranteed by the Constitution had *'proved inadequate to assure us equality in the pursuit of happiness',* as Roosevelt had put it. His remedy to declare an *'Economic Bill of Rights'* set the stage of institutionalising a Welfare State within the capitalist fabric, war time as well as peace time. Britain had a Labour Prime Minister post war. Concessions to the working class was necessary to prevent its radical shift to the left. The Keynesian economic measures, the practice of putting people back to work through government initiatives necessitated by the conjuncture capitalism found itself in the 1930s, (entirely of its making) came to be widely accepted post-war. Faith in the market was not lost but the free-market system was abhorred. It came to be widely believed that with adequate government intervention, the capitalist system was malleable enough to be rendered humane. It was widely held that Capital could be reined in by national governments. It was genuinely felt that world peace and tranquillity within the capitalist framework had at last been achieved. A belief that the capitalist system could reconcile itself with a Welfare State came to be universally subscribed, rendering Marx and Lenin obsolete for a while.

Capital Regains Lost Ground

Concessions from the capital to labour, when capitalism as an economic system was craving for legitimacy in the context of an alternative model finding success, was however short lived. Capital preferred to remain subdued for such time as was necessary and unleashed its unabashed tendencies to accumulate at a time of its choosing. Keynesian measures were administered a quiet burial and capital emerged to ride roughshod over the aspirations of mankind once a semblance of stability was achieved.

The rising oil prices and stagflation i.e., the simultaneous occurrence of runaway inflation and rising unemployment, provided the perfect pretext to roll back the Welfare State. The underlying causes of the crisis, the foremost being the US running a huge current account deficit due to the war in Vietnam, were glossed over. The monetarists who detested Keynesian welfare measures seized the moment. It was their moment of triumph. Keynesianism was held responsible for the imbroglio the world economy found itself in. As a panacea to the crisis plaguing the world economy, roll back of the Welfare State came to be subscribed to.

The tide of history had tuned in favour of capital. Thatcher and Reagan on either side of the Atlantic championed the systematic dismemberment of their Welfare States that had been built over the three decades following the great war. Capital regained its lost ground and, as in normal times, started to drive politics. The truce that was effected between labour and Capital was called off. Requirements of sound finance dictated that the government of the day withdraw from welfare schemes. With Keynesians purged from every financial institution and replaced with monetarists of the breed of those from Chicago school, owing allegiance to Capital, Darwinian struggle was restored to the capitalist system. With Darwinian struggle among the economic agents being the norm their objectification too was re-institutionalised. Labour was once again relegated to be a price taker. Rise in wage levels were no longer commensurate with productivity hikes, let alone being indexed to the commodity prices.

The Triumph of Capital and The Destruction of Politics

> 'Tony Blair and New Labour. We forced our opponents to change their minds.'
>
> **– Margaret Thatcher famously replied when asked what was her greatest achievement.**

> '[Thatcher] was immensely kind and generous to me when I was Prime Minister... Politically, certain reforms she made, for example, in Trade Union Law..., we kept the basic legal framework... We didn't renationalise many of the state industries that she privatized... I always thought my job was to build on some of the things she had done rather than reverse them... Many of the things she said... had a certain credibility... Whenever I wanted to ask her for advice, she would always give it... in a genuine, spirited way.'
>
> **– Prime Minister Tony Blair**

Even a political party that has won the mandate of the people on a plank of undoing the injustices of the incumbent, somersaults upon assumption of power and pursues policies in furtherance of entrenchment of the very policies that had caused the dismemberment of the vast millions. The rollback of the Welfare State is hardly contested.

Of late, even the rhetoric and election manifestoes of political parties, supposed to be at the far ends of the political spectrum, have become indistinguishable. Such is the narrowing down of the differences in the ideologies of various political outfits that there is hardly anything to choose from, thus, undermining the very choice that democracy ought to offer. The very *'Choice'* which is the cardinal principle around which the edifice of democracy is built being denied to the citizens marks the beginning of the *'destruction of politics'* in capitalist countries. British

Prime Minister Tony Blair is absolutely right when he says, *'We live in a post ideological society'*.

> *'If you have a Government that is elected, they need to do the hard work – because if they don't, they won't be around the next time the ballot box is open'.*
> **– Jean Drez, Indian Economist**

In a narrow technical term, a Government that refused to perform is replaced with, but the replacement is no better than the ousted.

Did Obama Disappoint?

> *'Our economy is badly weakened, a consequence of greed and irresponsibility on the part of some, but also our collective failure to make hard choices and prepare the nation for a new age'.*
> **– President Obama, Inaugural speech, 21st January 2009**

Not really. By locating the reasons for the financial meltdown on *'greed and irresponsibility'* of certain individuals, he refused to view it as an outcome of systemic issues of neoliberalism. It is very much in keeping with the entrenched view.

Caught in the vortex of the capitalist onslaught is every institution. The manner in which Capital conducts itself is such that no human force, how so ever organised, has ever put a check on it. History vindicates the helplessness of human efforts in the wake of the rising capitalist tide. No instrument of political power has offered sustained resistance to the self-aggrandizing nature of capital within a capitalist framework. Capitalism is so deeply entrenched that it cannot be suspended by merely voting in a socialist government. The entire nation's wealth stands usurped by a select few. With the various bilateral trade agreements and the strict conditionalities of the IMF and WTO that the government is bound to adhere to, the incumbent's hands are very much tied to formulate any policy towards implementing a just system.

PART 8

THE WAY FORWARD

Socialisation of Investment Sans Socialisation of Production is An Impossibility.

Aggregate measures like GDP growth or per-capita income in no way reflect human flourishing, but just the economic performance of an economy in which fewer and fewer people participate.

> 'I must frankly confess that I am a socialist and a Republican, and am no believer in kings and princes, or in the order which produces the modern kings of industry, who have greater power over the lives and fortunes of men than even the kings of old, and whose methods are as predatory as those of the old feudal aristocracy'.
>
> **– Jawaharlal Nehru**

> 'As an African statesman has observed to us, the fact that the world is a global village does not mean that it will be run by one village headman'.
>
> **– Remarked K R Narayanan, President of India, at the banquet in honour of the US President Bill Clinton on 21st March 2000**

Chapter 25: The Road Ahead

'The ruling ideas of each age had been the ideas of its ruling class, i.e., the class which is the ruling material force of society is at the same time its ruling intellectual force'.

– Karl Marx

'The better mind of the world desires to-day not absolutely independent States, but a federation of friendly inter-dependent States. .... I desire the ability to be totally independent, without asserting the independence'.

– Mahatma Gandhi

'The invisible hand deserves two cheers, not the three or four proposed by its zealot ideologues. Individual self-interest can be motivation for actions of great benefit to society but only if disciplined and channelled... the invisible hand theorem has to be modified by recognising externalities and public goods, where individual and societal interests diverge. These require treatment by Governments to protect collective interests'.

– James Tobin

'The purely rational economic man is, indeed, close to being a social moron'.

– Amartya Sen

Social movements should provide people with political and socio-economic means to change their lives in ways that are fundamental and not just limit themselves to securing some calibrated permission here and a few crumbs there from time to time. The only countervailing force that can checkmate the unstoppable march of capitalism is an informed and organised citizenry. A sturdy alliance of the citizenry with shared enduring convictions alone can take them from the quagmire they have found themselves in.

Figuring out the way forward necessarily entails a detailed analysis of the path traversed over the centuries with an emphasis on the immediate decades after WW II. How did the post-war consensus defer to the Washington Consensus? How did the rapid transition from welfare economics to corporate welfare jolt the millions living under democratic governments into meek submission without a protest against it? How were the Third World nations recolonised even while maintaining the pretensions of sovereignty? How could the democratically elected governments in Britain and the US administer the burial of Keynesian demand-side economics that uplifted vast numbers of millions from poverty, destitution and squalor in these countries and replace it with the supply-side economics virtually uncontested by the political parties across the spectrum? The realm of politics hardly witnessed any rhetoric, let alone real action to reclaim the lost economic rights that were painfully won in the aftermath of the Great Depression. The very people who stood to suffer being turned into willing collaborators in the furthering of their own dismemberment is appalling. GDP, per capita income, national income and such other aggregate measures of economic performance blur and at times, even mask the human suffering in an economic system in which fewer and fewer people participate. With the political process wilfully playing a second fiddle to the agents of the economy, a meaningful tussle between the two seems to be highly improbable.

The abject acquiescence of citizens to the agenda of neoliberalism in well-functioning democracies needs a closer analysis. Identifying the causative factors goes a long way in unshackling ourselves and steering a new path to a much more egalitarian, just and dignified world.

Rule by Consent of the Oppressed

> 'All previous historical movements were movements of minorities, or in the interests of minorities. The proletarian movement is the self-conscious, independent movement of the immense majority, in the interests of the immense majority.'
> – Chapter 1: Communist Manifesto

Capitalism with all its ills and vices was never in a mode of a retreat in its entire history. Yes, during the Great Depression, it found its very legitimacy questioned. But, still it could re-group, en-cadre and continue its relentless march. Even in a well-functioning democracy, a handful of minority capitalists could hold the political system at ransom and carry forward their agenda. Even during recessions and depressions, which the capitalist system is prone to, when the system seemed to have run out of steam, it is hardly contested, let alone replaced with a socially just system.

Marx contended that *'when ideas grip the imagination of the masses, they become a material force in and of themselves'*. As Victor Hugo stated, *'Nothing is as powerful as the idea whose time has come'*. But, then why did the *'spectre of communism'* that was supposed to be haunting Europe in the 19th century not find material expression in the advanced capitalist western nations of Germany or Britain as was predicted? The only prediction of Marx that did not turn right. After all the right *'philosophy had found its material weapon in the proletariat'*. The proletariat, in turn, had found its *'spiritual weapon'* in the Marxist philosophy. The world was pregnant with a revolution. But still, in the nineteenth or even in the twentieth century a revolution by the proletariat of the industrialised capitalist West seemed to be a far cry.

The trade union movement of the day was primarily interested in improving their conditions within the capitalist system rather than in a context transcending revolution. Metaphorically put, trade unions limited themselves to picking up crumbs thrown at them or that fell off the table rather than claiming their rightful place at the table. The populations living in abject conditions even now are hardly critical of their status quo. The Bolshevik experiment in a society that was predominantly feudal, un-skilled and illiterate, however successful, failed to bring about a series of revolutions across the capitalist world where the proletariat was better skilled, educated and organised. The clarion call for a World Revolution was not heeded. The Russian Revolution in retrospect was more an improbable aberration in the context of the disastrous turn that WW I took for the Tsar, than a sign of things to come.

Even in the post-WW II context, North Korea, East and Central Europe turning communist had got to do with the liberation of its people by the Red Army. But for the Bay of Pigs invasion of 1961 the nationalist movement in Cuba would not have turned Marxist-Leninist. Vietnam is no different. Despots still rule over millions across the globe. There is hardly any sign of resentment among the people against the tyranny.

It is almost uncontested that the state secures the obedience of the population by its monopoly over the instruments of violence which stands sanctified by constitutionally approved means. The brute use of force or any coercion by the State often breeds resentment that has the potential of assuming a revolutionary zeal, if stoked by a crisis within the apparatus of the State. A minor breach in the coalition ranks of the State would vent the pent-up resentment as was the case with the Russian Revolution.

Hence, individuals in power often rely on the consent of the ruled rather than resort to outright coercion of its subjugated class by brute force. The ruling class uses hegemonic ideas to gain domination over the subjugated classes. Through a host of institutions say media, religion and educational institutions, the ruling class lets its ideas and values spread and diffuse into the fabric of *common sense* of the society it presides over in such a convincing manner that they are subscribed to by the citizenry without an iota of doubt. '*Common sense*', guides the common man in making sense of and deciphering things around him. It explains and rationalizes the status quo around him. It helps him in '*explaining*' away things in his immediate private concerns.

Once the values of the hegemonic ruling class that rationalises its own hegemony over the subjugated class are socialised into the very fabric of common sense of the population through the State institutions, the ruled often consents into submission without being coerced. He fails to recognise, let alone reject the oppression, he is subjected to. At times he himself rationalises many of the injustices done to him. Submission by consent rather than coercion, bestows a near permanence to dominance of the hegemonic class. This way, millions of people become willing partners of their own belittlement and eventual ghettoization and complete dismemberment. The fact that the masses are not in a sense of resignation or despondency reflects the degree of their own socialisation with such hegemonic ideas.

Since time immemorial all the Kings had descended either from the Moon or the Sun or such other celestial object or had been destined by scriptures to rule over the people by the divine providence. Even in the highly industrialised Japan during WW II, the Japanese were ready to fight and to die for their Emperor who had caused so much harm to them. Even in a democracy the ruling elite resorts to such means. Supply-side economics which involves tax cuts to favour the captains of the industry are dressed up as measures to incentivise the rich to invest more in the economy, to stimulate and jump-start it in bringing more jobs to the jobless when in reality such tax cuts only serve the rich and lead to the roll back of the Welfare State. The unsuspecting hegemonized population is hoodwinked into believing that such measures would let benefits '*trickle down*' to them as well, though overwhelming evidence shows that their pie is getting smaller day by day.

A hegemonized people wilfully submit before the ruling class. Hegemony ensures that the very citizenry participates in its dismemberment and confinement on the periphery of the political process. Once hegemonized no attempt is made to take on the system. It may appear that the ruling class does not appear to use force to secure the consent of the population and to ensure its dominance but invariably force underwrites the appearance of consent.

Culture of Hegemony Formed the Bedrock of Colonialism...

> 'You will be hollow. We shall squeeze you empty, and then we shall fill you with ourselves'.
> – George Orwell, 1984

> 'The curriculum and organisation of schools often date back to a colonial past, when schools were meant to train a local elite to be the effective allies of the colonial state, and the goal was to maximise the distance between them and the rest of the populace'.
> – Abhijit V. Banerjee

Though India was the cradle to the greatest civilisation the world ever had, the British chose not to acknowledge its greatness. Going one step further, every attempt was made to belittle the same. In the words of Lord Macaulay who was tasked to *'enlighten the Indians'* through a pan-Indian education system *'...a single shelf of a good European library was worth the whole native literature of India and Arabia'.* He himself must not have subscribed to it. The education that he envisaged for India was to give the British government a better traction over the entire vastness of the dominion which the military could never attain. The medium of instruction was deliberately chosen to be English. Through education, the British wanted to create a pool of Indians who would be able to serve

British interests and be loyal to them. This class would be *'Indian in blood and colour, but English in tastes, in opinions, in morals and in intellect'*, he contended. The kind of acquiescence that such a subjugated citizenry yields to the hegemonizing colonial power is unparalleled.

Every institution the British founded in India was to reiterate the supremacy of the white race. Even Judiciary was no exception. The *Ilbert Bill*, which had come to be known after the legal member of the Council of the Governor General Sir Ilbert, introduced in 1883 in British India amending the then-existing Criminal Procedure Code, conferring the power to try accused Europeans upon Indian judges invited the ire of the Britons in Britain as well in India. The very spectacle of an accused white man appearing before a native Indian judge was appalling for many a coloniser. The Bill was viewed to undercut the very prestige of the white man, the cornerstone around which the British hegemony was built on.

The hegemony was reinforced through very subtle means. The British in India, as in any other colonies, relied on a handful of white officers to rule the millions. They were careful enough not to bring to India any of their native labour class to do menial jobs. Though it would have been a great relief for the officers to have their previous servants serve them in India, they chose otherwise. Instead, they relied on native Indian labour. The white man in India was to be seen solely in positions of power and prestige as that would go a long way in establishing the hegemony of the white race over the natives. Even the lowest ranking official of the colonial administration sat behind a desk with a paperweight and had an Indian orderly attending to him.

Hegemony of Finance Capital

The demise of the Soviet Union in 1991 yoked the Third World under the International Finance Capital. I had just entered my teens then. My generation grew up on the staple diet that the Soviet model except for the initial quantum jumps, was not sustainable, as it was inherently flawed as was evidenced by its implosion. Such was the propaganda even in India which stood to gain by the Soviet system and whose own state apparatus was closely modelled on the Soviet Union with its centralised planning bodies that my generation was very much '*convinced*' that the whole Soviet political apparatus was inching towards its inevitable collapse right from October. A counter-argument to the effect that had the Soviet system been fundamentally flawed, how come the Soviet Union braved all the odds and achieved tremendous success in every field of human endeavour beating the capitalist nations though starting late and working from feeble bases at the same time serving as a source of perennial succour to the very Third World impoverished by the capitalist colonial powers, seldom found listening ears. My country India started to **L**iberalise, **P**rivatise, **G**lobalise and opened up to Finance Capital in 1991–1992, close on the heels of the demise of the Soviet Union. The timing had never been that perfect. Any concern over the opening up of the economy from any quarter was summarily ignored as the meaningless utterances of holdovers of a bygone era. The spectre of many of the young executives selected from the campuses in the 1990s, the writer himself, with whopping salaries that put the senior most civil servant of the country to shame was convincing enough. 1994 witnessed two of our girls being crowned Miss Universe and Miss World. For a Third World country, it was kind of a coming of age. The entire Indian middle class was yoked into the consumerism of the neoliberal era.

The entire Third World which embraced neoliberalism was convinced that humanity had at last reached '*not just ... the passing of a particular period of post-war history, but the end of history as such; i.e., the end-point of mankind's ideological evolution and the universalisation of western liberal democracy as the final form of human government*', as Francis Fukuyama put it. The only viable alternative, it appeared, was to bow before western Capital. It was this hegemony that finance capital enjoyed that made its triumphant entry into every nook and corner of the globe possible.

Hegemonized Gorbachev Played Into the Hands of Western Capital

> *'There is plenty of everything: land, oil and gas, other natural riches, and God gave us lots of intelligence and talent, yet we lived much worse than developed countries and keep falling behind them more and more...*
>
> *We opened ourselves to the world, gave up interference into other people's affairs, the use of troops beyond the borders of the country, and trust, solidarity and respect came in response.'*
>
> **– Mikhail Gorbachev, in his farewell address on 25th December 1991**

Long before the demise of the Soviet Union, General Secretary Mikhail Gorbachev in all probability had been highly hegemonized. Gorbachev often lamented that the mainstream of West European civilisation never held the Russians in its bosom. Even in his last address to the people of the Soviet Union on 25th December 1991 he laments about falling behind the capitalist world without being mindful of the torturous past his nation and its great people had to traverse since October for having embraced an alternative path. While the former masters from the West left their colonies, it was Soviet Union towards which every developing Third World nations looked up to. It was never *'interference into other people's affairs'* as the last Soviet leader puts it. Internationalism formed the bedrock of the Soviet policy. The solidarity and the respect that he claims the Soviet Union won in response to compromising its own safety by abandoning the buffer zone to its West reflects his own deep-seated views of the West, borne out of a hegemonical relationship. Thatcher's mention of him as *'a man to do business with'* must have exhilarated the Soviet leader. The 1990 Nobel Peace Prize made Gorbachev play into the hands of the western Capital. The engagement Soviet Union had with the West, had an air of animosity which was a concern for the last General Secretary. It must be said that even during pre-Soviet days the West never engaged Russia on equal terms. While the West had embraced the Industrial Revolution in the eighteenth century, Russia under the last Tsar Nicholas II was a pastoral society even at the turn of the twentieth century. Tsarist Russia was viewed as just a colonial extension of the West with huge investments by its aristocracy. Russia with its century-old Romanov dynasty had the pretensions and prestige of a sovereign nation. But in effect, it was being courted for its wealth and was virtually a colony of the West. Alarmed by the rising power of Germany since its unification in 1870, the West relied on Russia to open a front in the East in the event of a war with Germany. To checkmate Germany they inked a treaty of mutual assistance with Russia. West's engagement with Russia was never on equal terms. To pursue its greed, the West wanted a slice of the Russian pie.

Shrugging Off the Yoke of Hegemony

> *'For 20 years we must stop this brain from functioning'*
> **– Intoned the prosecutor at Antonio Gramsci's trial in 1926.**

Antonio Gramsci, the most well-known Marxist after Lenin and Trotsky, was arrested by the police on Mussolini's orders in 1928. He spent much of his remaining life in prison. But, contrary to the fascist establishment's expectation, the most fertile brain in Italy did work on many challenges faced by the working class. Understanding hegemony with the aim of overcoming it was one of them.

Gramsci reasoned that the struggle between the classes in the realm of ideas precedes any meaningful struggle between them over the question of production. The ideas of the ruling classes having hegemonized the people had thus manufactured their consent. Working class in such a hegemonized state of mind do not even recognise their exploitation, let alone resent to reject it. The hegemonic culture that forms the very schema of the population, he reasoned, will have to be unlearned. They should build civic capacities to think differently, challenge the current narrative and articulate new ideas and visions. The working class will have to develop their own counter-hegemonic ideas that they truly believe in. Once such counter-hegemonic culture is developed and subscribed to, the people recognize the extend of their oppression and alienation. It is only through a battle of ideas that the long-established hegemony can be overturned. A population fights for an idea that they truly believe in.

The Indian freedom struggle is a case in point. The British were considered to be the benefactor by the majority of Indians, and this was not without any reason. The introduction of western medicine, the social reforms that the British administration undertook in a society riddled with superstitions and centuries-old inhuman practices won them the much-needed legitimacy of the common man. The prominent social reformers of the Indian subcontinent often looked up to the British to enact into law their aspirations of a just and humane society. 'Sati' the much-dreaded Hindu custom of a widow of a deceased husband being burned in the funeral pyre, female infanticide, child marriage to say a few of the social evils that plagued the Indian society were made punishable offences by the British. Widow remarriage was unthinkable in India but for the British enactments in this direction. The education that the British promoted was much more egalitarian even if it was meant to further colonial interests.

The intellectuals of the day, though appreciative of the zeal of reforms, could discern the inherent exploitative nature of the British. Their study of the drain of wealth from India and the crippling of the Indian industry for the benefit of the British threw light on the huge burden of the British rule. India was a rich agricultural country. The frequent famines the country witnessed under their colonial masters was a standing testimony to the 'Un-British rule' in India. When the British came to India India's GDP was 25 percent of the World GDP. By the time they left, it had shrunk to 4 percent.

India, thanks to the British systematic attempt to de-industrialise, missed the bus of industrialisation. Britain was the brown man's burden.

Mahatma Gandhi addressed the element of indoctrination in every relationship of hegemony across every walk of life. In every realm of civic life, he countered the hegemonic thought and practice the British had institutionalised. In the realm of education, he devised a scheme that facilitated the child's all-round development that blended the child with his socio-cultural milieu, rather than becoming excellent clerks and officers under the British Raj. In the economic front, he propounded the concept of trusteeship. He championed the cause of cooperatives and cottage industries. The social evils that were widely thought to have been sanctioned by a parochial and often perverted interpretation of the Hindu scriptures by a few and had become emblematic of the Hindu religion were systematically annulled by his encyclopaedic interpretation of the same. Without taking recourse to the legal and judicial institutions of the British, which would have in effect rationalised their presence, thus undermining the freedom struggle, his was an ingenuine way to get rid of the inhuman practices. Given the Indian context, an action of social reform divorced from religion would not have gained traction even among the masses who were marginalised by the institutions of religion. He fought the monstrosity that had crept into religion, not by shunning religion, but by remaining within the folds of the religion and engaging religion with increased intensity. It is to his genius that he could fight religious orthodoxy perpetuated by the priesthood locked in ivory towers while remaining deeply entrenched in religion and God.

Similarly, the intellectuals of the day should develop counter-hegemonic thoughts that would coalesce to form a culture. Whenever a society engages with a thought that is context transcending or that offers a new paradigm to conceive and assimilate, the society as a whole, stands elevated to a higher plane. In such circumstances, the citizenry summons for themselves the requisite energy, maturity and depth of thought to steer themselves to a new socio-economic order. Marxism, Keynesianism and Gandhism are such thoughts. With neoliberalism projected to be the final and inevitable stage of mankind, there is a genuine despondency and a lack of the '*utopian energies of the nineteenth century*'. Yet, another factor is that the constituency that formed the labyrinth of intellectual energy has been captivated by the material opulence that neoliberalism has offered. Enamoured by the prospects of a highly lucrative globe-trotting career, the intelligentsia has been harnessed by the very finance capital, thus, depriving the vast populations of a leadership in their struggle in opposition to capital.

Developing a Counter-Hegemonic Culture

> '*Awareness of our problems thus does not necessarily mean that they get solved. It may just mean that we are able to perfectly anticipate where we will fail.*'
>
> **– Abhijit V. Banerjee**

Capitalism in the neoliberal mould is structurally flawed in solving many of the issues that plague the world population. Except for a few short-lived bubbles, sustained growth does not appear to be in the pipeline. The issues that we face today are fundamentally different from any crisis capitalism had known till date. It is even ironic to expect neoliberalism to solve many of the ills it created. Finance has got to a point where no national government can tame it anymore. The legitimacy of a national government is confined geographically. The scope of finance capital is no longer national. With the internationalisation of finance the entire globe has become its playground. A government the writ of which is confined within its national borders can no longer hope to tame it according to its will. The best it can do is to bow before it and follow its dictates so that the nation will be considered worthy of investment.

Finance leaves a country the moment its government on behalf of its labour institutes safeguards such as minimum wages, maximum weekly working hours and humane working conditions. The neoliberal order even sets cap on the extent the national government can borrow from its Central Bank to finance welfare, developmental and employment generation ventures. Neither can the government raise the tax to finance its intervention on behalf of the labour, as finance abhors high taxes. Once yoked under international finance, the government finds itself in a quagmire it can never hope to escape. Unlike in the depression years where the government by judicious mix of taxes and fiscal deficits could jump-start the economy, governments these days find their hands tied. Japan and Germany were the first two countries that could extricate themselves from the Great Depression. The two countries' massive militarisation programme for world dominance triggered their respective economies into full bloom. With international finance dictating terms to the national governments such recourse which involves massive borrowing from the Central Bank to jump-start the economy is no longer possible.

With the entire terrain available for the marauding International Finance Capital, workers of different nations find themselves pitted against each other. Under the neoliberal order, labour market has been rendered a buyer's market. The stagnation of wages and, in fact, its downward fall in real terms and burgeoning unemployment are entirely of the making of International Finance Capital. Pursuing Keynesianism and reining in the reckless march of capital in the context of its internationalisation is an impossibility.

A Welfare State in a capitalistic framework is not possible, given the restrictions the International Finance Capital imposes on the national governments. The only possible way to build a Welfare State in such circumstances is to delink from the internationalised finance.

Delinking from International Finance Capital

Every institution has a raison de'tre for its coming into being. However noble the cause be, over the years every institution comes to reflect the mind-set of those to whom they are held accountable. Once under the yoke of the International Finance Capital, the Governor of the Central Bank of a Third World country will be perturbed not by the poverty statistics of his country but by the inflation statistics. The Finance Minister getting ready for another round of begging before the altars of finance capital will be concerned with the fiscal deficit rather than a deficit in housing, health care and infrastructure. From being the protagonist of the destiny of its own people, national governments find themselves as mere agents of finance capital.

The scenario of the working class, refusing to be pitted against each other, coming together and offering resistance against international finance is far-fetched. But, their governments, mainly those of the Third World countries, who stood to lose in neoliberalism as they were re-colonised back without firing a shot, acting in unison against finance is possible. But, the most preferred course of action for a singular government will be to retreat from globalisation on its own. To restore the national government's economic sovereignty, so that it can pursue an interventionist policy in the domestic economy to secure its citizens a modicum of welfare, it becomes imperative to de-link from internationalisation of finance. Instituting capital controls to check its sudden flight out of the country will empower the government to pursue policies on behalf of labour. Once the economic sovereignty is regained, the government can pursue appropriate taxation and fiscal policies to further welfare measures and employment generation schemes. Metamorphically, the resurrection of Keynesianism which has been administered a quiet burial is the need of the hour.

Managing National Wealth with the Aim of Providing Economic Bill of Rights

Scandinavia is often touted as the epitome of welfare. It is true it had the luxury of a history which Latin America, Africa and Asia were deprived of. But, the remarkable achievements in Human Development Indicators cannot be glossed over citing its history. The vision and the resolve of the leaders of these countries is exemplary. Norway is a telling example.

Oil was found in the North Sea in 1969. Right from the beginning the labour government of Norway was keen to leverage the oil wealth for the benefit of the entire nation. Thus was born the 10 oil commandments. Since the oil discovery in the North Sea, both Britain and Norway produced almost equal amounts of oil, say 40 billion barrels of oil. But, its impact on the two countries cannot be more different.

The Norwegian government always had a stake in oil exploration. It formed *Statoil*, a government-owned company to undertake oil production. Norway established a sovereign fund to invest the proceeds from the petroleum sector. It holds 1.5 percent of all the listed companies, as of 2024 and values at more than $1 trillion making it the world's largest wealth fund. The fund is worth $250,000 per Norwegian citizen. Within a span of two decades, Norway transformed itself from being a fishing and wood-cutting nation to an economic superpower.

Under Thatcher, Britain in the 1980s had been privatising perfectly solvent profit-making companies. By the time oil production had started in full swing in the North Sea, the British government had privatised British Petroleum. It was also the era of tax cuts. With no stake in oil production coupled with reduced taxes, Britain could not leverage the oil boom for national benefit. Margaret Thatcher squandered the windfall. Norwegians grabbed it with both hands.

From Stake-holder Capitalism to Social Economy

> 'Competition is the law of the jungle... But cooperation is the law of civilisations'
>
> – **Peter Kropotkin, Russian anarchist**

> 'A defeated argument that refuses to be obliterated can remain very alive.'
>
> – **Amartya Sen**

Many of the crises of the capitalist system is systemic. Each crisis has challenged the system in a deep and fundamental way. However the system continues to operate. In the present era of International Finance Capital, for those who preside over the economic activities from the Wall Street, the long-term benefit of preserving distant ecosystems hardly matters as the immediate windfall that comes from modes of production that are ecologically unsustainable are lucrative. Even the damage done to the environment in which the perpetrator and the victim coexist is seldom the cause of worry to the former. The greed for immense gain for oneself in the immediate future overrides the diffused loss shared by the general public of which they're also a part. This explains why the large monopolies are prejudicial to the genuine interests of the developing countries.

Industrialisation and its associated reckless mechanisation which resulted in job losses triggered worker cooperative movements in Europe, especially in France and England. As co-operatives are people-centred and not capital-centred and based on the premise of economic participation, they distribute wealth in a more egalitarian manner. Cooperatives believe in the dignity of mankind. They are engineered to enhance *use value* rather than *financial value* and ensure the safety and well-being of its employees who stand elevated as owners in the co-operative framework. The operational advantages of trust flowing from a sense of shared purpose are unique to cooperatives. The non-tradability of the cooperative share replaces the incentive for return on capital invested with an incentive to enhance use value. Cooperatives drive home the point that there is nothing like a trade-off between being profitable and serving social objectives.

Cooperatives have built-in resilience. Though to remain in business they should remain profitable. Their charter typically requires managers to plough back the bulk of their profits into the company to prevent layoffs in times of distress. It is the solution for stakeholder capitalism in which the knee-jerk reaction of any business at the very onset of a crisis is to fire employees.

What if the Residents of the Communities Truly Owned the Economic Base and Infrastructure of the Communities?

Mondragon Corporation based in the Basque country in Spain is one of the landmarks of the social economy movement, sheerly because of its scale. With verticals in the Finance, Industry, Retail and Knowledge it consists of 95 separate, self-governing cooperatives, employing around 80,000 people with 14 R&D centres. It is *'profitable, competitive and enterprising, capable of successfully operating in global markets'.*

The productive forces of an economy leveraged in response to the social needs in a manner that is conducive to the environment if organised in a cooperative framework can go a long way in ensuring the emancipation of the populations.

---

[36] The highest to lowest pay ratio of Mondragon cooperative in Basque, Spain is 6:1, while in any industry in the US, it is 350: 1.

The Iconic Indian Coffee House

The Indian Coffee House is a restaurant chain in India operated by Worker Cooperatives. With around 500 coffee houses across the length and breadth of the country, it is a standing testimony of how workers can run a profitable enterprise and shape their own destiny.

During the Colonial era, to promote the consumption of coffee in a predominantly tea-drinking nation, a Coffee Board was established. Post-Independence, by around 1950, the board, manned by the top brass of the Indian Civil Service, many of them British educated, started to register losses in consecutive years. It was decided to wind up the operations of the coffee houses to prevent further loss to the exchequer. Thousands of workers' lives were in the doldrums. It was then the veteran communist leader, AK Gopalan fondly remembered as AKG came forward and mooted the idea that workers themselves should assume ownership of the coffee houses and manage the operations of the entire chain of coffee houses. The initiative enjoyed the blessings of the then Prime Minister Jawaharlal Nehru. It is to be remembered that AKG was the leader of the opposition in Lok Sabha, the lower house of the Indian Parliament. The coming together of the two stalwarts of Indian Parliament, who battled it out whenever it was in session, was a heart-warming spectacle.

To assume the reins of administration from the officers of the elite Indian Civil Service and run the show was something that had not even crossed the minds of the workforce of chefs, waiters and cashiers of the Coffee houses. In a meeting conducted in August 1957 in the city of Bangalore, presently the IT hub of India, in an ominous reference to the USSR, AKG reminded that if the workers really willed, they could assume the reins of a great nation and turn it around. Under his guidance, the workers of the Coffee board formed the Indian Coffee Workers' Co-operatives and compelled the Coffee Board to hand over the outlets to the workers. The network of outlets was renamed as *'Indian Coffee House'*. Thus, the first

Indian Coffee House was born in August 1957 and started to operate in Delhi Connaught Place. From then on there was no looking back. In the legendary College Street Coffee House in the city of Kolkata, it was not uncommon to see the stalwarts of Indian cinema the likes of Satyajit Ray, Mrinal Sen, Sunil Gangopadhyay and many others engaged in discussions. Across the country, Indian Coffee House has turned itself into a venue for intellectual interchange. It has become the den of the intellectuals. Though multinational chains have entered India since the early 1990s, the Indian Coffee Houses refuse to yield ground. Presently there are 13 co-operative societies in the country to run the coffee houses. These societies are governed by managing committees elected by the employees.

AMUL! THE TASTE OF INDIA! How it Expanded its Operations During the COVID Pandemic

During the 2008 financial meltdown and COVID pandemic, as lay-offs and closures were the norm, cooperatives in every industry across the world showed high resilience. And in some instances, witnessed unprecedented spurt of growth.

The impact of the COVID lockdown was so heavy that it cost the milk producers of India more than 1123 million Indian Rupees every day. But Amul, a cooperative of milk farmers, increased its sales by INR 6980 million.

Amul is the story of the poor and marginalised milk farmers federating themselves into a cooperative structure along Gandhian lines. Amul which started off as a cooperative of unorganised and illiterate milk farmers in pre-independent India offers us many lessons on how to throw off the hegemonic colonial yoke, thus, leading to rural development and women's empowerment, catapulting a milk-deficient Third World former colony on to the roads of a White Revolution transforming it into a 'net exporter' of milk products.

The turnover Amul registered in 2022-23 Financial Year was 72 billion Indian Rupees. 80 percent of the profit reaches the pocket of the milk farmer toiling in the rural villages of the state of Gujarat. The supply chain of Amul collects 28 million litres of milk from 3.6 million farmers spread across 18,600 villages through 18,700 societies, and transport through 5,000 milk tankers to 200 chilling stations. After being processed into 750 plus stock-keeping units, the food products are being transported through 10,000 distributors to 1 million retailers.

During the COVID pandemic, when the Indian dairy industry was hit, Amul went on to increase its market share and recorded increased capacity utilisation and profits. Amul launched more than 100 new products across dairy and non-dairy categories during COVID times. It added 3.5 million more litres of milk every day and paid 8000 million INR extra to the milk producers. It increased its turnover by 6980 million INR in the first year of COVID! Almost all plants operated at full capacity. Some even at 115 percent. Such a supply chain resilience is unparalleled even among the fortune 500 companies. At times Amul even rented capacity from other private sector dairy units to cater to its increased processing needs.

AMUL, a PRODUCER COOPERATIVE shows the way to bring *'value for many'* of the poor and illiterate dairy farmers at the start of the value chain. That it spends less than 0.8 percent of its expenses on advertisements and marketing, in an industry where 10–15 percent is the world norm reflects the *'value for money'* that it delivers to the consumer at the other end of the value chain.

The 10 Oil Commandments that Saved Norway:

1. National stewardship and control must be secured for all activities on the Norwegian Continental Shelf (NCS).
2. Petroleum discoveries shall be utilised such that Norway achieves maximum independence from others as regards access to crude oil.
3. New business activity shall be developed with a basis in petroleum.
4. The development of an oil industry must be founded on necessary considerations for existing business activity, nature conservation and environmental protection.
5. Flaring of unusable gas on the NCS must not be accepted, with the exception of brief trial periods.
6. Petroleum from the NCS shall generally be landed in Norway, except in certain specific cases where socio-political considerations provide a basis for a different solution.
7. The State shall be involved at all appropriate levels, and contribute to the coordination of Norwegian interests within the Norwegian petroleum industry and the construction of a Norwegian, integrated petroleum community with national as well as international objectives.
8. A state oil company shall be established to safeguard the State's commercial interests and engage in appropriate collaboration with domestic and foreign oil interests.
9. North of the 62nd parallel, the chosen activity pattern shall be in keeping with the special socio-political factors associated with that region.
10. Norwegian petroleum discoveries may lead to broader perspectives on Norwegian foreign policy.

Conclusion

> 'There is a very clear dialectical relationship: imperialism exists because underdevelopment exists; underdevelopment exists because imperialism exists.'
>
> **– Salvador Allende, in his speech to the UN General Assembly, on 4th December 1972**

> 'When the productive social capital of any part of the world is obliterated, the potential value of private capital elsewhere is enhanced.'
>
> **– Michael Parenti**

The national government of the day is mandated by the social contract with the citizens to ensure their welfare. This social law is the supreme law of the land. In order for the government to pursue policies and actions to accomplish the same, it should never let itself be cowed by the finance capital. At times it may even have to act against the liking of the Capital. The full exercise of the political freedom by the national government to install social and economic democracy is a must in ensuring the welfare of its people. Against all evidence to the contrary, the advocates of market fundamentalism still preach the virtues of the market. They see the government and its involvement in the economy on behalf of citizens as the perennial source of all trouble. They still cling to the premise that the government alone is the epitome of inefficiency, parasitism and favouritism that retards human flowering and that it is the free market that unshackles the human into achieving his destined results.

The Third World in the aftermath of WW II and the decolonisation that followed it showed the political maturity to exercise the sovereignty in the course of socio-economic development. The role of the Soviet Union in facilitating the Third World to undo the wrongs of the past can never be over-emphasised. The collapse of the socialist bloc dealt a heavy blow to the nations of the Third World. Right lessons should be learned from the contrast between Russia's transition, as engineered by the international economic institutions owing allegiance to International Finance Capital, and that of China, designed by its own government. In short, the national governments, be those in the West or the East, should reassert themselves and restore their own authority, and be sovereign of circumstances they come to preside.

'We can have a democratic society or we can have the concentration of great wealth in the hands of the few. We cannot have both'.

BIBLIOGRAPHY

- *Glimpses of World History* by Jawaharlal Nehru
- *The Economic Consequences of Peace* by John Maynard Keynes
- *The General Theory of Employment, Interest and Money* by John Maynard Keynes
- *History of the Russian Revolution* by Leon Trotsky
- *Ten Days That Shook the World* by John Reed
- *Manufacturing Consent* by Noam Chomsky
- *Understanding Power* by Noam Chomsky
- *On My Country and the World* by Mikhail Gorbachev
- *Revolution from Above* by David M. Kotz and Fred Weir
- *Capital and Imperialism* by Utsa Patnaik and Prabhat Patnaik
- *A Theory of Imperialism* by Utsa Patnaik and Prabhat Patnaik
- *Capital in the 21st Century* by Thomas Piketty
- *A Brief History of Neoliberalism* by David Harvey
- *Empire* by Michael Hardt and Antonio Negri
- *Globalization and its Discontents* by Joseph Stiglitz
- *Neoliberalism - A Very Short Introduction* by Manfred B. Steger and Ravi K. Roy
- *We are Cuba, How Revolutionary People Have Survived in a Post-Soviet World* by Helen Yaffe
- *An Antonio Gramsci Reader* by Antonio Gramsci
- *The Second World War* by Antony Beever
- *The Most Controversial Decision Truman The Atom Bomb and the Surrender of Japan* by Wilson D. Miscamble
- *Five Myths about Nuclear Weapons* by Ward Wilson

- *In Retrospect. The Tragedy and Lessons of Vietnam* by Robert S. Mc Namara
- *To Kill a Nation. The Attack on Yugoslavia* by Michael Parenti
- *Red Shirts Black Shirts* by Michael Parenti
- *Shock Doctrine* by Naomi Klein
- *Conflicting Missions. Havana Washington and Africa* by Piero Glei Jesses
- *In Search of Enemies. A CIA Story* by John Stockwell
- *Overthrow. America's Century of Regime Change From Hawaii to Iraq* by Stephen Kinzer
- *Why Women Have Better Sex Under Socialism and Other Arguments for Economic Independence* by Kristen R. Ghodsee
- *I, Rigoberta Menchu. An Indian Woman in Guatemala* by Rigoberta Menchu
- *I Too Had a Dream* by Varghese Kurien

www.ingramcontent.com/pod-product-compliance
Lightning Source LLC
LaVergne TN
LVHW091541070526
838199LV00002B/150